THE FIRST WHIGS

UNIVERSITY OF DURHAM
PUBLICATIONS

The First Whigs

THE POLITICS OF THE
EXCLUSION CRISIS
1678–1683

BY

J. R. JONES

LONDON
OXFORD UNIVERSITY PRESS
NEW YORK   TORONTO
1961

Oxford University Press, Amen House, London E.C.4

GLASGOW NEW YORK TORONTO MELBOURNE WELLINGTON
BOMBAY CALCUTTA MADRAS KARACHI LAHORE DACCA
CAPE TOWN SALISBURY NAIROBI IBADAN ACCRA
KUALA LUMPUR HONG KONG

PRINTED IN GREAT BRITAIN
AT THE UNIVERSITY PRESS, OXFORD
BY VIVIAN RIDLER
PRINTER TO THE UNIVERSITY

PREFACE

THIS book deals with the Exclusion crisis of 1678–83 and with the forces welded together by the first Earl of Shaftesbury into the powerful political party for which the term 'Whig' was first invented. This is a subject which has been almost neglected, and the word party is one which historians have been dissuaded, or intimidated, from using. When first beginning work on this subject I naturally employed the approach and the techniques used with such success in the study of eighteenth-century parliamentary politics by the late Sir Lewis Namier. But it soon appeared that, with the very different political conditions existing before 1688, such an approach had serious limitations; a different set of historical questions must be asked. Whether they are the right ones, and whether they have been answered, is for the reader to decide.

My acknowledgements are due to Miss B. Behrens, of Newnham, who confirmed my first impressions that there was scope for this study, and to Dr. J. H. Plumb who supervised my research at Cambridge. I shall always be indebted for his guidance; he is not, of course, responsible for any of my conclusions. Professor H. S. Offler gave invaluable advice when this study was first submitted for publication, and I am most grateful to Dr. W. E. Saxton for his help while this book was in the press.

For reasons of economy and to avoid repetition I have not cited general authorities such as Ralph and Echard for established facts, but have confined references to original sources, manuscript and printed. If the reader wants a bibliography of pamphlet material he will find it in the only other recent book on this subject, F. S. Ronalds, *Attempted Whig Revolution of 1678–81* (Urbana, 1937).

October, 1960

CONTENTS

PREFACE v

LIST OF ABBREVIATIONS viii

1. INTRODUCTION 1

2. THE POPISH PLOT AND ITS EXPLOITATION 20

3. THE FIRST EXCLUSION PARLIAMENT 34

4. THE BREAK WITH THE KING 74

5. THE APPEAL TO THE NATION 115

6. THE OXFORD PARLIAMENT 156

7. THE DECLINE AND COLLAPSE OF THE FIRST WHIGS 183

8. CONCLUSION 211

INDEX 219

LIST OF ABBREVIATIONS

Addl.	Additional Manuscripts, British Museum
Barrillon	Baschet transcripts, Public Record Office; the dates of the dispatches are new style
BM	British Museum
Browning	A. Browning, *Thomas Osborne, Earl of Danby*, 3 vols. (1944–51)
Burnet	*A History of My Own Time* (1897–1900), ed. O. Airy
Carte	Carte Manuscripts, Bodleian
CSPD	*Calendar of State Papers, Domestic*
CJ	*Commons' Journals*
Grey	A. Grey, *Debates of the House of Commons* (1769)
HMC	*Historical Manuscripts Commission*
Harleian	Harleian Manuscripts, British Museum
Hatton Correspondence	Ed. E. M. Thompson, Camden Society (1878)
Kenyon	J. P. Kenyon, *Robert Spencer, Earl of Sunderland* (1958)
LJ	*Lords' Journals*
Luttrell	N. Luttrell, *A Brief Historical Relation of State Affairs* (1857)
Morrice	Morrice, MS. P, The Entring Book of Roger Morrice, Dr. Williams's Library, London
Prinsterer	Groen van Prinsterer, *Archives ou correspondance inédite de la maison d'Orange-Nassau*, 2nd series (1858–62).
PRO	Public Record Office
Shaftesbury Papers	Public Record Office
Sidney	R. W. Blencowe (ed.), *Diary of the Times of Charles the Second by the Honourable Henry Sidney* (1843)
State Trials	Ed. T. B. Howell (1816)
Tanner	Tanner Manuscripts, Bodleian

All dates in the text are old style, with the calendar year beginning on 1 January.

I

INTRODUCTION

I

In the study of the political, parliamentary, and social history of the seventeenth century the Exclusion crisis of 1678 to 1683 may at first sight appear to have been little more than an unproductive and relatively unimportant episode. Certainly, and rightly, it has been overshadowed by the far more significant events and developments of the two revolutionary periods, the so-called Puritan Revolution of the 1640's and the 'Glorious' Revolution of 1688. By comparison the Exclusion crisis was no more than an abortive revolution, inconclusive in its results since the first Whigs failed to achieve their objectives and the Stuart monarchy, victorious over them by 1683, collapsed five years later.

Unfortunately, most of the attention which the events of the crisis have attracted has been of the wrong sort. There has been a great deal of largely futile speculation on such topics as Oates and the Popish Plot, Godfrey's mysterious death, the Rye House conspiracy, and the Monmouth rebellion. The attempts to white-wash Charles II, James II, their ministers and mistresses, to portray them as devoted patriots and paternal governors, have acted as additional distractions. The result, and the consequence of trying to discuss and explain the history of the time in terms of person-alities (especially tempting since these lend themselves to bold black-and-white characterizations), has been the neglect of the really fundamental aspects of the crisis.[1] To explain it as the work of factious demagogues is misleading—Why should there have been such a serious crisis less than twenty years after the Restoration?

[1] For a survey of modern historical work on the period see J. P. Kenyon, 'Review Article; The Reign of Charles II', *Cambridge Historical Journal*, xiii. 1 (1957).

How was Shaftesbury able to agitate so effectively and to organize and receive such wide support? Again, during the course
of the crisis the words 'Whig' and 'Tory' were coined to describe
the opposing factions, a fact which raises several important
questions. Were these first Whigs and Tories parties? What was
the structure of politics at this time? Was it modified or changed
in the course of the crisis? Did anything resembling a party
system exist?

The historians of the nineteenth century assumed uncritically
that the first Whigs and Tories were parties, indeed, the ancestors
of those of their own time. Of course, such a view cannot seriously
be maintained today in the light of Sir Lewis Namier's work,
and the word 'party' has to be used with extreme care, and only
after careful definition. But Sir Lewis Namier's work has created
a new danger into which some historians have already fallen.[1]
It must be said at the start (and this is one of the main contentions
of this study) that the namierian approach will not give us the
answers to the most significant questions which must be asked if
we are to understand the crises and developments of the seventeenth century. The namierian technique is obviously useful,
indeed invaluable, in any analysis of parliamentary history. But,
since it works on the assumption that politics were, in the main, a
system operated by a small *élite*, the political nation, it would be
dangerous to rely solely (or even largely) upon it in the study of
periods like the civil war and the Exclusion crisis when great and
vital issues affected the nation and dominated the minds and feelings of almost everyone.

The first Whigs were, and had to be, a party, something more
highly organized and disciplined than a mere alliance or coalition
of small and autonomous groups. They possessed, and required,
organization in both Parliament and country, effective discipline,
and a wide popular appeal, stimulated and maintained by a large-
scale propaganda machine. In Shaftesbury they had the leader

[1] For instance R. Walcott, *English Politics in the Early Eighteenth Century* (1956),
uses the namierian technique with effect in his analyses of the politics of Anne's
reign, but nearly all his generalizations on the period before 1688 need very
considerable qualification.

with the necessary ability, determination, experience, and un-scrupulousness to weld them together into a force strong enough to challenge the King, the Court, the Church, and a powerful section of the political nation.

Issues were what mattered during the Exclusion crisis, issues on which the nation was divided with a bitterness and intensity unknown in the eighteenth century. In addition, the structure of politics differed in many and vital respects from that made familiar to all students of the eighteenth century by the studies and analyses of Sir Lewis Namier and those whom he has inspired and directed. Not the least of these differences is the fact that the structure of politics was extremely unstable, being constantly subjected to drastic changes. The Exclusion crisis, with its three elections in a space of two years, forms only a part—though an important part—of a longer period in which these changes occurred. When the parliamentary history of the years from 1660 to 1700 is examined it becomes evident that political techniques varied widely, that very few political interests endured throughout, or were not seriously affected by the major variations which occurred in the basic conditions of politics. To enumerate only the most important; the irregular elections and partial disqualification of former royalists in 1660; the municipal purges which preceded, as well as followed, the elections of 1661; the eighteen years of the Cavalier Parliament during which many interests withered or died from neglect or lack of electoral opportunity; the development of systematic management by Danby; the *Quo Warrantos* and the remodelling of the charters which first produced the 'Loyal' Parliament of 1685, and then facilitated James II's reversal of alliances, his large-scale interference with the electorate and his campaign to pack a subservient Parliament; the failure to restore the old charters in their entirety; the far-reaching effects of the regular elections which followed the passage of the Triennial Act and in many cases finally subverted the local influence of the gentry and destroyed the surviving independence of some boroughs.

All these changes, and their effects, form a subject on which it is hoped to present some conclusions at a later date, but it is clear that here we have no stable structure of politics, but one undergoing constant and major changes. Furthermore, the same period also saw society in process of transformation, and with inevitable political repercussions, although again the full extent and effects of the changes in land-ownership, the expansion of foreign trade, the accretion of capital, and industrial development at home, constitute a subject of magnitude and complexity which has yet to be fully explored. These economic and social changes form the background, and may be found to provide some of the causes, of the crises of the second half of the seventeenth century. On the political issues it is possible to be more definite and conclusive. The issues apparent during the reign of Charles II were not minor or temporary, but of fundamental importance, raised but not settled earlier in the century. By the late 1670's the Restoration settlement was already as irrelevant as the constitutional experiments of the interregnum. Basic issues had to be resolved once more. The forms, basis, character, and objectives of government had still not been decided before 1688, and all the explosive issues of earlier crises again came to the surface during the Exclusion crisis.

II

The Exclusion crisis took its name from the repeated attempts which Shaftesbury and the first Whigs made in 1679, 1680, and 1681 to pass a bill excluding James, Duke of York, from the succession. The immediate reasons were James's personal character, his religion, his inclinations to absolutism, his French connexions, and the alleged 'discoveries' of the Popish Plot, of which he was alleged to have been the intended beneficiary. But the basic causes of the crisis can be traced back a long way. The list of Whig reasons for the attack on James read like a summary of all the grievances and complaints which had been made against all the Stuart sovereigns and their ministers. As in the years before 1640, tension, suspicion, and distrust had been steadily mounting for years, caused by the sometimes oppressive and always provocative conduct and principles of the administration.

The dangerous policies of the Cabal in 1670-3 had revived all the old suspicions of the King and Court which had been temporarily and partially effaced by the bitter experiences of the nation during the civil wars and interregnum. A new generation, and many of the survivors of the old, came to believe that Charles, his brother, his Court, and his ministers could not be trusted to respect and protect either the religion, the properties, or the liberties of the nation. From this widespread and strongly felt belief it was easy to assert that there was in existence a definite and menacing 'design' or conspiracy against them, in favour of absolutism and Popery.

Despite the personal *bonhomie* of the King, his Court was becoming increasingly isolated and out of touch with the nation. The unfashionable and the poor naturally and strongly hated or envied its frivolity, luxury, culture, immorality, and ostentatious corruption—after all they ultimately had to provide the money for this flamboyant and parasitic growth. Even more serious and detestable were the Court's cultural, religious, and political affiliations and sympathies with France, connexions which were much more alarming and dangerous than they had been during the reign of Charles I. The political developments of this period must be related to the events across the Channel; now France had the largest and most powerful army in existence, and its victories in 1667 and 1672 had shown how effective it could be as the instrument of Louis XIV's policy of aggrandisment. Even more menacing was Colbert's construction of an entirely new and efficient navy, while his tariffs and aggressive commercial policies were damaging our trading and textile interests. Louis XIV had already become the personification of absolutism, and many contemporaries rightly feared that the Court at Whitehall admired the French mode of government as well as fashions in cooking, dress, music, and morals.

The newly revived fears of the existence of a design, for the introduction into England of both absolutism and Popery, did not altogether subside after the fall of the Cabal. Suspicions were only partially allayed by the ostensibly anti-French and specifically anglican policies which Danby pursued, because his success as the pioneer parliamentary manager, and particularly his attempt in 1675 to eliminate all opposition by the imposition of a test, seemed to threaten the independence of Parliament.[1] Moreover, suspicions, grievances, and resentments were all stimulated and exploited by his rival, Shaftesbury, who ceaselessly reiterated that religion, liberties, and properties were all under imminent danger. Even though this propaganda built up an atmosphere of fear and distrust it could not produce Danby's fall, since so long as the standing Cavalier Parliament continued in existence he was assured of working majorities in both houses.

Shaftesbury's activities did, however, contribute to the final explosion, they ensured that when proof was eventually forthcoming of ministerial duplicity and Papist plotting Danby would be irretrievably ruined and a dissolution forced. Oates's bogus discoveries, and Montagu's authentic revelations in the autumn of 1678 achieved these ends and, fulfilling Shaftesbury's predictions, the elections of March 1679 returned a House of Commons in which a clear majority were actual or potential supporters. Assured of their support by his tactics and declarations, Shaftesbury at last found himself in a position to dictate to the King. Charles had to sacrifice Danby, send James into exile, and reconstitute his Privy Council with Shaftesbury as its Lord President.

With this governmental revolution the Exclusion crisis began, the first Exclusion Bill being introduced into the Commons in May 1679. With Charles's resolution not to accept or concede it the struggle started between the Crown (not the Tories, for they were never more than royal auxiliaries) and those who were soon to be described as the Whigs. This struggle took place in three parliamentary sessions, in two general elections, and, what was remarkable and almost unprecedented, throughout the country during the intervals when no parliament was in session. Shaftesbury's long struggle against considerable odds was a testimony to his skill, determination, and ruthlessness, and to the strength of his support.

Whig strength depended on two main factors. The case for Exclusion appealed to a very large proportion of the nation;

---

[1] Browning, i. 152–3. All members and office-holders were to have to take an oath not to endeavour any alteration of the government in Church or state.

almost every section with serious grievances saw in the bill the means to achieving their removal or remedy. Shaftesbury showed himself extraordinarily successful in combining and unifying all elements of opposition, and in publicizing, dramatizing, and vulgarizing the issues at stake. Although Exclusion itself would not directly solve all problems he purported to show that its enactment would create conditions in which action could and would be taken to meet all problems—political, religious, and economic. This concentration on the one issue was a principal reason for his influence and success, and there is a striking parallel with later popular movements of the nineteenth century in which there was similar and effective concentration on one single issue.

The second reason for Whig success was the organization which Shaftesbury developed, and on which he was forced increasingly to rely as the spontaneous enthusiasm of the Whig supporters began to subside.

Before attempting an analysis of the first Whigs it seems best to give a brief chronological description so as to make clear the outlines of the crisis. The first Exclusion Bill received a second reading in the Commons in May 1679 by a substantial but not overwhelming majority. In order to stifle its progress, and as a sign of his determination not to accept Exclusion, Charles prorogued Parliament at the end of the month and dissolved it shortly afterwards. His action encouraged supporters to rally round the Crown, but the elections of August and September saw the Whigs strengthened, not weakened. For this victory Whig organization was largely responsible, and subsequently it achieved an even more important success by holding the party together, and maintaining its morale and enthusiasm, during the thirteen months which elapsed before Charles allowed this second Parliament to meet.

Charles intended these prorogations to gain time in which popular passions and excitement would subside, but when Parliament did meet in October 1680 the Whig hold was stronger than ever. Exclusion was at once re-introduced and this time passed through the Commons without serious resistance. Its rejection in the Lords, on its first reading, ensured a fight to the finish between the Whigs and the Crown. The second Whig Parliament was dissolved in January 1681 and, in the elections which followed, the party's organization reached its highest pitch of efficiency, reducing losses to a minimum. The Whigs went to the third Exclusion Parliament, which was called to Oxford in March, determined to persist in their demand for Exclusion, many believing that at long last the King was about to acquiesce.

Unknown to the Whigs the turning-point in the crisis had already been passed. Seeing that the Whigs were intransigent and having failed significantly to reduce their strength, the King preferred to become the client of France rather than the dependent of his own subjects. A secret agreement in February assured him of French support, and with this behind him he had no immediate need to call Parliament at all. The Oxford session was no more than a trap, called to give the Whigs the opportunity to discredit themselves. It lasted only a few days and the unexpectedly early dissolution was followed by a royal appeal to the nation against the Whigs, a clear indication that for the immediate future Charles intended to rule without Parliament.

Without Parliament the Whigs could not effectively mobilize the popular support which had enabled them to exert pressure on the Crown. In the last phase of the crisis, from March 1681 until the summer of 1683, their position gradually crumbled. The last, defensive success came in November 1681 when a packed Whig grand jury in the City threw out a fabricated bill of high treason against Shaftesbury. This success depended on Whig control over London; this they lost during bitter contests in 1682. By the end of that year most Whigs lapsed into a prudent inactivity, or made their submission. Shaftesbury fled to the United Provinces, a few of the more resolute began to talk, and perhaps to plan, violence. The Rye House Plot, 'discovered' in June 1683, merely completed the ruin of the Whigs. Without organization or recognized leaders, the Whigs as such ceased to exist. When Russell and Sidney died on the scaffold, contemporaries might be excused for thinking that the 'old cause' was dead.

III

From motives of prudence in an age when the informer and the professional perjurer flourished, few of the Whig leaders left behind much evidence of their political activity; as might be expected, the Shaftesbury Papers contain little of value.[1] But there is enough material for us to answer the question—Who were the first Whigs?

As might be expected in a party united largely by negative propositions, by what its members hated, feared, and opposed, the first Whigs constituted a rather heterogeneous coalition. In their social composition they were a cross-section of society with all types, classes, and sections represented—landed gentry, City and provincial merchants both wealthy and comparatively modest, lawyers, men of families which were to be ennobled in the near future and others about to decline or disappear from natural or economic causes. In short, the division between Whig and Tory, like that between royalist and parliamentarian a generation earlier, cut across geographical, social, and class groupings.

This study is not the place for a detailed survey of the biographies of all the individual members of the Exclusion parliaments, although it is partly based on such material, for the reason that political issues, rather than social interests and connexions, played the dominating part in the crisis. For its duration, a period of great tension and abnormal political rancour, the motive of self-preservation and the common cause of Exclusion welded the Whigs together into a coherent and highly organized body which can properly be described as a party. Their leader, Shaftesbury, was not a magnate in the eighteenth-century sense with captive boroughs at his disposal and a phalanx of dependent

---

[1] Events justified the destruction of both personal and political papers; Locke survived, Algernon Sidney did not. The two Whig leaders who left the largest amount of material, Wharton and Huntingdon, were not in the first rank. The Shaftesbury Papers contain little of value; one informative parliamentary list (J. R. Jones, 'Shaftesbury's Worthy Men', *Bulletin of the Institute of Historical Research*, xxx, Nov. 1957), a few memoranda, some letters on Scottish affairs, but no general correspondence.

members. On the contrary, he was first and foremost a party
leader, with influence that was national and political, and only
to a lesser extent regional, personal, and territorial. The Whigs
were bound together by adherence to his and the party's cause—
Exclusion: they were connected by political considerations, and
these often took precedence over personal, social, and family
connexions.[1]

Therefore, for the purposes of this study, it is more relevant to
analyse the component sections which the Whigs formed within
Parliament than to attempt a general examination of their
composition from the social angle. However, these groups must
not be defined too sharply; the differences which separated them,
and enable them to be distinguished, were always less important
than their common insistence on Exclusion, although had the
Whigs achieved their primary objectives they would certainly
have destroyed the unity of the party.

1. The 'old Presbyterians'

This was the oldest section of the party in two senses: it derived
from the minority which had opposed the Clarendon code in the
1660's, and its members were veterans, survivors from an earlier
age. They were to be distinguished from the majority of the
Whigs by a genuine and positive zeal for religious reform and
Protestant unity. All Whigs constantly talked of this, but most
meant it largely in a negative sense, as much political as religious,
meaning hostility to Popery and to those stigmatized as crypto-
Papists. But this section, sincerely sympathetic to the dissenters
although few of its members personally attended conventicles,
tried to effect toleration and a wide measure of comprehension as
real objectives and not merely as tactical or vote-catching moves.[2]

Politically these members shared the common mistrust of
ministerial and royal methods, remembering what they alleged to
have been the deliberate betrayal of the nation's liberties in the

[1] For instance, the so-called Sidney–Capel–Howard connexion mentioned by
Walcott (op. cit. 78–79) did not exist as a political, as distinct from a social, unit
during the crisis.

[2] Huntingdon's and Wharton's papers in the Carte collection are full of
memoranda and correspondence on religious and theological subjects.

years after 1660. They seem to have had little formal organization, and as in the past were loosely grouped around a few personal leaders, Holles and Wharton in the Lords, Sir Nicholas Carew, Boscawen, and Swinfen in the Commons. Indeed, many of them disliked, and resented, the primacy which his organizing ability and activities gave Shaftesbury within the party, and some suspected him of cynically exploiting the grievances of the dissenters for his own advantage.

2. The 'country Opposition'

A majority of the Whigs can be placed in this category, which again became an important factor in politics during the regroupings which followed the fall of the Cabal, under the leadership of Shaftesbury and Buckingham. Its title, 'country', implied the claim that it represented the nation at large against a small, corrupt fraction—the Court and its creatures. Like the title, its principles were traditional, those which had been evolved during the reigns of James I and Charles I: they can be summarized as honest administration and ministerial respect for the law, no favourites, the consultation of Parliament and the prompt redress of grievances, financial retrenchment and the furtherance of trade, insularity, and the defence of the Protestant religion. It is a fair comment to say that it was always easier for the 'country' to show that ministers were violating these principles than to put them into practice.

The 'country' combined in its ranks those elements which had as their driving force what has been aptly called the 'politics of resentment'. Some consistently and sincerely hated corruption. Others feigned indignation because the ministers neglected them. Many blamed the administration for their own poverty or particular grievances. Their backgrounds varied. One surprisingly large section, including some thirty members, came from formerly royalist families, or had been royalists themselves in their youth. The explanation for their change of front varied from person to person; some, like George Speke, had been disappointed in 1660 and complained that their services had never been recognized. Others, Essex and his brother Sir Henry Capel were the most

notable, had become progressively disillusioned with the Court
and its policies. Others had personal reasons; Sir John Coventry
never forgave the slashing of his nose by Court hooligans as
punishment for a gibe against the King; Roger Whitley was
engaged in a venomous local feud against Tory rivals. It must
also be noted that there were many examples of Tories with a
parliamentarian, or even cromwellian, past.

The causes of the Exclusion crisis were not identical with those
of the civil war, and individuals reacted not according to any set
pattern but as a result of their own attitudes of mind and their
own interests, and these did not necessarily coincide with those
of their fathers. For instance, few of the younger Whigs were
absorbed by religious questions, many (Thomas Wharton being
the most thorough-going) reacting strongly against a puritanical
upbringing.[1] If there were any real political significance in the
support of former royalists for Exclusion, it lay in the fact that
many were connected with the old middle group of moderates,
led by Lord Capel, which had at first reluctantly adhered to the
Long Parliament but had subsequently deserted to Charles I.
Two Whigs, Hotham and Carew, had had fathers executed for
trying to betray their trusts to the King.

Most, but not all, of the 'country' members can be described as
electorally independent, that is they owed their election to their
own efforts, influence, and interests. There were also a number of
dependents, those who owed their return to the control exercised
over boroughs by Whig magnates, but they were a minority,
not numerous enough to enable their patrons to dominate the
party. Few interests among the first Whigs compared with those
of the eighteenth century either in size or durability. Patrons could
certainly contribute to the success of Whig candidates, but very
few could consistently ensure success outside a limited range of
captive boroughs (places like Cricklade, Gatton, Bodmin, and
Tregoney). The Russells and the Whartons possessed far less
direct influence than after 1688; the former could rely on returning
seven M.P.'s, the latter at least four, to the Exclusion parliaments,
but both interests were to be virtually annihilated in 1685. The

[1] On the career of Thomas Wharton see J. Carswell, *The Old Cause* (1954).

most common interest among the Whigs, and the most consistently effective during this period, was not that of the aristocratic magnate but the well-entrenched local influence of provincial families—the Eliots at St. Germans, Sir Arthur Harris at Oakhampton, Yonge at Honiton, Grimstone at Colchester, Birch at Weobley (based on recent purchase), Cust at Stamford, Rudd at Higham Ferrers, and Wharton at Beverley.

3. The adventurers

A division occurred in the Whig ranks which is also to be found, in a more pronounced manner, during the next century. It lay between those members who, more or less disinterestedly, opposed both the governmental principles and the persons of the ministers, and those opportunists who attacked ministers in order first to supplant, and then to imitate, them. Power and money were their real objectives.[1]

This group among the Whigs included some outstandingly able men, notably Ralph Montagu, William Harbord, and Sir Francis Winnington. Apart from their greater unscrupulousness they were marked off from the majority of the Whigs by the fact that most of them had held office at one time and were accustomed to life at Court. By vigorous denunciations of ministers, by consistently advocating the most extreme measures, they tried to efface these facts—with some success, especially in 1680 when for a time they dominated proceedings in the Commons, and even tried to wrest leadership and the direction of policy from Shaftesbury. But it was impossible for them wholly to overcome the justified suspicions felt by many of the Whig rank and file, that these men were thinking primarily of themselves and would, if given encouragement, desert to the Court.

4. Monmouth and his circle

This section had close connexions with the adventurers—the two groups overlapped to some extent. In composition Monmouth's

---

[1] Men from this group provided Barrillon, the French ambassador, with most of his agents and contacts. They served him in ruining Danby and subsequently offered to betray Shaftesbury and the Whigs for money.

section was even more dissimilar from the Whigs as a whole. His support came from a personal interest of friends and a few opportunists who saw the possibilities in his cause from an early stage. Naturally these men were of very similar type to their leader—young, dissolute, and fashionable; Lord Colchester and Sir Thomas Armstrong, Monmouth's so-called evil genius, being in every way a contrast to the solid and unfashionable Whig M.P.'s.

This personal following started to push Monmouth's pretensions in 1679, but their success was at any time during the crisis largely confined to the common people, to whom he was the popular hero, as the western tour of 1680 showed. But very few of the Whig section of the 'political nation' ever countenanced or committed themselves to his claims. This is a point which must be stressed, since the Exclusion bills have come to be linked with Monmouth's claims to legitimacy and the succession. It is untrue simply to say that Monmouth was the Whig candidate for the throne; Shaftesbury and the Whigs naturally exploited his popularity with the masses, but they carefully and deliberately refrained from committing themselves explicitly and specifically to adopting and supporting his claims. The first Exclusion Bill of 1679 did not make him heir to the throne. When in the second bill, in 1680, Montagu and his associates deliberately left out the saving clause in favour of the legitimate succession, the reaction of the Whig majority was so unfavourable that the clause had speedily to be reinserted. Only once, and for a brief period, during the sudden crisis of August 1679, when Charles fell ill, did the Whigs definitely consider placing Monmouth on the throne.[1]

5. The radicals

They formed the opposite wing of the party from Monmouth and his associates, a factor which was to become apparent in 1685. This section derived from the levellers and the republicans of the

[1] At least until the Oxford session of 1681 when the clause was omitted. There is very little direct evidence on relations between Shaftesbury and Monmouth, but when Conway approached the latter on behalf of Danby, Monmouth would make no promises until he had consulted Shaftesbury; Addl. 28053, f. 140.

interregnum, some being survivors from that period. As had apparently been the case with them (although the evidence is not altogether conclusive) it was concentrated mainly in London, Bristol, and the textile towns of the west country. Driven underground after 1660, the radicals emerged again in London after 1672, under the protection of the Duke of Buckingham.[1]

The radicals were mostly obscure men of comparatively humble origins, and few gained, or even aspired to, a place in the Commons. But as the Exclusion crisis intensified so their importance steadily increased. Radicals manned the subordinate positions in the Whig political machine in the City and assisted in the organization throughout the country of mass petitions and agitation in 1679–80 and in the elections of 1681. The radicals were generally republicans, which in itself marked them off very sharply from most Whigs. Many were extremists, ready to plan the use of force. But it is hardly just to dismiss them as a mere 'lunatic fringe', devoted to plotting as an end in itself, since they represented a permanent force in the politics of the seventeenth century (although one that has generally been neglected), the demand for the redress of the chronic grievances of the common people. A great deal of attention has been devoted to the grievances of the lesser gentry, a class which opposed each successive administration on principle and from interest, but the permanent antagonism between governments and the governed was always far more acute at the foot of the social and economic scales. A radical like Robert Ferguson, the 'Plotter', like Lilburne before him, worked against every administration because he believed that all ministers were and must, under the existing system, be always oppressive, corrupt, and parasitic.

On the other hand, it is an exaggeration to describe the radicals as the only consistent, honest, and actively militant opponents of the Court. They had no leader capable of making them an independent political force, so they could never become more than

[1] The radicals re-emerged publicly in June 1676 when Jenks, a linen draper, spoke in the Common Hall calling for a new Parliament, for which he was taken into custody and examined before the Privy Council. *CSPD*, 1676–7, 253; Carte, 80, ff. 789–92. His *Case* was published in Amsterdam in 1677. See also, I. Morley, *A Thousand Lives* (1954), which overestimates the importance of the radicals.

subordinates and instruments of others. They shared in the common insistence upon Exclusion, but they had no hope of being able to gain support for the further political, social, and legal reforms which they alone advocated. Only in the last desperate phases, in 1683 and again in 1685, did the radicals exert much influence outside their own circles. Furthermore they were by no means all dedicated men; probably there were as many scoundrels and desperadoes among them as in Monmouth's entourage.[1]

6. Shaftesbury

He alone maintained contact with and control over all sections of the party. The first Whigs were his creation, Exclusion his policy. He had evolved the parliamentary tactics and organizational developments which made them a formidable force. But for all his originality and eminence Shaftesbury was to his contemporaries, and has remained, an enigma, perhaps because of that reserve and impenetrability which Richelieu had described as the most valuable gift for a politician. Certainly he has eluded his few biographers, and historians have either left him a blank, important but unexplained, or have followed the caricatures fashioned by contemporary Tories and hack-writers.

The most famous judgement on Shaftesbury is that of Dryden, in *Absalom and Achitophel*, but it does not bear close examination. Certainly Shaftesbury was ambitious and wanted power; he was as unscrupulous in his methods as any contemporary rival and he had apparently changed his coat often—almost as often as Dryden himself.[2] But he was not just a crooked politician on the make,

[1] Many of the radicals turned King's evidence in the trials which followed the Rye House conspiracy and Monmouth's rebellion. Some later collaborated with James II in his attempts to pack Parliament: J. R. Jones, 'James II's Whig Collaborators', *Historical Journal*, iii. 1 (1960).

[2] A more reasoned, though extremely hostile, sketch of Shaftesbury was written by Lord Peterborough in his little-known work, R. Halstead (pseud.), *Succint Genealogies* (1687), 432: 'he was as proud as Lucifer, and Ambitious beyond whatever entered into the designs of any Man; impatient of every Power but his own, of any Man's reputation; false to that degree, as he did not esteem any Promise, any Engagement, any Oath, of other use than to serve a purpose, and none of these of consequence to bind a Man further than it was his interest'.

out purely for himself—like Ralph Montagu—or an irresponsible frondeur, like Buckingham.[1] Dryden, of course, was out to smear Shaftesbury, but he made a fundamental mistake in believing, as had Clarendon, that the recurring crises and opposition to the Crown arose primarily from the machinations of a succession of wicked and ambitious men—Pym, Cromwell, and now Shaftesbury.

It is clear that Shaftesbury, like any other politician, wanted power, but not as an end in itself nor simply as the means of self-advancement, because he knew what he would do with it. He appreciated that the policies, principles, and sympathies of Charles and his Court directly endangered the religion and liberties of the nation, and that these would never be secure until the influence of the Court and Crown was drastically reduced and power and office permanently entrusted to men who possessed the confidence and support of Parliament and the nation. It was to bring this about that Shaftesbury introduced and fought for Exclusion.

Shaftesbury's real strength lay, as Burnet said, in his knowledge of England, and this is the explanation of at least the last phase of his career as the pioneer leader of systematic opposition. This dictum can be interpreted in two equally valid ways. First, Shaftesbury knew better than anyone else how to exploit the beliefs, prejudices, and fears of all classes, including the most humble or ignorant, even though he did not necessarily share them. Secondly, he represented more clearly and fully than any other leader, then or later, the cardinal Whig principle that governmental power should be vested in those who possessed the greatest weight in society. His extensive Dorset estates, wide commercial interests (which included mining, money-lending, shipping, and colonial proprietorship), his legal connexions, and his intellectual interests (Locke was his friend), all gave him natural and influential contacts with every section of the upper classes. His avowed sympathies with the dissenters gave him additional influence, and he deliberately set out to approach the radical as well as the mercantile interests in the City—approaches which were facilitated as well as symbolized by his residence in Aldersgate.

[1] See H. W. Chapman, *Great Villiers* (1949).

Shaftesbury had another asset in his political experience, which could not be rivalled by any other politician of his day, and few have ever shown themselves so quick and sure in profiting from their experience, and still more in adapting themselves to changing conditions and circumstances. All these factors gave Shaftesbury an acknowledged ascendancy in the party which was challenged, and unsuccessfully, only by the disgruntled but physically disintegrating Buckingham and the boundlessly ambitious Montagu.

Shaftesbury's ability as a judge and manager of men is shown by his choice of assistants and by the readiness of men of prominence and independence to serve as his lieutenants and subordinates. Lord William Russell, if he lacked eloquence and brilliance, was industrious, respected, and, above all, son of the Earl of Bedford. Sacheverel, Swinfen, Cavendish, the Hampdens, were all important and influential in virtue of their own ability or position, but they acted under Shaftesbury, discussing policy with him, transmitting directives, and putting them into practice in debates and at elections. Radicals on the one wing, peers on the other—all looked to him as their leader.

IV

From this brief initial survey it will be seen that although the Whigs were based on a combination of various groups, interests, and sections, they were united in their common insistence on Exclusion as the sole practicable means of self-preservation, as the sovereign remedy and security for their lives, liberties, properties, and religion.[1] To each section Exclusion also offered the preliminary means of obtaining their own particular objectives; to the older men it would above all safeguard religion; to the 'country' it meant the preservation of liberties; to adventurers it promised office and self-advancement; to Monmouth the opening

[1] As a result of their concentration on Exclusion, and the failure to obtain it, the Whigs passed only one major legislative act, the Habeas Corpus Act of 1679. See Helen A. Nutting, 'The Most Wholesome Law—the Habeas Corpus Act of 1679', *American Historical Review*, lxv. 3 (Apr. 1960).

of the way to the Crown; to the radicals the first stage towards sweeping political and social reforms. Each emphasized a particular aspect of the crisis; therefore if the first Whigs are to be understood it will be necessary to describe and examine the elements and events of this crisis which brought them into existence and went far to mould their character.

2

THE POPISH PLOT AND ITS
EXPLOITATION

I

THE existence, and practicability, of a design for the subversion of
the Protestant religion was generally suspected in the years after
1673. The fact that protestantism was the religion of an over-
whelming majority of the nation was not thought to provide
any security. In debate members recalled how easily the nation
had changed its religion at the bidding of the Tudor sovereigns.
They feared that, as under Mary, only a minority would remain
steadfast to their faith, and that eventually most would conform
to changes dictated by the Court.[1] The King's religion was a
matter for speculation, but by 1678 James was beyond doubt a
practising Papist. Although like him barred from office by the
Test Act, recusants filled Whitehall. With its Papist mistresses,
pimps, artists, musicians, servants, and even physicians, the Court
became abhorrent to all staunch Protestants, a constant irritation
as well as a potential danger.

The existence of this Court riddled with Papists and sympathizers provided Shaftesbury with his main argument, the danger
from Popery, but Danby's pursuit of an apparently anti-French
and anglican policy prevented it from being of decisive effect.
The years of unsuccessful attacks on the minister from 1674 to
1678 saw the development of a 'country Opposition' in both
Houses. This was in no sense a party, but rather a combination
of groups and interests, heterogeneous in composition, and held
together by hostility to the minister. Nevertheless, it can be
described as a real, if not always consistent, Opposition since it

[1] Sir Thomas Meres, 4 Nov. 1678. Grey, vi. 138.

THE POPISH PLOT AND ITS EXPLOITATION

opposed the principles of government as well as the person of Danby. The failure of this Opposition came rather from circumstances than from the actual defects of leadership and tactics. The standing Parliament gave Danby the opportunity to exploit the now anachronistic Cavalier loyalty of the survivors of those elected in 1661. Prorogations, adjournments, the powers exercised by the Speaker gave Danby an immense and permanent advantage. By bribery he could often detach hostile leaders; by patronage he kept his own supporters satisfied. If at times Danby could be checked, as with the political test of 1675 or in 1678 over foreign policy, yet there seemed to be no prospect of his power being brought to an end.

Even Oates's revelations of the Popish Plot did not destroy Danby's position. To suppose that Oates's so-called discoveries were a monstrous concoction which deprived the nation of its senses at one stroke, and automatically gave Shaftesbury the means to climb to power, is misleading and can only create a distorted picture of the crisis as a whole. By themselves these revelations might have had little effect. The country Opposition had continuously raised the cry of Popery since 1673 with little immediate effect although they had built up uneasiness in the minds of the people. The discovery of a Jesuit college in 1678 made little impression, despite the exposure by a parliamentary inquiry of magisterial connivance.[1] Nor was the fortunate murder of Godfrey (if that is what it was) the decisive factor. Oates's stories had such an effect because they appealed on different levels to every section of the nation, they confirmed assumptions about the Papists held by almost everyone, and they were coupled with the fear of absolutism and slavery. Only in Whitehall and among the clergy were sceptics to be found from the very first.

Oates deserves all the vilification which he has received from historians, but this chorus of denunciation is really a tribute to his undoubted if unsavoury talents, a mark of his success. He was no more vicious than the other informers of the age; his absurd stories of plots and silver bullets prepared and consecrated for the King's

---

[1] *A Short Narrative of the Discovery of a College of Jesuits* (1679). Carte, 72, ff. 378, 382. *CJ* ix. 466–70.

murder were intrinsically no more improbable than the fables of the Rye House in 1683. The panic which Oates caused was no greater than that of 1641, and it was to be surpassed in 1688 at the time of the Irish alarms.

The stories invented and spread by Oates and his imitators found eager acceptance from the ignorant and credulous, who were by no means confined to the lower classes.[1] They readily believed absurd tales of large Papist armies, mysterious movements by night, secret papers scattered in the highways, of projected invasions from France and even from Spain. The wildest rumours swept the nation. Fires were confidently attributed to Papist incendiaries unless clear proof existed to the contrary. A flood of pamphlets, many written by the informers, stimulated popular fears. Their contents, or even the titles alone, give us a picture of the fevered imagination of the time. Bedlow, second only to Oates as a discoverer, published *A Narrative and Impartial Discovery of the Horrid Popish Plot* giving an account of all fires since 1666 and describing himself as one 'lately engaged in that Horrid Design, and one of the Popish Committee for carrying on such Fires'.

Enterprising publishers used old stock again. *An Account of the Bloody Massacre in Ireland* was re-issued in December 1678. Sir William Waller, the Protestant magistrate, went even farther back with his *Tragical History of Jetzer*, a fraudulent Swiss visionary who lived as long ago as 1509. The title of another pamphlet explains itself: *The Jesuits' manner of consecrating both the persons and weapons employed for the murdering of Kings and Princes. A Narrative of Popish Plots* went as far afield as Bohemia, Mexico, and Peru in describing the bloody deeds perpetrated, and conferred a kind of proto-Protestant martyrdom on the Albigensians. Thomas Dawks, the publisher of the famous playing cards showing episodes of the Plot, also advertised *Sir Edmund Berry Godfrey's Murder made visible, with his character:* 'Dedicated to the Earl of Shaftesbury. With copper-plate of Popish cruelties in this murder;

---

[1] *HMC, Ormonde*, N.S., iv. 473. Sir Nathaniel Herne, a governor of the East India Company, proposed to evacuate his family from London for fear of a massacre by the Papists.

plain or painted, and with rollers, being a neat ornament for Gent's houses.'[1]

In the existing state of tension and excitement, Godfrey's death was confidently ascribed to the Papists. Oates could not easily be dismissed when he rounded up most of the priests resident in London. By the time Parliament met, on 21 October 1678, most people believed in the existence of an actual design to kill Charles, and wanted a thorough investigation to bring all those responsible to justice. From the start Charles and Danby were obliged to take the Plot seriously, although neither credited Oates and his imitators. Danby, who had exploited anti-Papist prejudices before, hoped that by joining in the attack on a now isolated and detested minority he could ride out the storm and preserve his position. Charles, who caught out Oates in his interrogation before the Council, believed that the informer was primed by Shaftesbury and Buckingham, but nevertheless he saw that the revelations must be treated as a matter for serious consideration.[2]

It is in fact most unlikely that Shaftesbury had any prior knowledge of the informers and their evidence. Many Opposition leaders expected that the whole affair would be 'slubbered over' because Papists, not fanatics, were involved. Others feared that the Plot might be a ministerial manoeuvre to find a pretext for the maintenance of the army raised during the summer.[3] Shaftesbury persisted with a policy of trying to detach James from his connexion with Danby in order to force a dissolution. But he quickly saw the advantages of the new situation. As he commented later: 'I will not say who started the Game, but I am sure I had the full hunting of it.'[4] When Parliament reassembled both Houses began to pursue their investigations, and once the initiative passed to the Opposition the Plot could be exploited for political advantage.

[1] Advertised on the back of a poetical broadsheet, *England's Overjoy at the Duke of Monmouth's Return* (1679).

[2] J. Pollock, *The Popish Plot* (1903), 77. Barrillon, 10 Oct. 1678, 5 Jan. 1679.

[3] Carte, 103, f. 236. Grey, vi. 266. Barrillon, 10 Oct. 1678, who was, of course, vitally interested in ensuring that the army was disbanded.

[4] L. Echard, *History of England* (1718), iii. 460.

By a display of parliamentary tactics learnt during the long years since 1674, the Opposition forced the Court on the defensive and began to undermine Danby's position.

II

The new session began symbolically, like the Long Parliament in 1640, with a motion for a solemn fast. More practically the Commons ordered an examination to discover whether Papists had obtained offices in defiance of the Test Act. They appointed two important committees; the first 'to consider Ways and Means for providing Remedies for the better Preservation and Safety of His Majesty's Person', the second to investigate Godfrey's death.[1] It cannot be said that these committees were packed; they were too large and included courtiers as well as Opposition leaders. No record exists either of those who attended or of proceedings, but enough can be learnt to show that they could be manipulated by skilful parliamentary tacticians. The quorum in committees was low, three or five members usually. Unless the House specified the place of meeting it could be arranged so that only those of known Opposition sympathies would be told where to attend. In one case Court members complained that a committee met 'in holes', a rather uncomplimentary description for the chairman's chambers in Gray's Inn.[2] The chairman, a man of importance since he presided over proceedings, convened meetings and reported to the House, was invariably a member of the Opposition. Moreover, as time went on the size of the committees decreased, their selection became more partisan, members being drawn almost entirely from the Opposition or personal enemies of the Lord Treasurer.

These committees proved invaluable as instruments for the exploitation as well as the investigation of the Plot. In its investigations the Commons followed an independent line, becoming a rival to the Privy Council since for obvious reasons informers

[1] CJ ix. 517, 518.
[2] Grey, vi. 370, 372, 21 Dec. 1678; the committee in question was the one named to draw up articles of impeachment against Danby.

preferred its sympathetic encouragement. Naturally the Opposition followed up its initial advantage. Courtiers could not object to the zeal with which the Plot was pursued, and found it difficult to prevent political capital being made out of the revelations. Danby realized his weakness, and his uncertainty was reflected in the Commons. Above all he hesitated whether or not to support the Duke of York. Although James showed himself slow to realize his danger, this was an issue which could not long be postponed since on 24 October the Commons committed a bill to prevent Papists from sitting in either House. From the start James was bound to incur suspicion since if the Plot succeeded he would be the beneficiary. With the discovery of Coleman's letters the situation became very much more serious.[1]

Contemporary Tories played down these letters, which were for the most part with the confessor to Louis XIV, on the grounds that they were several years old, that there was no evidence that James knew of their existence, still less of their contents, and that Coleman had been dismissed from the Duke's service. But he had written as if James did approve his design, and true or not this fitted in with the preconceived ideas of most Englishmen who assumed that Popery and absolutism were necessarily connected. Moreover, James had employed Coleman to influence M.P.'s, and although he had eventually dismissed him, Coleman had continued as secretary to the Duchess. His influence and usefulness survived, and Danby at least knew that he was carrying on a foreign correspondence. The discovery, deciphering, and production of some of this correspondence in the Commons must affect James. The letters seemed to show that he was following the principles of government associated with his religion, and confirmed the belief that these must be incompatible with the established form of government.[2]

So long as the Opposition pursued the investigation of the Plot it carried all before it. Even when, on 4 November, Russell

[1] Three of the letters were entered in the *Journals*; *CJ* ix. 525–9. The remainder were published in 1680 by order of the House under the editorship of Sir George Treby.
[2] R. North, *Lives of the Norths* (1826), i. 298. *Hatton Correspondence*, i. 138.

moved for the removal of the Duke from the King's councils and presence, it still seemed to be in control; Court members spoke uncertainly and ineffectively.[1] All objections to the printing of Coleman's letters—obviously a damaging move for the Court as well as James—were swept aside, Titus declaring that an attempt was being made to play down the Plot.[2] Sir John Coventry produced an argument often to be repeated; anyone who opposed the motion must either be popishly affected or bribed to vote against his conscience. But the boldness and confidence of the Opposition were premature. The despondency and uncertainty of the Court members reflected Danby's prolonged indecision, and when eventually he decided to support James the situation was at once transformed, and the Opposition checked.

As evidence of a definite policy, the King on 9 November, in addressing both Houses, promised his consent to any 'reasonable' bills for security in the reign of a Popish successor, but added the significant qualification 'so as they tend not to impeach the Right of Succession, nor the Descent of the Crown in the true Line'.[3] Although, apart from a single speech from Sacheverel, no mention had yet been made of Exclusion, the attacks being made on James could only lead to this conclusion.[4] On this occasion Sacheverel showed himself again bolder than the rest. He scornfully referred to these royal promises as 'a rattle to keep us quiet', and argued (as all Whigs in the near future were to do) that there could be no security unless the succession was assured to a Protestant. No other member openly agreed, the rest of those who spoke confining themselves to the comparatively innocuous topic of prosecuting the Plot. Once the Opposition went beyond this safe ground their quick flow of easy successes stopped abruptly. After an angry and prolonged debate on 18 November, Secretary Williamson was sent to the Tower, only to be released immediately by order of the King.

[1] Grey, vi. 133–49.
[2] Ibid., 149–51, 6 Nov.; the printing was moved by Sacheverel.
[3] *CJ* ix. 536.
[4] Grey, vi. 172–3, 9 Nov. Sacheverel's speech, in which he exposed the limitations of Limitations on a Papist successor, was interrupted by Secretary Coventry and the Speaker.

The decisive check came three days later in the debate on the proviso which exempted James from the disabilities laid on the other Papist peers by the new Test Bill.[1] Contrary to some expectations, Danby insisted on its retention, and for the first time the Court out-manœuvred their opponents. The Opposition leaders failed in an attempt to force an immediate division, and as one Court speaker took courage from another the members on the other side of the House maintained a glum silence. Not even shouts of 'Coleman's letters' could compensate for the weakness of the Opposition speeches and the irresolution of many of its members. In the first division of the session—this fact is an indication of previous Opposition dominance—the proviso passed by a majority of two. The Plot had given ample proof of the danger from Popery, but not until the threat of arbitrary government was as clearly established, and Danby implicated as well as James, could the Opposition assume complete control over the Commons.

III

Ralph Montagu's dramatic betrayal of Danby's secret correspondence with the French Court finally ensured the minister's downfall. This move had been carefully prepared, and must have been anticipated by Danby, who can have had no illusions as to Montagu's ambition and unscrupulousness. Yet he failed to prevent his enemy gaining election to the Commons. At Grinstead Montagu was unsuccessful, but at Northampton—where he possessed some family influence—he began to spend lavishly in order to gain the necessary protection of membership. Danby relied on the sheriff to return the official candidate, who was no less a person than Sir William Temple, brought back reluctantly from Holland to try to buttress up the minister's position. The sheriff did his work, but his fraudulent proceedings made it easy for Montagu's friends to reverse the return on petition, which was heard at a time when the Opposition still dominated the House. They handled the case efficiently and expeditiously. To save time

[1] Grey, vi. 240–53. *CJ* ix. 543.

and to gain more publicity it was heard at the bar of the House instead of being referred to the committee of elections and privileges. The indenture returning Temple was shown to be deficient, and with a weak legal case Danby's supporters offered little resistance. After a brief debate, without a division, the House unseated Temple and declared that Montagu had been duly elected.[1]

The ease with which Montagu's case succeeded was an ominous indication of Danby's unpopularity. In the actual betrayal Montagu and his associates were to show themselves equally astute and skilful.[2] The blow had been prepared at the instigation of Barrillon, the French ambassador, who with his master regarded Danby's policy as incompatible with the long-term interests of France. At first the conspirators intended to reserve the attack until later in the session, but their hands were forced when Danby anticipated their move by making counter-revelations about intrigues between Montagu and the Papal nuncio at Paris. But in debate the Court spokesmen showed themselves inept in comparison with the coherence, eloquence, and effrontery of their opponents. Ernle, one of the old Cavalier school, bungled his task, and his revelations were answered with withering sarcasm by Powle and Clarges, at this time still Opposition leaders. Speaking with foreknowledge, having carefully rehearsed their tactics, Montagu's friends out-manœuvred the Court from the very start. Their speeches cleverly prepared the way for the production of the incriminating secret papers which Montagu had retained after his dismissal as ambassador in Paris, and which they alleged Danby wanted to seize and destroy. Once the House decided to send for these papers the Opposition became masters of the situation. Doubt had already been thrown on Danby's anti-Papist zeal; now they convicted him of secret collusion with France at a time when he had asked for supply in order to go to war against her. As Cavendish explained: 'it will appear by those Papers, that the war

---

[1] HMC, Ormonde, N.S., iv. 471. HMC, Egmont, ii. 76–77. CJ ix. 537. Grey, vi. 186.
[2] Barrillon, 24, 27 Oct. 1678, reporting his conversations with Montagu. For the debates, Grey, vi. 337–59.

with France was pretended, for the sake of an Army, and that a great man carried on the interest of an Army and Popery.'[1] The facts that this army still existed, and that the Court seemed reluctant to disband it, made this argument all the more convincing. Furthermore, nobody had forgotten the army raised in very similar circumstances in 1672. Disregarding speeches by courtiers the House voted that there was matter for an impeachment of the Lord Treasurer.

Danby's counter-attack on the following day proved ineffective. Charles Bertie produced letters incriminating members of the Opposition in intrigues with France, but the House refused to enter them in the *Journals*, as had been done with those which Montagu had produced. Naturally those affected, knowing their own vulnerability, tried by every means to disparage these allegations. Their task was greatly facilitated as, by a tactical error, the evidence chiefly incriminated Lord Russell, the far from brilliant but solid and respected heir to the Earl of Bedford. Although he, like his friends, had been guilty of intrigues with France during the first part of the year, the accusations against him seemed less convincing than his character. His entirely dishonest denial was immediately and generally accepted. As Capel—an associate— said, there was no harm in trusting Russell with matters concerning France. Another argued against entering the letters on the ground that they might mislead posterity, since future generations would not know Russell as contemporaries did. Instead of retrieving the position this counter-attack still further weakened Danby, for without regaining the initiative it incensed the Opposition leaders still further against him. Afraid of exposure they could not feel safe until they had silenced or destroyed the Lord Treasurer.[2]

The committee appointed to draw up the impeachment against Danby consisted of his bitterest personal and political enemies.[3] When the articles were reported to the House there followed a prolonged, tense, and fiercely contested debate before the Court

---

[1] Grey, vi. 347, 19 Dec.   [2] Grey, vi. 359–64.
[3] *CJ* ix. 560. Seventeen of the members can be accounted Danby's enemies, including Sacheverel, Montagu, and Sir Thomas Clarges.

interest was finally defeated by a combination of the country
Opposition, personal enemies, and those who now thought it
time to desert a failing cause. The motion to recommit the articles
was defeated by 179 to 135, candles were voted, so as to prolong
the debate, by 165 to 115, and the work 'traiterously' was retained
by 179 to 141. A last despairing motion to adjourn failed by 143
to 170 and impeachment on the fourth article was finally voted
by 143 to 119. With this succession of defeats Danby's dominance
over the House came finally to an end. After this debate the desertion of Court members could be expected to increase, the Opposition had regained the ascendancy.[1] Danby had to recognize these
facts. On 30 December 1678 the Cavalier Parliament was prorogued, never to meet again.

Danby had in the past frequently used prorogations to gain
time and disorganize his opponents, but now his enemies were
too strong for him to hope to regain his influence. The Opposition
leaders remained together in London, preparing for the new session
due to begin in February. Danby could not prolong the period
before Parliament met, since supply was urgently needed to
disband the army, which in many places was already getting out
of hand for lack of pay. The purge of those office-holders who
had voted against him added to the number of Danby's enemies.
In these circumstances it seemed that there was nothing to be lost
by risking a dissolution, since in another session the existing
House would certainly prove to be intractable. On the other
hand, negotiations with a moderate section of the Opposition,
who it must be emphasized were not in fact its real or most
influential leaders, promised that part at least of Danby's position
could be saved.[2] Therefore with the King's announcement of a
dissolution on 24 January 1679, the long life of the Cavalier
Parliament came at last to an end.

[1] *CJ* ix. 562. The most prominent among those who voted against Danby, and
suffered dismissal, was the Solicitor-General, Winnington.
[2] Barrillon, 9 Feb. 1679. These moderates, led by Holles, Boscawen, and Sir
Thomas Littleton, promised money which was urgently needed. They insisted
that Danby must be dismissed but they would allow him to escape impeachment.

IV

In the upper House Shaftesbury proved to be far less successful. The Lords, after agreeing with the Commons for an address to the King for a fast and for the expulsion of all Papists from London, heard the informers frequently. The committees appointed by the two Houses worked together. But while the Lords investigated the Plot thoroughly the Opposition peers found it much more difficult to exploit the situation and never achieved an ascendancy comparable to that gained in the Commons at the start and in the last few days of the session. They were numerically inferior to the Court, since apart from the bishops there were many peers who would support Danby so long as he retained the King's confidence.

This comparative weakness of the Opposition was reflected in the more varied and flexible tactics which Shaftesbury employed, as compared with the more direct methods of his lieutenants in the Commons. At first he continued to negotiate with James in the hope of separating him from Danby, and so securing a dissolution—a tactic which had almost succeeded in 1675.[1] But this policy could not long be combined with the all-out attacks on the Papists, and eventually on James himself, which were being made in the Commons, and when Danby at last decided to support James—and in doing so exposed himself to the fury of the Protestant militants—Shaftesbury went the other way and placed all his reliance on exploitation of the Plot.[2]

The investigations did not lead to an initial stampede of the House, as had been the case in the Commons. Their chief result was the acknowledged ascendancy of Shaftesbury within the Opposition, rather than over the House as a whole. At this time Southwell described him as 'the great giant that speaks to all, and they say with strange freedom and admirable eloquence'.[3] His particular care was to see that the committee for examinations should work in harmony with the corresponding committee of the Commons. He took a leading part in the interrogation of witnesses and prisoners, some of whom were later to complain

[1] Barrillon, 26 Sept. 1678.   [2] Barrillon, 3, 17 Nov.
[3] Carte, 38, f. 678.

that in doing so he had treated them with excessive severity. By
the end of the session Shaftesbury had no rivals, but he did enjoy
the support of several peers of great ability. Essex, Halifax, and
Winchester were the three members of the subcommittee of the
Lords, their appointment giving the Opposition a considerable
advantage.

Essex, comparatively straightforward in character, but slow
by temperament, appeared genuinely alarmed by the Plot.
Experience rather than ability gave him his place as one of the
leaders, and certainly he had less skill if more scruples than either
Shaftesbury or Halifax. There was no trace of the supposedly
sagacious and disinterested Trimmer in the session of 1678.
Halifax showed himself prepared to go to the most extravagant
lengths in his hatred of Danby and distrust of the Court. He was
one of the few who, after Oates's impudent and baseless accusations, voted for the removal of the Queen from Whitehall.[1] The
attitude of Winchester might seem surprising in view of the
traditional loyalty of his family, but he had for long been associated
with the country Opposition. Finally, there was the most extravagant and inconsistent, but at the same time the most popular
of all peers, the Duke of Buckingham. In the past he had been
Shaftesbury's closest political associate, in some respects his rival,
but by his foolishness and indolence he was rapidly dissipating
what remained of his influence and his fortune. Realizing that
at best he would be no more than a subordinate in the Opposition,
his connexion with Shaftesbury became more and more tenuous,
and he and Shaftesbury openly quarrelled.

The first serious rebuff to the Opposition peers came on 11
November, when the House resolved not to agree with the
Commons in their address for the printing of Coleman's letters.
On the other hand, the bill to disable Papists from sitting in either
House represented a success of some importance, since naturally
those peers could be expected to support the Court. But the
proviso exempting the Duke of York did not encounter as much

[1] HMC, 12th Report, ix (Beaufort), 82. He was one of those who voted to agree
with the Commons to address for her removal, but he did not sign the Protest, LJ
xiii. 392.

opposition as in the Commons. Even after Montagu's disclosures destroyed Danby's position in the Commons he still retained a majority in the Lords. On 23 December the peers rejected a motion that he should withdraw, being under the threat of an impeachment. Three days later they decided to insist, in contradiction to the vote of the Commons, that money voted should be paid into the Exchequer, not the Chamber of London. This was tantamount to a vote of confidence in the Lord Treasurer, and the impotence of the Opposition was again demonstrated on the 27th when the Lords refused to commit him in custody.[1]

These defeats were in sharp contrast to the run of successes achieved by the Opposition leaders in the Commons, but they cannot be described as decisive. If the failure of Shaftesbury to secure a majority in the Lords was, as most historians have assumed, the decisive factor in the defeat of the Exclusion Bill and the failure of the Whigs, then it is clear that Shaftesbury must have been doomed from the start. In fact Shaftesbury's whole policy depended on the Commons, not the Lords. If he could acquire and exploit complete mastery in the lower House, then he could hope to bring the King to terms, to force Charles to accept him as minister. Once he gained chief office Shaftesbury could expect a change in the situation in the Lords. Admittedly the bishops supported Danby as the champion of anglicanism, and would not readily desert him, but many of the Court peers had in the past invariably supported the minister, whoever he was, who possessed the King's confidence. Once Shaftesbury became minister he could expect that a majority would come into existence to support him regardless of the measures which he might advocate. Moreover, his position appeared to be all the stronger since there was no peer among the courtiers with the confidence, ability, and influence to replace Danby and block Shaftesbury's way.

[1] *LJ* xiii. 349, 392, 434, 441.

3

THE FIRST EXCLUSION PARLIAMENT

I

THE decision to dissolve the Cavalier Parliament, taken only after considerable hesitation, was a calculated gamble. This 'standing' Parliament, with its patiently constructed majorities in both Houses, was the basis of Danby's position as Lord Treasurer. Recognizing that this was so, its dissolution had been Shaftesbury's primary political objective ever since 1674. Nevertheless, the decision to dissolve was in the circumstances inevitable. In the last few days of the session Danby had lost control in the Commons, and there was little chance of his reconstructing a majority, since the prorogation and the purge of those members who had deserted him had infuriated the House and added to the number of his personal enemies. There was no possibility of governing without Parliament. Money was still urgently needed to disband the army, and none would be forthcoming from France until this was completed. To prolong the prorogation would merely lead to accusations that the Plot was being hushed up, and probably to charges of direct personal complicity.

At the same time Danby was not yet convinced that his political career was finished, and he expected, despite the dissolution, to hold on to some of his power and to continue to enjoy his profits and perquisites. Although he might have to surrender his office as Lord Treasurer, he expected to retain a share of effective power by means of several expedients. First, in order to divert attention from himself, he planned an attack on Buckingham who was, as always, vulnerable through his follies.[1] This was a tactic which Arlington had used with success in 1674. Secondly, realizing that

---

[1] *HMC, Ormonde*, N.S., iv. 329. Ossory to Ormonde, 22 Feb. 1678–9.

the association was damaging, Danby broke with the Duke of York, and was largely responsible for the royal order sending him into exile. In doing so he was probably influenced by learning that James was trying to save himself in the same fashion, by negotiating with Shaftesbury and offering to assist in the overthrow of Danby.[1] Finally, an agreement was reached with several moderate leaders of the Opposition which promised a satisfactory start to the new session. In return for the dissolution and James's exile, which could be expected to be an advantage to them, these moderates promised to vote the King supply. They made it clear that this would mean Danby's dismissal, since nothing would be voted so long as he remained at the Treasury, but they undertook that the impeachment and all further proceedings against him would be abandoned.[2]

The whole basis of judgement which led to the decision to dissolve, and to the conclusion of this bargain with the moderates, was totally unreal. These moderates, led by the veteran Holles, were not the real and effective leaders of the Opposition. They constituted a group rather than a party, members in the main representing the older generation and a pattern of politics which was rapidly becoming obsolete. Holles and his friends were former Presbyterians. In the past they had worked with Shaftesbury, but they still placed much greater emphasis on purely religious issues than he did. They lacked the cohesion, understanding, unscrupulousness, and tactical skill which enabled the Opposition speakers to dominate the proceedings in the House of Commons. Formerly they may have represented the opinions of the inarticulate 'country' members, but after the session of 1678 they were unable to compete with the far more energetic and coherent lead of future Whigs like Harbord, Bennett, and Sacheverel. The fact that they could not influence elections on a large scale is of much less significance; this was out of everyone's power in the first of the three Exclusion elections. Nevertheless, although the elections were not fought on strict party lines of division, the effect was to be a party triumph and the domination of the new House by

[1] Addl. 28053, f. 133. Robert Brent to Danby, 21 Jan. 1678–9.
[2] Barrillon, 9 Feb. Burnet, ii. 188.

the future Whigs. The more extreme leaders were re-elected;
many of the new members were promising material for them to
work upon.

The King seems at one stage to have expected that the results
would be comparatively favourable, and although others were
less optimistic, few courtiers foresaw their actual effects.[1] On the
other side, Shaftesbury had for long expected that elections
would favour his cause and associates, not because of any elaborate
organization ready for elections, but because of favourable
circumstances. The country Opposition had always claimed a
monopoly of anti-Papist zeal, and in the continued excitement
caused by the Plot this was an electoral asset of some value in
places with a wide franchise. For many years by-elections had
shown that opinion had changed considerably since 1661, and
that the balance of local interests had often altered. Many of those
elected in the early years of the Cavalier Parliament had since lost
their local standing, quarrelled with their neighbours or patrons,
or become too poor to seek re-election. Others had neglected
their interest or slighted the voters, assuming that the Parliament
would be eternal. Those who had accepted pensions and places of
profit often found themselves under intense attack, since lists had
been published of those alleged to have sold their honour and their
country to Danby and abetted his infamous designs.[2]

Moreover, there was comparatively little that the King or his
ministers could do to prevent these changes being reflected by the
elections. Danby's position depended on the Cavalier Parliament.
As long as this 'standing' Parliament continued he could use Crown
influence and patronage within the two Houses, using existing
family interests and groups as the basis of his working majority.
This was easier, cheaper, and safer than attempts to intervene in
by-elections so as to secure the return of favourable members.
Danby did so on occasion, but there was a risk of alienating local
interests. In any case, there was not the slightest possibility of

[1] Carte, 39, f. 13. *Hatton Correspondence*, i. 170–1.
[2] One pamphlet, *The Seasonable Argument*, had been published in Holland in
1676; another, in *Unanimous Club of Voters*, did not appear until after the first
elections of 1679.

Danby being able to 'manage' or 'undertake' a general election. There was not enough money to ensure success in more than a few boroughs. There did not exist as yet the network of electoral agents, influence, and Treasury boroughs which eighteenth-century ministers were to possess.

At this time the direct electoral influence of the Crown was limited. Formerly, the King and the great ministers of state had often claimed a right of nomination. In the Cinque ports the Lord Warden had attempted to name one baron in each port as late as the elections of 1661. But when the deputy mayor of Dover asserted, in these first elections of 1679, that the lieutenant of the castle had a right to one place, his claim did not survive a petition and examination by the partisan committee of elections and privileges.[1] Elsewhere the Crown could control the return of members in not more than a dozen places, and in these it often found its power subverted by the activities of the committee of elections. There was castle influence also at Windsor, exercised mainly in the choice of mayor, who as returning officer could ensure a favourable return. He did his best in 1679, and refused to accept the election of two strong opponents of the Court by the 'rabble.' But the courtiers whom he declared elected were unseated by the committee, and Charles had to bear the affront of two hostile members for his 'own' borough.[2] The maritime towns were more trustworthy; as a large-scale employer of labour the Crown had considerable though not necessarily preponderant influence at Harwich, Queenborough, Rochester, and Ports-mouth, where it was exercised through the Governor. In the Isle of Wight, where the boroughs were small and dependent, the governor had a measure of control over the results. In Lancashire the chancellor of the duchy exercised influence; four of his relations and dependents sat in the first Exclusion Parliament. The Paymaster to the Forces secured a seat at Kingston-on-Hull as a result of recommendation from Monmouth, who was the governor. The latter, as Chancellor, also succeeded in gaining the election of his secretary for Cambridge University. These two

[1] T. Papillon, *Memoirs* (1887), 128.
[2] A. Sidney, *Letters* (1742), 22–23.

men were elected as a consequence of the offices which Monmouth
held, not because he was as yet recognized as the popular champion—the 'Protestant Duke' and associate of Shaftesbury. This
is emphasized by the fact that neither was re-elected later in the
year, although for opposite reasons. The University, which in a
mood of characteristic subservience was to burn Monmouth's
portrait (a Lely too), would not have tolerated the candidature of
an exclusionist; at Hull an official became unacceptable.

Apart from this handful of members the Crown had to rely
on the efforts and influence of Court members, and in the intense
competition for seats few even of the most loyal were willing to
leave vacancies to be filled by carpet-baggers from Whitehall.
Pepys was deputed to secure a place for Sir John Ernle at Portsmouth, but although Legge, the governor, was a particularly
staunch courtier, he clearly resented this interference and refused
to make a place for him.[1] The Earl of Ranelagh, whom Charles
wanted in the Commons because of his ability as a speaker, failed
in his pretensions at Ludgershall.[2] But most of the courtiers
expected no help beyond general letters of recommendation
from the King as testimonials to their loyalty. These he was
strangely reluctant to issue, but they were not in the circumstances
likely to be much of an asset.[3] Nor could Danby do very much.
He was by the time of the elections fighting for his life, and in no
position to devote all his time and energies to the almost impossible
task of influencing elections on a large scale. He did try to block
the return of those chiefly concerned in his impeachment,[4] but as
self-proclaimed champions of religion and liberty these Opposition leaders were all re-elected, although Ralph Montagu had to
migrate to Huntingdonshire. Indeed, Danby found great difficulty
in obtaining the election of his own sons and connexions. He
wrote to the Duke of Newcastle asking him to use his influence
in Nottinghamshire, and to Fairfax in Yorkshire, but in both
cases without success.[5] Latimer managed to bribe the electors

[1] J. R. Tanner (ed.), *Further Correspondence of Samuel Pepys* (1929), 342–9.
[2] *CSPD*, 1679/80, 90. HMC, *Ormonde*, N.S., iv. 317.
[3] HMC, *Ormonde*, N.S., iv. 311. *Hatton Correspondence*, i. 172.
[4] HMC, *Ormonde*, N.S., iv. 315.
[5] HMC, *13th Report*, ii (*Portland*), 153. Stowe MSS. 746, f. 7.

at the venal town of Buckingham, but Dumblane fell victim to the committee of elections and was unseated.

The importance of this lack of a clear lead from the minister must not be exaggerated. Danby could not dictate either to patrons or to boroughs; to have done so would merely have added to the number of his personal enemies. Hence, although there was despondency when the returns came in, by no means all the courtiers or pensioners were defeated. The confusion among the ministers was comparatively unimportant. Even though Pepys discovered it was a time when pretensions based on a Court dependence met with little advantage, many of the pensioners had an impregnable interest in their boroughs.[1] Cornwall again returned a substantial Court majority, not because its small boroughs were in the possession or gift of the Court and held by carpet-baggers, but as an accurate reflection of the traditional loyalty of the Cornish gentry who represented them. Political conditions in some parts of the country were such that they were relatively unaffected by the excitement caused by the Plot. In County Durham the Papists, a fairly large minority, were alleged to have been released from custody by the sheriff on condition that they voted against the Vane interest and for the Court candidates.[2] This should be compared with the attitude of the freeholders in Hertfordshire who, on seeing that one of their candidates was being supported by the Papists, abandoned him, put up an alternative, and elected him instead.[3] Cambridge town elected two officials, the Master of the Ordnance and LordAlington who, as Major-General of the forces raised the previous year, might have been expected to be unpopular. The dissenting interest in the town, however, despite the asset of a very strong candidate in Roger Pepys, who had represented the town in the last Parliament, was not sufficient to prevail against the influence of these two local magnates combined with the university interest.[4]

These elections were primarily a series of contests between

---

[1] Tanner, *Further Correspondence of Samuel Pepys*, 338.
[2] Dean and Chapter of Durham, Hunter MSS. 24. *CJ* ix. 576.
[3] Carte, 228, f. 134.   [4] Tanner, 39, ff. 171, 176.

such local interests. In contrast to the elections to the two later Exclusion parliaments they were not fought systematically on party lines, for such divisions did not as yet exist outside the two Houses of Parliament. Even among political opponents there was not always such bitter feeling. When Edward Seymour went down to the west to arrange his election he broke his journey at White Lackington,[1] the home of George Speke, who was to become perhaps the bitterest of all Whigs; such a visit would have been unthinkable to both men a few months later. Under these conditions the very considerable changes in representation which the elections produced were inevitable, and often of no particular political significance. In some places there had been no opportunity to gain election since 1661, and, baulked for so long, many individuals, groups, and family interests were determined to contest as many places as possible. In Wales, where family feuds and loyalties played an even larger part, often with extreme violence, there had never been so many contested elections.

There are few signs of systematic electoral organization on either side. On the Court side a few forceful lord-lieutenants were able to exert effective influence. The most successful was Lord Yarmouth, who procured the election of his son at Norwich, issued circular letters, and through his subordinates succeeded in the county election—only for his candidates to be unseated by the committee of elections.[2] In Oxfordshire there was a strong partnership of Lord Abingdon and Bishop Fell.[3] Opposition successes were mainly the result of favourable circumstances. Many members who had been eliminated from the Commons in 1661 were now able to return, since their past history and former parliamentarian and presbyterian sympathies were no longer a liability and disadvantage. Those who had opposed Danby in the last Parliament could exploit their record of hostility to the principles of Popery and arbitrary government with which he was

---

[1] *HMC, 15th Report*, vii (*Somerset*), 106.

[2] There is a copy of this letter in Mr. Ketton-Cremer's possession at Felbrigg Hall, Norfolk. An extract from it in *CSPD*, 1679/80, 59, is wrongly attributed to Secretary Williamson. On Norfolk politics at this time see my article, 'The First Whig Party in Norfolk', *Durham University Journal*, Dec. 1953.

[3] Bodleian, Clarendon MSS. 155, f. 39.

alleged to be associated. Often rumours were spread as to the unsoundness of opponents' religion. Thus Pepys found at Castle Rising that his prospects had been damaged by rumours that he was a crypto-Papist, although at Aldborough it was a courtier, the ingenious Reresby, who tried to 'smear' a rival in this way.[1]

No clear pattern can be expected, or discovered, in the borough elections. In most of them, and especially in the smaller ones and those with a limited franchise, everything depended on local conditions. The Berties, close relations and associates of Danby, found that their interest at Stamford had disappeared. The reason was not the fact of their unpopularity, but the decision of Lord Exeter, the virtual proprietor, to use his influence on behalf of others.[2] At Exeter the defeated candidate, the Recorder, claimed that his opponent was sympathetic to the dissenters, and that they and his other supporters had behaved riotously. Yet there were no principles at stake between the two interests, for the man who was denounced in these terms was in fact to vote against Exclusion.[3] As Lord High Steward of Oxford, Buckingham recommended the re-election of the former member, Broome Whorwood: 'hee has deserved soe well that I cannot beleeve you will thinke of putting anybody into his place.'[4] Characteristically, Buckingham at least did have second thoughts, and wrote again withdrawing this nomination and telling the city to elect one of their own number. This made no difference; Whorwood was returned and was also to sit as the city member in the two later Exclusion parliaments. Many of the changes were voluntary and agreed; at St. Germans the older generation retired to be replaced by younger members of the Eliot family. Others changed their constituencies. Montagu, finding that he had little chance of success at Northampton, accepted an invitation to stand in Huntingdonshire, where his family had a great deal of influence. His friend, William Harbord, who had played the leading part in managing the betrayal of Danby, was desperately anxious to

[1] HMC, *Various*, ii. 394–5. The rival, Sir Godfrey Copley, was later to vote for Exclusion.

[2] HMC, *13th Report*, vi (*Fitzherbert*), 13.

[3] HMC, *Montagu of Beaulieu*, 174.

[4] Lady Burghclere, *George Villiers, Second Duke of Buckingham* (1903), 365–6.

secure re-election and so to gain the protection of membership. As a result of his efforts he found himself returned for two boroughs—Thetford and Camelford.

Some Oppositioners

The Opposition did succeed in winning some clear-cut and spectacular victories in the counties and the larger boroughs which had a wider franchise. The election in the City of London was particularly important, many looking to it for a lead to the rest of the country. Here the Opposition won a resounding success. Only one of the former members, all supporters of the Opposition, was seeking re-election. The Court realized that it was out of the question to think of gaining all four places, but put forward one strong candidate, Sir Joseph Sheldon, an alderman, a rich merchant, and brother to the late Archbishop of Canterbury, and it was hoped that he would defeat and exclude the most obnoxious of the Opposition candidates, Sir Thomas Player. But he was unable even to challenge a poll and had to desist so as to prevent the revelation of the pitiful weakness of his support. Even more striking was the triumph of Sir William Waller, the priest-hunter, at Westminster, where the large electorate was already noted for its turbulence and independence. Apparently he had made few preparations, which may have been the result of his financial embarrassments, so that at first few appeared for him. It was reported that in a day from being no bigger than a man's hand his interest soon covered the heavens, a convincing demonstration of the popular demand for the most rigorous prosecution of the Plot.[1]

Many of the Opposition victories in the county elections were an indication that they possessed more popular support than their rivals. Lord Bruce complained that the Russells failed to honour a previous agreement to share the representation of Bedfordshire.[2] They certainly did fail to give him their support, but the real reason for his defeat was the belief of the electors that in the last sessions he had given his vote consistently for the Court, and that his father did not give sufficient credit to the Plot. In Surrey,

---

[1] *HMC, 13th Report*, vi (*Fitzherbert*), 13. A public subscription was later raised to clear off Waller's debts so as to enable him to continue his magisterial and political activities.   [2] Ailesbury, *Memoirs* (1890), 33.

despite the fact that he retained a considerable personal interest, Lord Longford lost a heated and expensive election to two supporters of the Opposition—Arthur Onslow and George Evelyn. The former came from an old Roundhead family with a great parliamentary future before it, but the latter had not at first intended to stand. He had actually been invited to stand by a section of the gentry and freeholders who were determined to prevent Longford's election because he was a prominent courtier.[1]

The number of contested county elections in 1679 was an indication of the intense passions aroused and the violence of partisan feeling. In the past county meetings had often been held, at which candidates were selected in advance to whom the gentry then pledged their united interest and support. As a means of sharing the representation between rival interests this procedure had obvious merits. It obviated the necessity for a poll, it forestalled riots, violence, fraud, and lasting bitterness, and it made election to Parliament very much less expensive. But in 1679 good feelings and unanimity were not often to be found. The competition for vacancies was too intense, animosities were increased by becoming political as well as personal, and many were not prepared to accept a decision of the gentry as final, but resolved to defy them and to challenge a poll.

This is what happened in Leicestershire.[2] A preliminary meeting was held for the purpose of fixing on candidates 'to unite in the Election, that so trouble and charge might be prevented'. This, it might seem, had been achieved when it was decided to nominate two strong candidates in Lord Roos, son of the Earl of Rutland, the greatest proprietor in the county and an adherent of the Court, and Lord Sherrard who was inclined to the Opposition. But their appearance on the day of the election, with a majority of the gentry and clergy behind them, did not prevent a contest. A poll was challenged by Sir John Hartop, who as both stepson and son-in-law of Major-General Fleetwood, was rightly regarded as a sympathizer with the dissenters. Allegedly he had no support from the gentry, but he was backed by a substantial body of the

---

[1] HMC, Ormonde, N.S., iv. 317, 341. HMC, 14th Report, ix (Round), 485.
[2] PRO, State Papers, 29/411, f. 120. CJ ix. 597.

freeholders in belligerent mood. The two lords claimed that they behaved in a riotous and insubordinate manner, and that in any case Hartop was at the foot of the poll. Nevertheless, he petitioned against Roos's return, the committee ordered a new election between the two, and in this second contest Hartop was declared elected. He was also to represent the county in the two following Exclusion parliaments.

As might be expected, because of its size and population, an attempt was made in Yorkshire to prevent the trouble, uncertainty, and expense of a poll. Here, again, unanimity was lacking, and the hopes of the Court party were frustrated, not by a revolt of those who had not been included in the arrangement, but by the intrigues which went on among those who had convened the meeting. The principal gentry were summoned to the 'George' at York 'for the purpose of choosing fit members'. Some of those invited were also requested to forbear using their influence in boroughs where they had an interest until afterwards. The meeting itself was preceded by intense bargaining and intrigue, and the issue was settled beforehand by the construction of an impregnable interest. The leading contestant with the most favourable chances of success was Lord Fairfax, whose support was sought by each faction in turn. Among those who applied to him was Danby, who as a Yorkshireman was anxious to secure the return of his son, Latimer, for the county in order to bolster up his prestige. Danby's agent, Sir Henry Goodricke, wrote to Fairfax: 'I know t'would be a testimony of your kindness so well employed, that it would be a great endearment of our whole country to my Lord Treasurer, who has a most particular esteem for your Lordship and an earnest desire to have his son your partner.'[1] He promised Fairfax personal support, and held out the bait of a borough seat for one of Fairfax's relations, but it was most doubtful if these promises could be fulfilled. Association with Danby would not in the circumstances be much of an asset. Instead, Fairfax preferred, after some hesitation, to join his interest with that of the second candidate, Lord Clifford, son of the Earl of Burlington. The whole series of negotiations shows how personal

[1] Stowe MSS. 746, f. 7.

and indefinite were the politics of these elections. Fairfax was slow to join with Clifford, although they were both to vote for Exclusion and to campaign together against the Tories and the Court interest in the two next elections. Moreover, when Fairfax went up to London for the session he was greeted by the King with extreme cordiality, in an obvious attempt to secure his support at Westminster.[1]

Once Clifford and Fairfax had agreed to join their interests, all further bargaining, and the meeting of the gentry itself, became superfluous. The third contestant, Sir John Kaye, who had the reputation of a courtier and was later to stand as a Tory, was forced to desist. The convenors of the meeting announced that he had generously decided to retire in order to avoid a contest. They tried to compensate him by finding him a seat elsewhere, but when they wrote to John Wentworth asking him to reserve one of the places at Aldborough their request was disregarded.

The Buckinghamshire election also shows the lack of systematic pattern and organization in these elections. Lord Wharton's correspondence shows how haphazard were the steps which led to such an apparently clear-cut and decisive victory for the Opposition as the return of his son, Thomas, with John Hampden as partner.[2] Although the two families were related, and had for long been close political associates, there was no prior agreement that they should combine their interests to contest the county election. Independently both Lord Wharton and Hampden approached the Lord Lieutenant, Lord Bridgwater, suggesting that he should nominate his son and promising him their support, obviously in the hope of gaining reciprocal support for their own interest. Bridgwater did not in fact intend to press the candidature of his son, but in recognition of the respect which they alone of intending contestants had shown him, he promised Wharton and Hampden his conditional support. The fact that they were both avowed opponents of the Court does not seem to have been regarded as important. With this promise Wharton and Hampden

---

[1] HMC, Various, ii. 393. Bodleian, Fairfax MSS. 33, f. 109.
[2] Carte, 79, ff. 168–9, 171, 173, 175–6. See also J. Carswell, The Old Cause (1954), 53–54.

began actively to prepare for the election, the latter writing to all his friends and telling Sir Thomas Lee, the member for Aylesbury, to meet him when he came down to the county.

Nevertheless, when on 31 January Lord Wharton wrote to his son, who in political if not in any other matters seems to have obeyed parental instructions, the situation was still very uncertain. Hampden's family, who were all along the less resolute, doubted the chances of success. In this, as in other Buckinghamshire county elections, everything depended on the place of the poll. If it was at Aylesbury, an Opposition stronghold and close to the Wharton and Hampden estates, success could be expected, but for that very reason it was likely that the sheriff would transfer it to the town of Buckingham, which is at the northern end of the county and was known to be favourable to the Court interest. All that Wharton could suggest was to offer the under-sheriff a bribe of 20 guineas. Should this be unsuccessful, and if Hampden decided not to attempt the county election, it would be useless to stand alone. In those circumstances Thomas Wharton would have to make a strategic retreat. His former place at Wendover would be needed for Hampden, but a seat at Malmesbury was being held ready for him in case of need. With another at Westbury it was regarded as a refuge for unsuccessful members or friends of the Wharton family.

In fact Hampden succeeded in getting hold of the writ for the election, and found that the under-sheriff would serve him. This upset the calculations of the Court interest. Danby had intended to put forward his son, Dumblane, but now that conditions would be unfavourable it was he, and not Wharton, who had to retreat to a safe borough, in his case Corfe. To ensure success the Wharton and Hampden families began systematically to enlist all the influence and interest at their disposal. Lord Wharton assured his son of the support of many of the leading men of the county. He wrote to some of the borough members in the county, and persuaded his friends and legal connexions in London to write down in support of his son's interest. The latter was to inquire whether Lord Lovelace had any influence in the shire: if he had then he was to be canvassed. An approach was made to the Duke of Buckingham, who wrote promising his support: 'I thank you with all my heart for giving me this occasion of showing my kindness both to you and young Mr Hampden, for whom (though I have not the Honour to be acquainted with him) I have a very great esteem upon the report I hear of his ingenuity and worth.'[1] He undertook to be present at the day and place of election. The result of all these preparations was an easy victory. Hampden and Wharton were returned, and for the latter there now began the long connexion with the county seat, first as member until he was called to the Lords, and then as the great Whig magnate and parliamentary manager.

A last example of this lack of systematic organization, and the dependence upon purely local factors, of these elections can be seen in the correspondence of John Swinfen, another close associate of the Hampden family.[2] In the Cavalier Parliament he had for long been prominent as an opponent of the Court and a champion of the dissenters. The difficulties which he now encountered in securing re-election at Tamworth were not the result of unpopular religious or political opinions but those of managing a greedy electorate from a distance. Moreover, the agent whom he employed was a clergyman, and his partner was Thomas Thynne who, not to be confused with his namesake and relation 'Tom of Ten Thousand', had recently gone over to the Court and was to earn a peerage by his strenuous efforts against Exclusion. Yet he preferred to join his interest with that of Swinfen, the reputed 'Presbyterian', rather than with an apparently much more desirable colleague, Sir Andrew Hackett, the son of the late Bishop of Lichfield. Money was the argument which convinced the voters. At the beginning Swinfen's agent feared defeat, 'many having complained that they could not drink on your account'. But when, as a result of intense canvassing, a joint account at the public houses, and by securing the influence of the local gentry, a majority was assured in the corporation, election was certain. It was not necessary to contend, as had been suggested, that the franchise lay in the inhabitants at large rather than in the restricted members of the corporation. This would have been a last resort.

[1] Carte, 79, f. 179.　　　　[2] Addl. 29910, ff. 84–85, 86, 90–91, 99.

It was likely that in view of his reputation the committee of
elections would have favoured Swinfen, as it did other Whigs,
but this course would have involved not only the expense of the
petition but also the treating of a large number of townsmen both
in this election and on all future occasions.

II

The lack of political definition, which contributed to the un-
systematic character of the elections, made it extremely difficult
accurately to assess the results. Contemporary estimates varied
considerably. At first some courtiers believed that the new House
would not be as bad as they had feared, but with the succession of
unfavourable returns they became more despondent than the
facts warranted. Immediately afterwards Barrillon wrote that
the Court would not have more than thirty or forty votes in the
Commons. This, a gross underestimate, has misled many historians.[1] It was true that, as the elections had been held while the
excitement caused by the Plot was at its height, there had been a
considerable slaughter of suspected or known pensioners. It would
be hazardous to attempt to evaluate the results, for many of the
new members were obscure men, a high proportion of whom
were to abstain from voting in the Exclusion Bill division, and
so cannot be identified on that basis as Whigs or courtiers. For-
tunately, we have a contemporary, detailed, estimate of the very
highest authority, since it was compiled by Shaftesbury himself.
He drew up a list of the new House, placing marks against the
names of all but a few, indicating their known or probable
political opinions. That he was able to do so, and with a high
degree of accuracy, was a tribute to his comprehensive knowledge
of the country and the gentry, on which as Burnet said his power
depended. Shaftesbury found that he had a commanding majority,
composed almost equally of old and new members. All his
principal lieutenants had been re-elected. But the Court faction had
not by any means been annihilated. It was still a substantial, and

[1] Barrillon, 6 Mar. 1679. Ranke, for instance, in his *History of England* (1875),
iv. 72–73, without giving a source, says not more than 25 or 30.

potentially influential, minority, and a number of royal officials remained to lead it, if no longer to control the whole House.[1]

Yet this Court minority was for the first few weeks of the session entirely negligible. The belief that it had been annihilated appeared to be borne out by its initial ineffectiveness. This was the result of the tactical superiority of the Opposition together with the favourable ground on which they chose to fight the Court. In a House of which many members were ill-informed, undecided, and uncommitted, the resolute and boldly aggressive policy and tactics of the Opposition enabled it to dominate the proceedings. Its leaders were careful to preserve continuity with the work of the old Parliament in the investigation of the Plot, and they were given a great advantage from the very start of the session by the dispute over the appointment of the Speaker with which it began.

The refusal on 7 March to accept Edward Seymour once again as Speaker was in its effects a major blunder, but in the circumstances Danby could not allow a free choice. More than ever he needed someone in the Speaker's chair on whose support he could absolutely depend. The powers of the chair were very considerable; members of the Opposition had in the past complained that they were oppressive. The Speaker could influence proceedings by his choice of motions and of members wishing to speak in debates. With a potentially unruly House it was essential that he should be prepared to obey royal orders of adjournment or prorogation promptly and without question. Finally, it was on the Speaker that the King, unofficially as well as officially, depended for knowledge of what happened in the Commons. A man of almost unsurpassed arrogance, Seymour, while never at any time a member of the Opposition factions, had quarrelled with the Lord Treasurer during the last few days of the Cavalier Parliament. As a personal enemy he would be outstandingly dangerous because of his ability and experience, and also because of the very high view which he had of the position of Speaker, and the arbitrary use which he had made in the past of his powers.

[1] J. R. Jones, 'Shaftesbury's Worthy Men', *Bulletin of the Institute of Historical Research*, xxx, Nov. 1957.

These he had employed in the service of the minister; now it was certain that they would be directed against him in the future.

The rejection of Seymour's nomination and the attempt to foist an alternative candidate, which the Court representatives characteristically bungled, insulted the new Commons, exciting and inflaming both old and new members at the very start of the session. Birch, a veteran Opposition spokesman, described it as 'an unlucky stumble at the threshold, before we get into the House', but in fact the incident was a godsend to the Opposition.[1] The dispute greatly increased animosity against Danby, making it more difficult for Court members to defend him. It gave Opposition leaders an ascendancy over the new House which they knew how to exploit.

The eventual choice of a compromise candidate, Serjeant Gregory, was in itself an advantage. The Opposition supported Seymour's case as another stick with which to beat Danby, but they had little in common. A few weeks later Seymour was one of the main opponents of Exclusion, and had he regained his position as Speaker his influence would have been thrown against the Opposition, as so often in the past. In contrast Gregory proved to be a mild and sympathetic Speaker, who allowed members much more latitude than the arrogant Seymour. Furthermore, the heated and vociferous reaction of the Commons on this occasion certainly deterred the King from attempting to exercise his prerogative to veto the choice of Speaker in the two later Exclusion parliaments, when the Commons elected the partisan Whig and exclusionist, William Williams.

Once the dispute was settled and Parliament reassembled, the first step taken by the Opposition leaders was to ensure that their new colleagues were instructed in knowledge of the Plot. By this means they would be encouraged, and the House enabled, to renew the proceedings and measures which had been in progress at the time of the prorogation, a course which had been followed at the start of the Long Parliament in 1640. The *Journals* of the last session were inspected and in their speeches members recapitulated the accusations which had been made. As Sir John Knight ex-

[1] Harleian MSS. 6274. Grey, vi. 407. Bodleian, Firth MSS. c. 2, ff. 14–15.

plained; 'You see, by Coleman's letters, that the King and Parliament have been betrayed for these seven years last past, and I would have them reviewed again.' Sir Thomas Lee added, with surely an underestimate of the publicity which all the details of the Plot had received: 'Gentlemen that were not here then, and who live in the country, will scarcely believe what they will find.'[1] A committee of secrecy was appointed with very wide terms of reference to pursue the Plot more effectively, and in fact to facilitate its exploitation for partisan purposes. As the session advanced its powers were increased, and on occasion it was to use them with extreme harshness.[2] The members were carefully chosen. Vaughan, Titus, Sacheverel, Capel, Ellis, Maynard, Powle, and Treby were all long-standing and prominent leaders of the Opposition. Two new members, Sir Thomas Player and John Trenchard, were soon to give evidence of their extreme Whig views. The recent dispute earned Seymour, by now incensed against Danby, his place. Equally bitter at being displaced was Winnington, the former Solicitor-General who had been dismissed for voting against the Court. The last member, Meres, had actually been the Court candidate for the office of Speaker during the dispute, but as an experienced turn-coat and opportunist he had already begun to swim with the tide. The activities of a committee with this composition were bound to be favourable to the Whigs, and in fact its reports were used carefully and with skill to influence proceedings in the House. The two crucial debates of 11 and 21 May were both to be preceded by reports concerning the papers which the committee held connected with the Duke of York.

At the beginning of the session the Duke was hardly mentioned, the House concentrating its attention and attacks on Danby and the five Papist peers who had been arrested on suspicion of being implicated in the Plot. As long as attention was confined to these innocuous subjects the House remained united, or at least there was no real sign of dissension. After he had been given a pension and promotion in the peerage, as well as his pardon, virtually no one was willing or bold enough to defend Danby. On this

[1] Grey, vii. 5–6.   [2] CJ ix. 571.

occasion his cupidity had overcome his political judgement. All sections, from extreme Whigs to those courtiers whom he had slighted or neglected, joined in the attacks upon him. The Commons showed a savage determination to ruin the fallen minister, to strip him of all his property, and many of the more extreme were genuinely intent on his execution, not only as a form of vengeance but as a deterrent to future ministerial wrong-doing. But there was a significant difference in the basis of the attacks made upon him by the various sections. Sir Robert Howard, a personal enemy, described Danby as a bad steward: on 22 March he had moved for an address to the King promising that if the 'evil council' were removed the Commons would join their interest with his. The implication was that everything would flourish again once Danby was dismissed. Sacheverel's attack in the same debate was based on very different reasoning. His hostility was constitutional and political rather than personal; he said: 'I am not of opinion that to remove ministers from the King will better our condition unless those maxims of state they govern by be removed. Whoever comes in to be a minister follows the same maxims of state.'[1] This speech implied that fundamental and far-reaching constitutional and political changes were necessary. Few were bold enough openly to disagree. Barrillon believed that the introduction of new legislative pro-posals was the result of pressure on the old leaders by the new, rasher, and more extreme members, but the parliamentary de-bates do not bear out this contention. Rather there was a sur-prisingly wide agreement and absence of dissent, that the mere removal of Danby was by itself insufficient security, and that it must be supplemented by legislation.[2]

In the first place the Opposition used their ascendancy to attack Danby's associates. Most of his former followers lay low, and allowed the Opposition to initiate a wide inquiry into the methods by which he had held power for so long. When an address was voted against Lauderdale only a single official, a relation and a fellow Scot, dared to defend him.[3] In order to

[1] Grey, vii. 50–52. [2] Barrillon, 20 Apr.
[3] Grey, vii. 188–99, 6 May.

prevent a repetition of Danby's management of Parliament by bribery and systematic prorogations, demands were made that in future all grants of supply should be strictly appropriated. Church reform was all the more essential because of the help which the bishops had given, and were still ready to give, to the minister. The army, in view of Montagu's disclosures, was regarded as the instrument for the establishment of an intended arbitrary government, such as had already been introduced by that means in Scotland. To disband it was not enough; precautions must be taken to ensure that another should never be raised, and the royal Guards were to be replaced by militia detachments.

The most vital safeguard for the liberties of the nation was, of course, Parliament, but it was essential to ensure that its meetings should be regular, and not at the discretion of the King or his ministers. This was to be achieved by a bill which was introduced on 26 March for the regulation of elections, which went very much farther than its title suggests and would have produced considerable constitutional changes.[1] It contained provisions against writs for payment of wages to members, a practice by this time almost obsolete, but one which could be used as a threat to ensure re-election as the price of withdrawal of the demand. An attempt was to be made to suppress the frauds of returning officers, at this time by far the most common form of electoral offence. The first of the more radical clauses affected the franchise. In the shires this was to be vested in householders and inhabitants having £200 in fee, clear of debt. This recalled the reform of the franchise in the Instrument of Government, and its importance need hardly be stressed. The electorate would be much smaller but more independent. Corruption would be more difficult, and the cost of elections would be reduced. The borough franchise in most cases was to be vested in those inhabitants who had been resident for a year, were rated for poor relief, and paid scot and lot. The remaining provisions were even more far reaching. Candidates convicted of treating or bribery were to be declared incapable of election to that Parliament. The place concerned was to lose its

[1] The Bill for Regulating Abuses in Elections of Members (1679). Copy in Bodleian, Godwyn 1247.

right of representation, which was to be transferred at the discretion of Parliament either to the county at large or to another borough within its borders. This would have gone far to perpetuating Whig ascendancy in the Commons. The other provisions would have prevented the packing of boroughs either by the Crown or by the local Tory gentry, but the condemnation of boroughs, and the choice of places to receive their right of election, would have been at the judgement of the House and the committee of elections, which was already being used with strictly partisan justice to unseat courtiers and to declare Whigs returned. Most important of all there was never again to be another 'standing' Parliament which, like the Cavalier, could form the basis of ministerial management on the grand scale. The bill declared: 'no Parliament shall hereafter have Continuance in any manner, by Prorogation, or Adjournment, or Session . . . for above the space of two years . . . but at the end of the said two years shall be ipso facto dissolved.' It was a mark of the domination of the Commons by the Opposition that these important proposals should have received a second reading on 5 April without the Court being able to challenge them seriously either in debate or in a division.[1]

The obvious effect of these provisions, and the other proposals put forward during the first weeks of the session, would have been to give Parliament a greatly increased and possibly predominant share in the government of the country. At the same time it would have been difficult for the Crown to rally opinion against them and to appeal directly to the nation, as was to happen over Exclusion. These might be proposals for changes in the constitution, but it was plausible for the Whigs to claim that they were intended to preserve the liberties of the people against subversion. Yet, with the exception of the Habeas Corpus Amendment Act, all these proposals proved abortive. These various expedients, although excellent in themselves, were all regarded by the Whigs as palliatives, as of no more than secondary importance. By themselves they were entirely inadequate to provide security for the liberties and religion of the nation; this, it was thought, could be

---

[1] *CJ* ix. 585. There is no report of a debate on this matter in Grey.

achieved only through the exclusion of the Duke of York from the succession. Just as Danby's dismissal was regarded as totally insufficient unless his maxims of state were abandoned as well, so the temporary exile of the Duke of York was entirely worthless.

The Whig leaders could not have avoided the fundamental question of James's position as heir to the throne and his apparent connexion with the Plot, even had they wished to do so. The negotiations they had engaged in with him were futile; to have come to any agreement would have meant political suicide. The problem had already been debated in the previous Parliament, and Sacheverel, with characteristic if premature boldness, had even then raised the question of the succession. The arguments contained in the memorandum which Shaftesbury drew up early in 1679 show why he decided to concentrate on Exclusion.[1] He saw James as the active agent of arbitrary government during his brother's lifetime. The assertion that a definite design existed was one which most members would have accepted. Shaftesbury's animus against Danby was not merely that of a rival kept from power for so long, but also the result of a genuine belief that Danby had attempted to make the King absolute, and had only just failed to do so. James's participation in such a design was easily explained—he would be the future beneficiary. As a Papist he must establish his brother as an absolute King if he was himself to succeed peaceably without bloodshed and confusion. In all this his brother was, Shaftesbury remarked, extraordinarily complaisant and acquiescent. Hence it was not surprising that even though James had been sent into temporary exile he retained his influence at Court, and this could be expected to increase when he eventually returned.

The introduction of the bill to exclude James from the succession was therefore the logical outcome of his character, which was known to be arbitrary, arrogant, and unforgiving, his religion, and his alleged connexion with the Plot. On 27 April a debate, started with a consideration of how effectually to preserve the King from the Papists, was turned into a concerted onslaught

[1] Shaftesbury Papers, VI A, 334, 'State of the Kingdom', 6 Mar. 1678-9. In the handwriting of Thomas Stringer, one of his household.

on the Duke.[1] Even an apparently attractive proposal for the expulsion of all Papists from London was ignored, although it was moved by a member of the Opposition. For the first time James was openly and generally attacked without reserve or respect for his birth, position, or past services. Bennett, who had become prominent in the last weeks of the Cavalier Parliament as a spokesman even more extreme than Sacheverel, declared that the Plot could not have been carried on without his approbation, and quoted Coleman's letters as proof. Some members talked ominously of securing a Protestant succession. By now even the project of an Act of Association, on the model of the one passed at the time of the murder plots against Elizabeth, was regarded as a mere palliative.

The debate showed that to many members Exclusion, and nothing else, was the sole acceptable and valid security. But although the trend of the debate was towards such a measure the vote of the House was not explicit. It ran: 'that the Duke of Yorke's being a papist, and the hopes of his coming such to the Crown, has given the greatest Countenance and Encouragement to the present Conspiracies and Designs of the Papists against the King and the Protestant Religion.'[2] This was cleverly phrased. The Duke was not stated to be guilty. The courtiers were not given an opportunity to oppose the motion, but the implication could be developed later. The vote passed unanimously. Nevertheless, it was the prelude to Exclusion, and to the final and irrevocable division of the House. Later the same day the fatal vote passed, ordering the committee of secrecy to prepare and draw up 'an Abstract of such matters as concern the Duke of York, relating to the Plot, contained in such papers and writings as they have in their custody'. This was as far as the demoralized Court members could be driven. Their failure to oppose this vote exposed their impotence; this demonstration of the superiority of their opponents must have had some effect on waverers and the uncommitted. But they were bound to resist any further advance towards Exclusion, such as this vote implied. Otherwise

[1] Grey, vii. 137–52. His reports accord very closely with the version in Harleian MSS. 4053. [2] *CJ* ix. 605.

they would become accomplices in what they believed would be illegal, a defiance of divine law and subversive of the monarchy and the constitution.

III

By the time the committee reported, on 11 May, the House of Commons had divided into two factions between whom compromise and accommodation were impossible. At last a revived and reorganized Court leadership began to challenge Opposition domination over the Commons. These leaders were new recruits for the Court interest, for at the end of April a group of the most eloquent and able members of the Opposition defected.[1] Their secession weakened the Opposition, but not decisively or for long, since some of these men had already begun to lose their influence because of their moderation and caution. But their adherence greatly strengthened the Court interest which had been badly led up to this time, indeed hardly led at all. Previously, the Court had been forced on to the defensive by the aggressive and confident Opposition. Now at the same time it gained new leaders, and was provided with a clear, reasoned line of policy as a practicable and positive alternative to Exclusion.

For this change in the fortunes of the Court interest Charles was himself responsible. Previously he had accepted Danby's advice with results that had been disastrous, even if inevitably so. The prorogation of the Cavalier Parliament had been enforced by loss of control over its proceedings, but the relief which it had brought had been temporary. The crisis had been postponed, but at the price of its intensification. The dissolution had turned out to be an unmitigated catastrophe because the results of the elections had not been foreseen. The new House of Commons had been provoked at the very outset by the dispute over the Speaker. The Court policy had been one of both obstinacy and weakness, concessions had eventually to be made, 'yet the thanks are lost for want of some expedition or frankness in the manner of

---

[1] The most able and prominent among them were Sir Thomas Clarges, Sir Henry Capel, Lord Cavendish, William Harbord, and Henry Powle.

granting'. It was out of Danby's power to save his position, but where he can be condemned for lack of statesmanship is in his selfishness in not seeing that his retention of power and his policy were involving the Crown in his own ruin. The final, and in the circumstances quite gratuitous, provocation was the generous treatment which he received when he resigned his office. The pardon which he was given was by itself enough to rouse the indignation of his political and personal enemies. But to reward with a pension and promotion in the peerage the man whom the Commons were impeaching, and who was alleged to have embezzled the King's money on a large scale, was insulting and dangerous. It threatened to associate the King in the hatred and detestation felt by almost all for the dismissed minister.

After his fall Danby continued to offer the King advice from the Tower, quite apart from pleading his own case. It has been noted how well informed he was despite his imprisonment, but the policy which he was advocating remained unrealistic.[1] Danby urged the King to take a strong line. During the summer he advised that the prosecution of the Plot should be taken out of the hands of Parliament, that a new session should be called outside London, and (surprisingly in view of what had happened in 1642) that Charles should also leave the capital. His other suggestions would have led to an immediate head-on collision with the Whigs under the most unfavourable circumstances, and possibly to civil war. To have secured the Tower (and it would have been difficult to have done it in secret) would have set the City in an uproar. To have attempted to secure the arms of all the old parliamentarians and to have renewed the persecution of the dissenters, would have produced tumults in every town in the country. There were already rumours of coming military action against the City, of mass arrests of Whig leaders, and these were prolonging the excitement originally caused by Oates's revelations. Ominously the danger was now thought to come as much from the Court as from the Papists, and had Danby's advice been followed popular hysteria, especially in London, would once again have reached fever pitch.

[1] Addl. 28042, f. 19. Pollock, *The Popish Plot*, 390–1.

In contrast the policy which Charles followed, and for which he was in the main personally responsible, was based not on coercion and repression, but on conciliation and flexibility. During the next few months, more than at any other time in his life, he was to show himself a master of 'king-craft' or, put less fancifully, an able and totally unscrupulous politician. His intention was not to strike at, or destroy, the Opposition, but to disarm its leaders of their best arguments, to sow dissension between them and their rank and file. Charles took measures to ease the tension, not in order to produce a permanent settlement but so as to strip Shaftesbury of his assets of national excitement and political ferment.

There can hardly be a bigger contrast than that between the measures which Charles took to stave off disaster and the policy which had led his father to ruin. Charles I had at the very start surrendered vital prerogative powers, and by doing so had crippled himself in the struggle against Pym. His son was determined never to concede any vital power even temporarily, but he was ready to make concessions in non-essentials, whereas his father had had to be coerced and had made them so grudgingly as to provoke suspicions of bad faith. Charles I had alienated many by his stiff pride and obstinacy; his son was on the surface all things to all men. Later historians may be excused for having underestimated him, since most contemporaries were also deceived by his easy-going good nature and inveterate indolence. Among them was Shaftesbury. He regarded the King without hostility, at least in 1679, but with some contempt. Charles, he considered with a cutting qualification, had he 'been so happy as to have been born a Private Gentleman had passed for a man of good parts, excellent breeding and well natured'. But as a King he was found wanting, and dismissed as the puppet of others. Shaftesbury believed that power had fallen into the hands of a most unholy trinity— 'His Brother, his Minister and his Mistress play the game into one another's hands, and perfectly govern all matters.'[1] No one would rely on his word; his affairs were in the last extremity for want of money.

[1] Shaftesbury Papers, VI A, 334.

Shaftesbury can be excused for this harsh and mistaken judgement. In his own experience, an education in politics such as no
other politician even of that time possessed, the King had almost
always been weak. He had easily been induced to discard Clarendon, to whom he owed so much. The Declarations of Indulgence
had been withdrawn, the ministers and the policy of the Cabal
abandoned with the exception of Lauderdale. Danby had been
accepted and supported for so long because he took on his own
shoulders the wearisome work of administration and dealing with
the troublesome Parliament. Charles had invariably given way
to serious pressure; apparently he had never possessed principles,
still less shown himself ready to exert himself to defend them.
There could be no better proof of his indulgence and lack of
principle than the fact that he had for so long tolerated Buckingham.

In reaction to the classical—'Whig'—view, some more recent
historians have gone to the other extreme, describing Charles
as the personification of king-craft, a master of political tactics
who skilfully played Shaftesbury and his supporters before finally
destroying them. There can be no doubt that, in contrast to his
father and brother, Charles was extremely intelligent and clever.
But there was a limit to what cleverness could achieve during the
Exclusion crisis. Although the King retained his prerogative
powers he could not use them during the summer of 1679 against
those whom he was now increasingly regarding as the enemies of
the Crown as well as of his brother and the ministers. He possessed
other, and eventually decisive, advantages, the protection of the
Guards, the fund of old Cavalier loyalty which although overlaid
by fear of Popery was bound to revive, and the unswerving
support of the Church. Yet he was still obliged to play for time,
and in order to do so he had to make concessions even if in bad
faith. With the time which he gained Charles was able to rally
support against Exclusion, and he was the real founder of the
Tory party. Later in 1679–80 he succeeded in ruling for sixteen
months without calling Parliament, and in ejecting the Whigs
from all positions of influence in the central and local administration. Nevertheless, he was still checked by Shaftesbury, and his

policy was only partially successful in lessening tension. Despite all the advantages which the King enjoyed, Shaftesbury was able to defy him and to continue to do so until foreign intervention altered the balance of power. The Whigs were not to be defeated until the King chose to become a French dependent in preference to reigning as the servant of the most astute of his subjects.

The King's first move in his bid to wrest the initiative from the Whigs came with the announcement on 21 April of the reform and reconstitution of the Privy Council. Most historical attention has been concentrated on its constitutional implications and on the problem of the authorship of this scheme of reform. To contemporaries it was the changes of membership that were surprising and important. Sir William Temple, who claimed that the idea had originated with him, believed that it would provide a permanent solution to the problems of government.[1] As a means of reconciliation it included members both of the Court and of the Opposition. This was intended, in the immediate future, to restore confidence in the King; more permanently, it was intended to put an end to the monopoly of the King's council and favour either by a single minister, or by a cabal or small coterie. The wealth of the councillors was to redress the balance of economic forces; since the time of Harrington a theory of political analysis had held that the preponderance of Parliament, and especially of the Commons, was the result of its preponderant share of the nation's wealth. The defects of the scheme are obvious. Thirty were too many effectively to discuss business, and quite apart from other considerations made the development of some inner ring of councillors inevitable. Inclusion of politicians of differing views did not put an end to their dissensions. The councillors were neither willing nor able to supply from their estates or capital enough money to enable the King to carry on the government.

In practice the new Privy Council was never given a chance to succeed. Whatever Temple's original intentions the King regarded it as a political instrument to be used in his struggle

[1] Sir W. Temple, *Memoirs* (1714), 318–23.

against Shaftesbury and his party. Had the remodelled Privy Council been accepted as a permanent constitutional device it would have amounted to sharing political power between the King, his ministers, and independent politicians who derived their authority from their strength and position in Parliament. Charles was not willing to share effective power in this way with those whom he detested as being forced upon him. Moreover, Exclusion was totally unacceptable to him, and by the end of April Shaftesbury was moving to a complete acceptance of its necessity. If Exclusion did pass into law the power of the next king would certainly be diminished. In addition Shaftesbury and the Whigs would insist on supplementary laws in order to ensure that the act was effectively executed, so that Charles for the rest of his life would be reduced to the status of a figurehead, a doge of Venice. In his speech announcing the reform of the Council he had declared that he would always be guided by its advice, but in fact (as he was frank enough to tell Ailesbury) he distrusted many of its members and resolved not to take them into his confidence.[1]

The tactical advantages which Charles derived from the reform of the Privy Council were considerable. By the appointment of certain of its leaders he succeeded in causing dissension among the Opposition by feeding the suspicion of the rank and file, a long-established feeling, that many of their leaders were careerists or would abandon their principles as soon as they accepted office. The announcement received an extremely tepid welcome; the bonfires in the City had been ordered by the lord mayor.[2] In the Commons members were either disappointed or suspicious. Many were resentful that they had not themselves been included. Montagu, for example, whose ambitions were almost limitless, had expected to become a councillor, and was disgusted that his former colleagues had not insisted on his inclusion before they would accept themselves. From a man of his character this is surprisingly naïve. Those who had never any chance or hope of appointment were wary, remembering all those in the past who had attacked the Court in order to gain a higher price for their

[1] Ailesbury, *Memoirs*, 35.　　　　　[2] Barrillon, 4 May 1679.

silence.[1] Many had feared the 'infection' of their leaders even before the announcement was made. When their suspicions were confirmed they took action. On 1 May leave was granted for the introduction of a bill by which a writ was to be issued for a new election whenever any member was preferred to an office or place of profit by the King.

The new privy councillors were in a most invidious position. Not being in the inner ring of ministers they did not share the King's confidence or know what were his intentions. Their former colleagues in the Opposition treated them with something like contempt, especially when they had the thankless task of asking for supply to fit out a fleet.[2] Powle's performance was as embarrassed as it was halting and ineffective. He was at once attacked by Sacheverel and Garroway. The latter had already discounted the effects of the new Council, and affected to believe that there was still a danger of misappropriation. Powle had to intervene that he did not intend to 'argue for miscarriage, which has been great and intolerable . . . but it is not your duty to leave the Crown in this misfortune'. Upon this Whorwood charitably observed that Powle would have shared the opinion of those who refused supply had it not been for his appointment. Speeches from other councillors, that the alternatives were money or ruin, proved to be unavailing. The final speech, from Capel who argued that common safety demanded the provision of a fleet, was drowned in cries of 'No, no'.

This debate, on 14 May, made it clear that those who had accepted office had forfeited their former influence. To the belief that they had sold themselves to the King was added the fact that these new councillors and their associates, with the single exception of Russell, were now advocating a policy that was unacceptable to the other Opposition leaders. Although there is no direct evidence, it seems that there must have been a serious crisis in the Opposition leadership during the first days of May. The new

[1] Grey, vii. 197. Garroway on 6 May.
[2] Grey, vii. 265-78. Throughout the crisis most Whigs consistently ignored foreign affairs, and regarded all ministerial proposals for a Protestant foreign policy as a trap or diversion from Exclusion.

councillors and their friends included many of the most able and
staunch leaders of the old Opposition. Not all of them had been
moderates. William Harbord and Winnington, although the
latter had deserted the Court as recently as December, had proved
as extreme and intransigent as anyone. They, it is true, were merely
opportunists, who apparently believed that Exclusion was premature, and that to support it would antagonize the King and
make future preferment impossible. But most of the others, men
like Sir William Hickman and Sir Thomas Clarges, both friends
of Halifax, were actuated by higher motives. To them the
reform of the Council, and of course their own appointment,
were the first signs of a change of heart on the part of the
King.

Further evidence of the King's sincerity was forthcoming on
30 April when at last explicit and comprehensive alternatives
were put forward to bring about security for religion and the
liberties of the nation.[1] Hitherto the King had merely promised
safeguards: there had been no positive proposal which could be
canvassed in order to win over the uncommitted and all those
who felt that Exclusion was a rash and irrevocable step. On behalf
of the King the Lord Chancellor now offered very considerable
concessions which were to take effect in the reign of his successor.
The powers of a Papist king were to be limited and circumscribed.
He was to have no control over judicial and ecclesiastical appoint-
ments. Parliament was to continue in session, or was to reassemble,
on his accession. But there was the significant qualification that
these concessions were not to extend to 'alter the Descent of the
Crown in the right Line, nor to defeat the Succession'.

This alternative policy, of 'expedients' or 'limitations', was
apparently attractive to the new officers and councillors. There
is no evidence that it was particularly welcome to the old courtiers,
who were consistently to leave its discussion and recommendation
to the new leaders whom they now received from the Opposition.
It is clear that there must have been many who shared the views
of the Duke of York himself, who in exile believed that these
concessions were the prelude to his abandonment.[2] It is also

extremely doubtful, at this time as later, whether the King was sincere in these offers. Nevertheless, the new councillors made them the basis of their speeches on 11 May, when the Whigs moved explicitly for the exclusion of the Duke of York.[1] Powle followed the King's arguments very closely, advising caution and delay. He professed that he would be satisfied if an act should be brought in to secure Parliament and the continuance in office of place-holders, judges, and (curiously) bishops, after the death of the King. Capel argued for a Triennial Act, and warned the House of the consequences of Exclusion. This was the theme elaborated by other speakers, a promising tactic since so many especially of the new members were uncertain and uncommitted, and might be frightened more easily than persuaded. Hickman pointed out that Exclusion would entail a break with both Scotland and Ireland, and so bring about a state of perpetual war. A further danger was presented—that foreign princes would intervene in defence of the right of the legitimate successor. The argument was introduced, to be elaborated in the future as one of the chief Court arguments against Exclusion, that it would be tantamount to the establishment of a Commonwealth. This, too, might be expected to deter most members, as it is doubtful whether there was a single republican in the House.

The Opposition leaders, faced with the loss of many former colleagues, and afraid that they might lose their own influence, could not afford to accept any of these arguments and warnings. Caution and moderation at this stage might be misconstrued as hesitation and lack of confidence. In this debate of 11 May the most violent speeches came from the new members, as if there was competition in extremism to gain prominence and influence. A veteran, Sir John Knight, rather plaintively exclaimed 'something must be done, but I dare not venture to propose what'.[1] An old leader of the country Opposition proposed merely that James should not return from exile without the consent of Parliament. The hotter members had no hesitation in rejecting such a proposal as insufficient. Pilkington confidently and extravagantly

---

[1] Grey, vii. 237–60. Bennett and Paul Foley, two new members, were particularly violent. See also *HMC, Ormonde*, N.S., v. 95.

demanded that, on the contrary, James should return 'that
we may impeach him of High Treason'. Another member for
the City, Sir Thomas Player, then moved for 'a Bill for excluding the Duke of York by name, and all Papists whatsoever, from
the Crown of England'. After this even a proposal that all Papists
should be banished failed to divert the attention of members.
Arguments that Exclusion would entail bloodshed and civil war
were dismissed by Paul Foley, who declared with apparent
equanimity; 'do what you can, all may come to blood, but you
will secure the Protestant Religion by making the Duke incapable
of the Succession by Act of Parliament.'[1]

Nevertheless, this debate on Exclusion was not nearly so one-
sided as those earlier in the session. Speeches against Exclusion were
slightly the more numerous, and those made by the new councillors were more cogent and closely reasoned than those of the
Whigs. But although the Court faction now possessed both leaders
and arguments, the conclusion of the debate showed that it
was still insufficiently organized. The leaders decided to force a
division, those in favour of the bill having to go out of the chamber to be counted. There followed a dramatic scene in the gathering
gloom of a Sunday evening; as the House emptied the Court saw
by the light of candles that their own numbers were steadily
dwindling. Realizing the effects of an overwhelming defeat before
they were properly organized and prepared, the Court members
hastily rose from their places, refusing to be counted, and so
yielded the question without revealing the extent of their weakness.[2]

This was a grave error in tactics, to have attempted to challenge
the Whigs prematurely and apparently without due preparation.
Its effects on the timid, undecided, and calculating must have been
considerable, going far to destroy the new impression of confidence and strength which the Court speeches had revealed. But
these signs of a Court revival were not neglected by the remaining
leaders of the Whigs. They at once began to pack committees,

---

[1] Grey, vii. 238, 240–1, 256.
[2] Ibid. 260. Harleian MSS. 4053, ff. 34–35. Sunday sittings, a most unusual
practice, were a sign of the gravity of the crisis.

selecting only those on whom they could depend. Of the eight members who had spoken in favour of the introduction of the bill, six were appointed to the committee which was to draft its provisions. Five of the remaining seven members were known to be staunch Whigs, and there was reason to believe that the remaining two were wavering and might easily be persuaded.

IV

For the next two years Exclusion was to be the single dominating objective of the Whigs on which they were to concentrate all their energies. This meant that, when all their attempts to pass it into law had failed, they had nothing to show for Whig supremacy in three successive parliaments with the exception of the Habeas Corpus Amendment Act. This neglect of all other legislation was deliberate. To use it as a criticism of Whig statesmanship and political acumen is to misunderstand Whig method and purposes. This concentration on Exclusion was based on arguments which were irrefutable provided that Whig assumptions were accepted. Exclusion was not only necessary if religion and liberty were to be secure, it was the sole effective means by which that security could be obtained. If Exclusion could not be achieved, then all other legislation would be useless and dangerous, since if other expedients were accepted the nation might be lulled into an illusory sense of security.

The arguments for the exclusion of James from the succession were based on necessity, on the immediate political situation rather than on any profound or detailed political theory. By contrast with the later years of the crisis there was at first comparatively little in the way of pamphleteering justifications. The case against James was a simple one. He was believed to endanger religion and liberty for three reasons. The arguments were drawn first from knowledge of his character, then from his religion, and finally from the use which he could be expected to make of the royal powers should he ever become King.

Shaftesbury described James as a man 'heady, violent and bloody, who easily believes the rashest and worst of councills to be most sincere and hearty'. All those who had opposed or abused him, still more those who attempted to exclude him from the succession, could expect his inveterate hostility. James was known to have been the consistent advocate of severity and repression in the past, and his later conduct as the King's representative in Scotland was to confirm Whig suspicions as to the nature which his revenge would take. The first argument for Exclusion was therefore based on the principle of self-preservation. James had not always been so feared and hated. His services in the Dutch wars were still sometimes quoted in his defence, and he still had friends among a section of the dissenters. The main reason for his unpopularity, the arguments which were the most difficult to refute, were drawn from his religion. The conversion was in itself technically treasonable, his new faith was, of course, detested. Obviously the succession of a Papist, in the days when the principle of *cuius regio eius religio* was still the general rule on the Continent, must endanger the Protestant religion. Furthermore, as Shaftesbury said, Popery and arbitrary government were sisters going hand in hand, the two were necessarily connected.[1]

Of this there was direct and particular proof. Although James had disavowed Coleman few could believe that the correspondence with Louis XIV's confessor and other leading Papists abroad could have been carried on by a simple secretary without James's knowledge or connivance. But, even if there was no direct proof of his implication in the Plot against his brother, James was obviously the beneficiary. This argument had all the more force since few contemporaries believed that otherwise James would outlive his brother. But in addition to the Plot most people were convinced that there was also in existence and execution the 'design' to make the King absolute. James had been closely associated with Clifford, the Dutch war, and the Declaration of Indulgence, although these were not subjects on which Shaftesbury could safely enlarge. Later, James was said to have assisted

---

[1] Shaftesbury Papers, VI A, 334. The Whig suspicions that limitations would prove illusory and ineffective seemed to be confirmed when James was granted a dispensation, before he left for Scotland, by which he was excused the oaths (Barrillon, 25 Dec. 1679; *HMC, Ormonde*, N.S. iv. 569).

Danby in his efforts to introduce an arbitrary form of government. Shaftesbury concluded: 'His Interest and designs are to introduce a Military and arbitrary Government in his Brother's time; which can only secure a man of his Religion a quiet possession of his Beloved Crown.' This was a portent of what could be expected if James succeeded. No expedients or limitations would be effective once he became King and could use his prerogative powers against his enemies.

Exclusion was intended entirely as a means of defence against James. Most of those who voted for the second reading of the bill were not so much concerned with the question who was to succeed if it passed, as with the immediate and urgent necessity of securing themselves against James. For them the situation was still precarious. Should the Papist plotters succeed at last in assassinating the King, then their cause would triumph, and James as King would be quick to take vengeance on all who had opposed and affronted him. Although the policy of Exclusion has come to be associated with the proposals to put Monmouth on the throne, there is no real evidence that this was the intention of Shaftesbury and the major part of the Whigs when the bill was introduced in the Parliament of 1679. On the contrary, the clause in this first bill was explicit; the Crown was to go to the next in line of succession as if the Duke were dead, that is to his elder daughter. It must be added that, as Barrillon was quick to see, this was not a watertight guarantee of her right. The bill might be passed with this safeguarding clause, but once the Whigs were secure in power it could then be amended in favour of some other candidate. But if such were the intentions of the Whig leaders, the rank and file were kept in ignorance, and were far from supporting Monmouth's pretensions.[1] One report said that there was no member 'so mad as to design the Duke of Monmouth'. This was an exaggeration, since a few personal friends were already pushing his claims, but they possessed little credit or influence. Later, in 1679, after Monmouth's disgrace, a prominent and well-informed Whig could still express wonder at the movement in his favour. His comment shows that he believed Monmouth to be

[1] *HMC, Ormonde*, N.S., v. 95.

an instrument in the hands of others rather than a pretender in his own right.[1]

X The Whig leaders pressed Exclusion as the first step towards security. There was no alternative. The King's attitude made the project of a royal divorce impracticable, and a plan to prove the Queen's complicity in the Plot, or Godfrey's murder, was still less likely to succeed. But although all Whigs were satisfied that Exclusion was necessary, the generalities which they used to justify it did not convince everyone, even though the excitement caused by the original disclosures of the Plot had not subsided to any significant extent. It is hard to avoid the conclusion that Exclusion was rushed forward with insufficient preparation. This House of Commons, in contrast to the two which followed, contained many neutral or uncommitted members, who were not yet convinced that Exclusion must come, although they were equally suspicious of the indefinite promises made by the King.

The existence of this large group of undecided members, many of whom were in fact to abstain from voting on Exclusion, made any estimate of the opinions of the House uncertain and difficult. At the start of the session Shaftesbury had marked only a few as doubtful, on account of their obscurity, and had confidently classed the rest as opponents or supporters. This had been on the basis of their past record and sentiments towards Danby. But the fall of the minister and the introduction of Exclusion transformed the whole political situation, and as criteria these former tests were now no longer relevant, as the desertion of the new privy councillors showed. What mattered now was not the past but the present attitude of members towards the radical proposal of Exclusion.

When the second reading became due on 21 May the tactics which they employed showed that the Whig leaders were aware of the danger of their position.[2] Once again a report was made of Coleman's letters and other correspondence concerning James and the Plot. A long and effective attack on the bill was made by

[1] BM, Portland Deposit, 711E, Portfolio 1. Edward Ashe, who had voted for Exclusion and was a friend of Sacheverel and Treby, wrote in Dec. 1679; 'knowing that the parliament intended not his (Monmouth's) succession, I cannot imagine how the popular be so zealous, except they be set on by some wiser than themselves.'   [2] Grey, vii. 313–14. CJ ix. 626.

Sir Thomas Clarges, the former Opposition leader who, only a fortnight before, had joined in the general attack on Lauderdale. No attempt was made to meet his arguments. If he was answered the House might become involved in a long debate in which the number and weight of the speeches might, as on 11 May, be in favour of the Court. With cries of 'the bill, the bill', the reading was pressed, and at last the Court forced a division. The result, 207 in favour of the second reading and 128 against, was only superficially a victory for the Whigs. The Court, for all the accession of strength after the reform of the Privy Council, was still a minority, comparatively small, and with apparently little hope of wresting control over the Commons from the Whigs. Nevertheless, the number of abstentions was disturbing. Some members had leave of absence, but the majority, as the figures for Shropshire and Oxfordshire show, must have been deliberate and concerted. Significantly there was a higher proportion among those whom Shaftesbury had regarded as supporters than among the presumed courtiers. Whig arguments had failed to move them, and if any large number of them seceded to the Court then the Whigs would find themselves in a minority. This was at least possible. Barrillon reported that many members had stayed away from the House, not daring to appear in order to oppose the bill, but that had it been its final reading they would have come to vote against Exclusion.[1]

The size of the Court minority, and the number of abstentions, showed that the Commons was now sharply and permanently divided into two factions. The Whigs could no longer represent themselves, as they had done with some plausibility when attacking Danby and investigating the Plot, as speaking for a virtually united House and nation. The result was to encourage the King and the Court faction in the House of Lords. At no time during the session were the Whig peers in a commanding position in the upper House. The strength of the Court peers was to be seen in

[1] Barrillon, 1 June 1679. Wherever reference is made to a member voting for or against Exclusion the authority is the list on the Exclusion division from the Morrice MSS., D. Milne and A. Browning, 'An Exclusion Bill Division List', *Bulletin of the Institute of Historical Research*, xxiii. See also the other list, K. Feiling, *History of the Tory Party* (1950), 494-5.

the tenacious defence which many of them put up on behalf of Danby. In the last few days of the Cavalier Parliament the Lords had rejected the motion that he should withdraw, and they had refused to commit him. Even after the outburst of indignation caused by the news of Danby's pardon and pension, the upper House refused to go to the same lengths as the Commons. The peers first insisted on their own act of banishment, and then on amendments which in effect mutilated the proposal of attainder made by the Commons. Danby's lists show how evenly divided was the House on the issue of his guilt or innocence. With the exception of the Bishop of London he could depend on the consistent support of the episcopal bench, and Whig attempts to prevent the bishops from attending in capital cases did not secure a majority. No pretext could be raised to prevent their voting against Exclusion, as they were certain to do, but even so there was certain to be a majority of peers against the bill. Not all the personal enemies of Danby were opponents of the Court once he had fallen, still less members of an organized and systematic Opposition acknowledging Shaftesbury's leadership. Halifax, Newport, Robarts, Rochester, and Fauconberg could all be classed at the start of the session as 'country' peers, but although for various reasons they voted for the attainder they were not consistent opponents of the Court. When it ceased to be a question of animus against the fallen minister, the Opposition could depend in political matters on no more than a minority of between twenty and thirty peers.[1]

For these reasons the prospects for Exclusion in the Lords were not such as to encourage haste. Instead of proceeding at once to the third reading in the Commons the Whigs sought first to consolidate their position. This was done by intimidating their opponents in order to shake their resolution and to impress the King and the peers with the fact that the strength of the exclusionist party was unshaken, and their hold on the Commons as strong as ever. This bold front concealed a measure of despondency or fatalism on the part of some Whigs. They were troubled at the

---

[1] *LJ* xiii. 594. The regular Whig vote is seen at its maximum on 27 May 1679, when twenty-seven peers signed a protest against the presence of bishops in capital cases.

dissensions between the two Houses, and still more by the attitude of the King, although they took some comfort from the belief that he was under the influence of evil men, and might still throw himself into the arms of his people. Most members expected an early prorogation or dissolution, but they were determined to prepare for the trial of strength with the Court in the elections which would follow. The attempt to force royal officials to disclose the amounts and recipients of money distributed by Danby for political purposes was intended to destroy the credit of Court members.[1] But although Sir Stephen Fox proved to be less resolute than had Charles Bertie earlier, the disclosures which he made were less spectacular and useful than had been expected. Nevertheless, the incident did show that the Whigs were still intransigent. Certainly no further supply could be expected. There was, therefore, no reason why Charles should continue the session. Once the trial of the five Papist peers began, it would be virtually impossible to dissolve or prorogue for fear of exciting accusations that they were being saved from condemnation by the King and his ministers. On the other hand, the increase in the strength and ability of the Court faction in the Commons may have led the King to hope that a new House would prove to be more tractable, and it certainly could be no worse than the present. On 27 May Parliament was prorogued and Charles followed with a dissolution before it was due to meet again.

This decision to dissolve was one of the turning-points in the Exclusion crisis. This was an irrevocable step, one that made any compromise impossible. The newly reconstituted Privy Council was dealt a fatal blow. The last shreds of confidence between the King and the Whigs were destroyed, and events now moved on to an inevitable crisis that could be resolved only by the capitulation of the King or the destruction of his opponents. Shaftesbury was now convinced that 'things must be worse before they can be better'. He realized that he would have no power, and that his position as Lord President of the Council would be illusory, until he could exert enough pressure on the King to compel him to concede all that he demanded.

[1] *CJ* ix. 629. HMC, *Lindsey*, supplementary volume, 270.

4

THE BREAK WITH THE KING

I

DURING the summer of 1679, despite the division of Parliament into two sharply hostile factions, the exclusionists or Whigs and the courtiers who were soon to be styled the Tories, there were two factors which caused political uncertainty, not least about the King's policy and intentions. The first was the continued existence of the reconstituted Privy Council with Shaftesbury as its Lord President, although its members were divided on almost all political questions of importance, especially over Exclusion. The second cause of uncertainty was the anomalous position occupied by Monmouth, who retained all his offices and influence although his pretensions as successor were being canvassed by his friends, to the alarm of his uncle in exile on the Continent.

The new Privy Council had originally been intended as the instrument of reconciliation, which would make possible a compromise between Court and Opposition. Shaftesbury had accepted nomination because, being appointed Lord President, he believed at first that this meant the concession of real power to him. He was in an unprecedentedly strong position. Danby had been able to control a parliamentary majority because he was the Lord Treasurer and royal confidant. Shaftesbury, on the other hand, had become Lord President because he was a party leader with such strength in the Commons that he could hamper all administration and block grants of supply indefinitely. With his appointment he had apparently acquired a commanding position, if not exclusive power, for he was not prepared to accept responsibility without being able to wield effective power. This was the position which, to the Duke of York's amazement, he appeared to have attained when the new Council was announced. James at once tried to come to terms. Through intermediaries, who included Lord Townshend, a moderate member of the Opposition, he proposed an agreement. James promised that he would oblige Shaftesbury, 'for now that he Lord Shaftesbury being well with the King, the Duke will easily be brought to live well with him, his chief exception to him being upon the King's account'. This approach was not so foolishly optimistic as might at first sight appear. In the past Shaftesbury had been as adept and unscrupulous an intriguer as any other member of the Cabal. He had abandoned the Court and its policy to put himself at the head of an Opposition faction, but he might now be tempted by the fruits of office to reverse this course, to discard the Opposition once it had served its purpose. Moreover, secret negotiations had taken place between James and Shaftesbury in the spring, when the latter working through the agency of George Pitts had made or offered several inducements in an attempt to detach James from his connexion with Danby. Further, obscure negotiations had also been conducted at much the same time through the dubious agency of Mrs. Celier, the Papist midwife. Now James again employed Pitts, but since January the situation had changed so much that there was even less chance of success.[1]

Shaftesbury's refusal to entertain James's approaches is not the less important because we can now see that it was inevitable. James was assuming that Shaftesbury was, like most contemporary politicians, a careerist, on the make, an aspirant for office who would be satisfied with his salary, patronage, and perquisites. This was totally to miscalculate his purpose. Shaftesbury had already experienced the insecurity of a tenure of office based on the King's favour, since he had seen Charles leave the ministers of the Cabal to shift for themselves. He appreciated the fact that for a minister divorced from popular support the favour of the Court, as well as of the King, would be necessary. From a selfish point of view there could be no security for him if he had to rely on Whitehall. His nickname with Charles and James was 'little sincerity', which for them signified cant, hypocrisy, and humbug, but in fact Shaftesbury never really pretended to be a courtier. He was ill

[1] *HMC, 11th Report*, v (*Dartmouth*), 32; James to Legge, 8 May 1679.

placed by character and reputation to win the favours of mistresses, buffoons, worthless hangers-on, and subterranean figures like Prodgers, the King's pimp. Moreover Shaftesbury, despite what his detractors have said, was a statesman as well as a politician. Burnet's phrase, 'his strength lay in his knowledge of England', is the key to his personality, his attitude to politics, and his policy towards the King. His connexions and sympathies were with the unfashionable country squires and City and provincial merchants, classes far removed from the modish vice and Papist inclinations of Whitehall. Shaftesbury knew that he would never be willingly or permanently accepted by Charles or the courtiers, but the appearance or belief that he had become intimate with them would be dangerous to his reputation in the country. Already in 1674 he had refused an offer of high office unless certain conditions were satisfied which would give him exclusive power, security of tenure from Court intrigues, and a free hand to pursue a policy of suppression of Popery.[1] On that occasion the King had naturally preferred to accept Danby as his minister, but now it seemed for a short while that Shaftesbury had been granted his demands.

Therefore when Shaftesbury accepted office in 1679 he was careful to make it appear to the nation that he did so only as its servant. To show that he had not abandoned either his principles or his supporters he declared that he served as the 'Tribune of the People'. This concern is evident in his speeches, which were intended to ensure that he did not forfeit his popular credit. He made an outright attack on the principles as well as the methods of the Scottish Government, stigmatizing it as an absolute rule, in addition to demanding the removal of Lauderdale.[2] He spoke in the House of Lords with great vehemence on behalf of the much-despised Quakers so as to show that he was still the defender of popular liberty.[3] When, as an additional tribute to his new importance, Ormonde was persuaded most unwillingly to write to

[1] Shaftesbury Papers, VI B, 441. Memorandum by Thomas Stringer, part of the materials which he collected for a biography of Shaftesbury.

[2] Browning, ii. 85, 87–88.

[3] Barrillon, 4 May. He reported Shaftesbury as saying: 'tout haut que s'il avait cru ne pouvoir rien obtenir dans une chose de telle conséquence, il ne serait point rentré dans les affaires.'

him in congratulation on his appointment, Shaftesbury did not
reply. It would be dangerous to give support to one so vulnerable as Ormonde. In any case Shaftesbury was probably thinking
already of possible charges against him, of neglect to secure Ireland
against the designs of the Papists.[1]

There is no evidence to show exactly when Shaftesbury decided
to stake everything on the Bill of Exclusion; there is no specific
mention of it in the memorandum which he drew up at the beginning of the session.[2] But the fact that many Whig members in
the Commons had openly declared in favour of trying to pass such
a measure made it inevitable that Shaftesbury should lead the
agitation if he were to remain in control of the Opposition. Not
to have done so would have left him as a minister dependent on the
King's favour, to be discarded like Halifax once the crisis abated.
Only Russell of the other councillors followed him, and the split
which developed between these two and the rest of the Council
was of very great significance. Hitherto Shaftesbury had been
primus inter pares of the country Opposition. Now as his ascendancy increased within a more coherent and disciplined party so he
alienated his former colleagues, quite apart from the fact that they
disliked the policy of Exclusion. Shaftesbury's strength and primacy were rapidly becoming such that all the other ministers were
forced to unite against him. Exclusive power for him would mean
subordination or loss of office for them. In their very different
ways both Halifax and Sunderland saw how dangerous Shaftesbury was, and sought to secure themselves against him.

The adherence of Halifax was the most important benefit which
Charles derived from his reform of the Privy Council. Previously
he had been as intransigent and extreme in his opposition as
Shaftesbury himself. Both had pursued and exploited the Plot
with equal skill and ruthlessness, despite the fact that they had
little more in common than hostility to Danby. During the first
few weeks of the new Parliament they continued to work together. Both possessed influence in the Commons, but of very
different kinds. Halifax had friends there, but his reputation derived mainly from his past activity against Danby and the Court.

[1] Carte, 118, f. 198; 70, ff. 487, 495.   [2] Shaftesbury Papers, VI A, 334.

Shaftesbury added to reputation the leadership and management of a party of which the very idea was abhorrent to Halifax. Although Charles had been most reluctant to accept him, the entrance of Halifax into the Council was soon to lead to his adherence to the Court now that Danby had gone, and to a final estrangement from Shaftesbury.

Whatever part was played by personal animosity and jealousy, the irreconcilable breach between them derived first from their different opinions on Exclusion, and also from their very different conceptions of office. Halifax and Shaftesbury differed on the conditions under which they were prepared to exercise power as well as on the uses to which they wanted to put it. Shaftesbury soon found that his titular presidency of the Council brought him less power than that exercised by those ministers who possessed the King's personal favour. Halifax became one of the King's chief confidential advisers, and as such he entirely forfeited the reputation which he had acquired with the Opposition in the Commons. Shaftesbury could not have imitated him even had he wished to do so. His whole position rested on the support which he derived from his control over the Opposition in the Commons by which he had virtually forced himself on the King. In the language of the next century he had forced the King's closet. Knowing that the King disliked him and his policy, Shaftesbury had at all costs to retain parliamentary support. Rather than risk the loss of popular support he preferred to court dismissal.

The first bitter clashes which broke out at the Council over Exclusion were intensified after the prorogation of the first Whig Parliament.[1] Shaftesbury denounced those whom he held responsible—Halifax, Essex, and Sunderland—in the most violent terms. The fury of the ordinary Whigs was not lessened by the fact that they had expected it. Shaftesbury occupied himself with preparing for the next session, which would certainly prove to be turbulent, and showed himself in a constant ill humour at Council meetings. The situation was gradually, but it seemed inevitably, deteriorating when there occurred the first of two unexpected crises which were to alter the whole political position.

[1] Temple, *Works*, i. 337-8, 339.

II

The revolt of the Covenanters in June 1679 seemed at first to be extremely dangerous. Despite their lack of effective or unified leadership, and the turbulent undisciplined fanaticism of many of the followers, they were a formidable and desperate party in Scotland. The situation was ominously reminiscent of the time of Charles I's Bishops' wars. The misgovernment of Lauderdale, the King's representative, had for long been a favourite topic for the Opposition, and even moderate supporters of the Court joined in their protests.[1] Consequently many were readier to attribute the rebellion to the cruelty of Lauderdale's rule than to the wickedness of the rebels. Many of the Scottish aristocracy, under the leadership of Hamilton, who was already in contact with Shaftesbury, used the outbreak as an argument in interviews with Charles for Lauderdale's removal. It seemed that, like his father, Charles could not rely on the co-operation of his subjects to suppress the rebellion. Parliament, if recalled, was not likely to vote money. Many Whigs ostentatiously refused to serve. In the City extremists went so far as to start a petition calling for negotiations with the Covenanters.[2] But in contrast to his father Charles did not have to depend on the unwilling assistance of his subjects, and the ease with which the rebellion was suppressed was a striking illustration of the greater strength and resources of the monarchy after 1660. The revolt was put down, and disaffection energetically and permanently repressed by the use of Scottish resources. Lauderdale had been careful to preserve in good order the relatively large standing army which formed the basis of royal authority throughout the reigns of Charles and James. Furthermore, there was by now a considerable King's party in all parts of the country except the south-west, particularly among those members of the aristocracy with Highland influence and associations. The rebellion was

[1] Grey, iii. 24–33; v. 358–67. Early in 1679, hoping that Danby's imminent dismissal could be followed by a change in the Scottish administration, a section of the Scottish Opposition renewed relations with Shaftesbury. Shaftesbury Papers, VI A, 325, 338; VI B, 428. J. R. Jones, 'The Scottish Constitutional Opposition in 1679', *Scottish Historical Review*, xxxvii, No. 123 (Apr. 1958).

[2] Sidney, *Letters*, 113, 123.

soon over, the Covenanters being dispersed by the battle of Both-well Brig on 22 June.

The swift downfall of the rebels and the re-establishment of royal authority by a decisive victory was undoubtedly a surprise and a disappointment to both Hamilton and Shaftesbury, although there is no proof of the latter's alleged complicity with the rebels. The real interest in what proved otherwise, at least so far as English history is concerned, to be no more than an incident was the part played by Monmouth as the commander of the royal army. His appointment put Shaftesbury in a dilemma. He did not want the rising suppressed before he tried to make capital out of it, but he was not averse to seeing Monmouth's prestige and influence increase by his command. This may have been calculated by the King, but in the event Monmouth did not lose any popularity from his victory because of the wise and lenient policy which he pursued afterwards. Moreover, his appointment emphasized the fact that he was still not definitely committed to any single faction. It showed that he continued to enjoy his father's confidence and favour, and it alarmed James who believed that he was about to be abandoned.[1] Suspicions were reawakened as to the King's intentions: it was still possible to believe, or to affect to believe, that Charles did not mean what he said when he announced that he regarded Exclusion as unacceptable. This sign of trust in Monmouth strengthened the belief that, as he was apparently indifferent to the fact that his son's pretensions were being canvassed, he might still declare in his favour.

Monmouth's pretensions were nothing new, but previously they had been vaguer and little short of chimerical. As far back as 1667, before there was any question of his personal popularity, there had been a project to have him acknowledged heir to the throne by persuading Charles to declare that he had been married to Lucy Walter, Monmouth's mother.[2] When he grew up Monmouth was soon on very bad terms with his uncle, but this was originally a personal antipathy, apparently produced by amorous rivalry. Even when James began to fear his nephew's ambition,

---

[1] HMC, 11th Report, v (Dartmouth), 34–35, James to Legge, 7 June; 36–37, 25 July.   [2] Browning, i. 55–56.

and to set himself the task of preventing Monmouth's nomination
as General, he does not appear to have considered him as a serious
rival. The Plot began to alter the situation. It made James bitterly
and widely unpopular except at Court, but only among the
ignorant and credulous did Monmouth's pretensions gain any
consideration. The influential and important were indifferent or
hostile to the claims put forward on his behalf. In November 1678
Monmouth was said to be not without hopes of being declared
Prince of Wales, but when it was reported that his health was
being drunk as such in the City the courtiers were contemptuous.
The reaction to the attempt to increase his standing was discouraging. With Monmouth's connivance the word 'natural' was deliberately omitted from his commission, 'to our very dear and faithful
son'. There were immediate protests. When Cavendish, a personal
friend and later a Whig, made a sharp attack on this subterfuge
the Commons applauded. Before James was sent abroad Charles
made his own attitude clear when he formally and solemnly
declared that he had never been married to any woman but the
Queen.[1]

This did not mean that Monmouth was in disgrace or disfavour.
Although an opponent of Danby he continued to hold many
offices. On occasion he voted for the Court. In January he joined
with his uncle in deploring and opposing the disbandment of two
regiments.[2] The members whom he recommended in the elections of 1679 were friends and officials. Yet although Monmouth
was not identified with the Opposition, or committed to its support during the session of 1679, he was already beginning to show
signs of the precipitancy and indiscretion which were ultimately
to prove fatal to him. At the start of the session Monmouth was
intriguing with both Shaftesbury and Essex.[3] The details are not
known, but they are more likely to have been for the dismissal of
Danby than to gain support for Monmouth's pretensions. Essex
was at this time confident that the King could be trusted, and as a
result was given both an appointment and a place in the inner ring
inside the new Privy Council. He was not likely to have discussed,

---

[1] Barrillon, 24 Nov., 1 Dec. 1678. Grey, vi. 225. Burnet, ii. 203.
[2] Carte, 103, f. 241.   [3] Ibid., 39, f. 21.

still less countenanced, at this early stage Monmouth's still chimerical claims. As the session advanced he, like Halifax, lost his credit
with the Commons, and after the prorogation a sharp break
occurred between him and Monmouth. Similarly, Monmouth
quarrelled with Sunderland. As these links with other politicians
were weakened or cut altogether, so his connexion with Shaftesbury became progressively stronger. But there is no evidence to
suggest that at this stage Shaftesbury had any serious intention of
putting Monmouth forward as the Whig candidate for the succession.

Those who did canvass the idea of Monmouth's rights to the
succession were few in number and extremist in their views. Although the notion was gaining a measure of popular support
among the ordinary people, the importance of Monmouth's advocates must not be exaggerated. Most of them were personal
friends of the Duke, young hotheads, extravagant and in some
cases desperate for want of money. In contrast to the major section
of the Whigs they were essentially of the fashionable class of
courtiers, whose opposition was that of opportunists or frondeurs.
Sir Thomas Armstrong busied himself in the search for the famous
Black Box, said to contain the evidence of Charles's marriage to
Lucy Walter. Another friend to show himself active was Lord
Gerard. With others they canvassed members of the Opposition
in an attempt to induce them to name a successor in the Exclusion
Bill, who presumably was to be Monmouth. Ralph Montagu
offered, as usual for a price, to get Monmouth to work in the
French interest, and proposed that his pretensions should receive
support from Louis. With over-elaborate machiavellianism he
explained that this might well lead to a civil war, which he assumed would be in the interests of France, as had been the Wars of
the Roses. These members did not possess enough influence to enable them to carry the Whig majority in the Commons. But their
activities, and the popular sentiment which they succeeded in
arousing, were not unimportant. By his failure to check or repudiate them, Monmouth was slowly antagonizing both the King and
the privy councillors with the exception of Shaftesbury and Russell.[1]

[1] Carte, 39, f. 72. Browning, ii. 83. Barrillon, 30 Jan. 1679.

Shaftesbury's position as Lord President of the Council, and his advocacy of Exclusion, had already forced the other ministers to band together in order to preserve their influence. Monmouth's prestige and his favour with his father still further alarmed them, for it would be exercised whenever possible on Shaftesbury's behalf. The ministers could not revive a connexion with James; since they had been responsible for his exile they did not trust him, and any association with him would merely cause them to be included in his unpopularity. The only alternative to Monmouth was the Prince of Orange, and it was to William that the ministers began to look. Some of them, Temple for example, were already in his confidence, and in Henry Sidney they had a trusted channel of communication.

Barrillon, the French ambassador, who was always anxious to prevent William from acquiring any influence or interest in England or at Court, believed that Sunderland, Essex, and Temple considered they had enough credit with Charles to persuade him to declare in favour of the Prince should it prove to be impossible to maintain the right of the Duke of York.[1] This may have been at the back of their minds, but as Mary's husband William was already in a favourable position should Exclusion pass into law. The purpose of the negotiations with William was more immediate. All those who feared that the partnership of Shaftesbury and Monmouth threatened them with impotence and subordination combined in order to introduce William as a counter-weight. If he could be persuaded to come over to take his place in the Council and the Lords, then his influence with the King might replace that of Monmouth. Comparatively ignorant of English personalities and institutions, William would be as dependent on his advisers as Monmouth was on Shaftesbury. Moreover, these ministers would not only recover their position, they could also expect that William would stiffen the King's resolution and prevent him from capitulating to the Whigs.

The ministers and their associates were united in their dislike of Shaftesbury and Exclusion, but there was not much else in common between them. Temple, the most statesmanlike but least

[1] Barrillon, 15 May 1679.

influential, thinking of foreign affairs and the danger from France, wished to conclude an alliance with the States-General, and in this he was supported by Halifax and Essex. The more unscrupulous were thinking mainly of their own selfish interests. William Harbord, a former friend of Monmouth who in return for office deserted the Opposition and voted against Exclusion, declared that he was in favour of the Prince, and spoke of making him Protector in case of James becoming King. As a pensioner of Barrillon he was in fact playing a double game. So too was Sir John Baber who, although a member of the moderate Holles group which Barrillon believed was suspicious of William, approached Sidney. He suggested a reconciliation, complaining that in the past William had been unfriendly, and put all the blame for parliamentary factiousness on Shaftesbury.[1]

The most accomplished of those playing a double game, or in his case one even more complicated, was Sunderland. To him power, and the money which went with office, was an end in itself. He thought of all questions of policy and administration as less important in themselves than from a consideration of how they were likely to affect his tenure of office. The first essential was the retention of the King's confidence. But in view of Charles's character and inconstancy this might be insufficient. In addition, but if possible without antagonizing the King, Sunderland always attempted to propitiate or come to an understanding with the individual or group which he considered to have the greatest actual or potential strength. Therefore when, at the end of April, Shaftesbury seemed to have become predominant and Halifax and Essex combined against him, Sunderland was in contrast very careful to remain on the best possible terms with the Whig leader and Lord President. He told Sidney that he found it impossible to work with Shaftesbury, by which he probably meant that he found he could not manage him, but this did not put a stop to the negotiations.[2] Nevertheless, the intrigue with Shaftesbury was a

[1] Sidney, i. 3-4, 8-9.
[2] Negotiations were still continuing in July, Sidney, i. 28. Kenyon, 25-26, 29, stresses Sunderland's relative inexperience at this time, but the lines of conduct which he was to follow throughout his later career were already apparent.

last resort, an insurance against his becoming all powerful. Shaftesbury was already the recognized leader of the Whigs and monopolized Monmouth, so that Sunderland could never hope to be
more than a subordinate to them in the event of Whig ascendancy.
At the same time Sunderland was careful not to sever his connexion with James, even though his fortunes were at their nadir,
many thinking it possible that he would be abandoned, and
there was no immediate prospect of his return from exile.

Sunderland's third line was to encourage William and gain his
confidence. Through the agency of Sidney he sent advice urging
William to come over, and recommending that when he did he
should set up a 'party' by entertainment and personal soliciting.
Of course, such an interest would have been as much at Sunderland's as at William's disposal. Instructions were sent that William
ought to write to the Duchess of Portsmouth, as she was unsatis-
fied, and make some application 'for that she will be of great use
to us, particularly against the Duke of Monmouth'. Sunderland
stressed the part which she had played in changing the Privy
Council, and declared that the Prince must make use of her if he
intended to do anything with the King. Here again, his advice
was self-interested, for the royal mistress had for some time joined
her interest with Sunderland's. In contrast Shaftesbury made no
great effort to secure an understanding with William: his motives
in omitting to do so must for lack of evidence remain a matter
for conjecture. Sidney was expressly instructed to inform William
that Shaftesbury was not of 'our' party, but that as a tool he would
be invaluable in virtue of his control of Parliament. To think of
using Shaftesbury as an instrument was somewhat optimistic, but
his indifference was apparent in the cold and general remarks
which he made when Sidney went to take leave of him. He declared that he was in favour of an alliance against France, and said
of William that 'if he would continue a good Protestant we would
do him right'.[1]

The dissolution, announced on 12 July, did not put a stop
to the plans for a visit from William. When he got to The
Hague Sidney continued to urge him to go over when the new

[1] Sidney, i, 10, 15, 19, 20–21, 28. Kenyon, 29.

Parliament met. But while the ministers in their preparations for the new session looked to The Hague for assistance, Charles was making an effort to avoid having to allow it to meet. He renewed the negotiations for French help which had proved abortive in the spring. Complaining that he was reduced to such a condition that he had to meet Barrillon in private, he pleaded that it was in Louis's interest to save him, for if he did not do so all authority must pass into other hands. He hinted that he might be forced, although against his inclinations, into hostility against France, and accord with her enemies. He excused himself for the continued persecution of the Papists, regretting that he had ever thought it would appease the Commons. Without French assistance there would be no alternative but submission to domestic enemies who would never be satisfied with less than complete power.[1]

Charles was not alone in thinking his position precarious. Buckingham believed that his only plan would be to save himself by abandoning those near to him one by one, and that when Parliament reassembled the Court would have to follow the wishes of the House of Commons. Shaftesbury's expectations were being fulfilled at least in part. Things were steadily getting worse. The first Whig Parliament had been dissolved in order to gain time for tempers to cool, to show that the King could dispense with a Parliament even if only for a time, and to make possible an attempt to undermine the position of the Whig leaders. But the violence of the Whig reaction to the dissolution, and the probability—soon to be confirmed by the first election returns—that the new Commons would be even more extreme than the last, made it clear that the brief respite had been purchased at a high price. The King had done no more than postpone the crisis. Soon a decision would have to be made as to whether Parliament should be permitted to meet. The situation was already fast deteriorating when the whole crisis was suddenly intensified, and as suddenly resolved, by the King's unexpected and momentarily dangerous illness. The outcome was a complete ministerial and political revolution which entirely changed the course of events. The uncertainties of the summer were dissipated. Monmouth's anomalous

[1] Barrillon, 16 Feb.; 13 July; 3, 31 Aug.

position was brought to an end. The new Privy Council was destroyed. The result embittered still further the spirit of the elections, and within the next few months the whole nation, even down to the lowest classes and most remote districts, was to be divided into two irreconcilable factions.

III

When Charles fell ill on 22 August, and for a time seemed to be at the point of death, the ministers were forced to abandon their long-term projects. There was no time to send for William, and even he might be useless in the crisis which would follow the King's death. Dangerous rumours spread that the King had actually been poisoned, and had he died few would have believed that it was due to natural causes. Probably Shaftesbury and Monmouth would have attempted to stage a *coup d'état*. Shaftesbury was still Lord President of the Council, while Monmouth was in London and in command of the Guards, many of whose officers were his friends. The ministers were panic-stricken at the prospect of civil war. The Whig leaders had been bitter enough at the prorogation, but the decision to dissolve the first Whig Parliament possessed them with fury. Shaftesbury swore that he would have the heads of those who had advised the King to this action, and in the seventeenth century this was not a figure of speech. Russell warned them that the first vote of the new Parliament would be to declare them enemies of the King and kingdom. Now these threats were remembered. From an almost panic fear of losing their heads should their enemies become masters of the situation, Halifax and Essex sent word to the Duke of York to return. By the time he arrived Charles had recovered. But the events of this sudden if short crisis forced Charles to realize how far Monmouth was pursuing and hoped to pursue his claims, and how near the country had come to civil war.[1]

Previously Charles had not openly disapproved of Monmouth's intrigues. One courtier discovered in August that frequent meet-

[1] HMC, *Ormonde*, N.S., iv. 531. Kenyon, 30–32. Temple, *Works*, i. 337–8, 344–5.

ings were taking place between Shaftesbury and Monmouth. From what he could gather the discussions were on how best 'to set up the title to the Crown, after the Duke should be banished, which they resolved certainly to do, or not to grant any thing to the King'. What astounded him was the presence at these surreptitious meetings of the Earl of Bath, acting as agent for Danby, who in his desperation was making an attempt to come to terms with the Whigs. Most astonishing of all, when on a friend's advice Cholmley acquainted the King with his discoveries, he found that Charles 'was no stranger to the Duke of Monmouth's meeting there'. This inactivity was a measure of the gravity of the crisis. After his illness Charles could not remain so tolerant, and the influence of his brother was in favour of more energetic action being taken. During the crisis the Whigs had not been inactive, and Monmouth's pretensions had been put forward quite openly.[1]

Charles's illness and the prospect of his death had put the Whigs into a dilemma as acute as that of the ministers. They could not stand passive. All their arguments for Exclusion had been based on the need to prevent the Duke taking his revenge and then proceeding to subvert religion and liberty, as he would if he came to the throne. Now, with Exclusion baulked by the dissolution, his succession seemed to be imminent, and the Papist design on the point of being fulfilled. Self-preservation forced the Whigs to do something, although the actual details are obscure. Some military plan, it is not clear what, was prepared. Sir Thomas Armstrong was very active. In the City he conferred with Jenks, the leader of the more extreme London Whigs and a former associate of Buckingham. Some popular demonstrations seem to have taken place, perhaps as a result. Furthermore, Armstrong was reported to have gone to the Earl of Oxford, acting as if he was authorized by Monmouth, to ask him to intercede with the King for the succession. But even if this was, as some believed, a 'made' story, Monmouth's pretensions could no longer be disguised or ignored. More as a check than as a punishment the King required him to

---

[1] Carte, 39, f. 68; Cholmley, 24 Sept. BM, Portland deposit, 711E, portfolio 1, a newsletter of 18 Sept.; but see also *CSPD*, 1679/80, 240, 244. *HMC*, *7th Report*, 472, for the approach to the Earl of Oxford in May. Barrillon, 21 Sept.

go abroad, but this still did not amount to disgrace, for Monmouth retained his offices which were to be exercised for him by deputies, and received an affectionate reception from his father when he went to take leave.[1]

Those who convinced Charles that he could no longer ignore Monmouth's claims but must discourage them by actions as well as declarations, now formed a new group or junta consisting of the Duke of York, the Duchess of Portsmouth, and Sunderland. Although Sunderland had not been responsible for the recall of James, it was he and not Halifax and Essex who profited from it. He now benefited from his foresight in having maintained a connexion with James during his exile, while the other ministers found themselves virtually in eclipse. With James's return his interest was bound to revive: courtiers who had previously felt demoralized rallied round him. For a short period Charles listened to the vigorous advice offered by his brother. During the early summer James's fortunes had been so low that even the faithful Feversham had told him that his only resource would be to return to the Church of England.[2] A chimerical project had been started to solve the problem of his position by having him elected King of the Romans. Once back at Court, with Monmouth in his turn sent into exile, James again became a person of influence and importance. The Duchess of Portsmouth, terrified at the prospect of an attack by the Commons, renewed her understanding with him. Sunderland at once rallied to the support of the rising power, showing once more how fully he possessed the flexibility necessary for a successful minister and courtier of Charles II.[3]

Nevertheless, he remained cautious. Sunderland was careful as before to keep several policies in progress at the same time. He did not sever the links with the Prince of Orange, telling Sidney that he must set him right and explain 'how all that hath been done could not be avoided'. He went even farther to reinsure himself. After Shaftesbury's dismissal in October, Sunderland continued to negotiate with him, offering to help him to recover his

[1] Barrillon, 25 Sept.
[2] Sidney, i. 12.
[3] Ibid. 176. Barrillon, 2 Oct. Kenyon, 31–32.

office.[1] This astuteness had its reward. James's return increased
Sunderland's influence. But although he owed his return to them,
James was exceedingly cool to Halifax, Essex, and the others. He
believed that they were men who 'did not love a monarky as it
was in England'.[2] In particular he was indignant at their consideration of limitations. He suspected that Halifax aimed at the
complete ruin of the Catholics, and more immediately he feared
that Halifax was attempting to persuade Charles to send him overseas once again.

This new ascendancy of James, Portsmouth, and Sunderland
was reflected in a more determined and firm royal policy. Sidney
and William were unfavourably impressed with the assurance
with which James declared that Parliament would not be allowed
to meet. Temple was in particular disfavour. He had opposed the
King's policy in Scotland, and he was held responsible for William
who, it was now alleged, had been setting up for himself. Halifax
and Essex found themselves held responsible by the nation for
the King's actions, but in fact in no position to influence him.
Excluded from his confidence they were no more than 'other
Men's dupes, and did other men's works'. Their credit with the
people and the members of the new Parliament would be ruined;
their power was shown to be illusory.[3] In a position similar to that
of Shaftesbury they did not have as reserve the party support
which he was free to mobilize again after his dismissal. The dis-
advantages of being merely the King's minister now became
apparent—a problem which Halifax was to encounter again after
1681, and which he made no real attempt to solve. With the worst
of the crisis apparently past, and under the influence of his brother, Charles could now temporarily regard Halifax as dispens-
able and disregard his pertinent but unpalatable advice. Until
the King's necessities once again became pressing, and his position
critical, Halifax was to remain in a kind of retirement, without
formally breaking with the Court and carefully keeping himself
strictly apart from the Whigs.

[1] Sidney, i. 181, 184. HMC, Ormonde, N.S., iv. 558.
[2] HMC, 11th Report, v (Dartmouth), 36. J. S. Clarke, Life of James II (1816), i.
594.   [3] Temple, Works, i, 345.

Essex was driven farther by his loss of influence. His abandonment of the Court was generally attributed to ambition; it
was said that Shaftesbury had won his support by a promise of the
Lord Lieutenancy of Ireland.[1] This allegation had some basis in
fact; Essex was engaged in a complicated intrigue for the removal
of Ormonde. His main motive, however, was his suspicion of the
King, and fear of the Duke of York and arbitrary government.
Essex had always been a firm believer in the Plot. As a former
leader of the moderate Opposition the attacks of his former colleagues were particularly wounding. His approval of the prorogation and dissolution had produced accusations that he had deserted
his old principles as well as his friends. His ability and parsimony
at the Treasury had been construed as part of a design to enable
the King to live without Parliament. Yet he retained his principles,
and the return of the Duke of York and his influence in favour of
a firmer policy was bound to alienate him. In July, when he was
the object of Whig denunciations, Essex had expressed his suspicions of arbitrary government and had attacked Lauderdale and
his methods. When Charles announced a modest reinforcement
of the Guards by raising another company of musketeers, Essex
protested vehemently that this would 'give great cause of jealousy
to your people and prevent the good effects which your Majesty
hopes for, this next session of Parliament . . . there is nothing I do
more apprehend than a mistrust men may have, that any design
is on foot of governing by an army'.[2] This protest shows that the
cleavage with the Court was implicit even before the return of
James. Essex's main concern was to establish harmony between
the King and his people, to restore mutual confidence. Having
broken with Shaftesbury for this reason, he now began to fear
the danger from James. It was becoming apparent that Charles,
under his brother's influence, in dispensing with his new ministers
was reverting to the old principles of government which had
for so long been opposed by the 'country' in the Cavalier
Parliament.

The test of the King's sincerity was whether he would allow
the new Parliament to meet at the appointed time. The independ-

[1] Ibid., 348, 350.   [2] Sidney, i. 37–38.

ent councillors, Temple, Essex, Capel, and Powle, were all in
favour, but when they expressed their views in Council they
were abruptly silenced by the King.[1] The decision to prorogue
the new Parliament before it was due to meet finally destroyed
the new Privy Council, and with it all chance of compromise.
Temple absented himself from its meetings. Essex resigned as
first Commissioner of the Treasury. He was to continue as a councillor for another year, but in January the other independent
members resigned. In reply to the request from Russell, Cavendish, Capel, and Powle for leave to withdraw, Charles answered
'with all my heart'.[2] Thus the King's determination to resist Whig
demands, to fight them to the finish, and to require an equal resolution from his councillors, caused the return to the Whigs of
those leaders who had for a time trusted him, accepted office, and
voted against Exclusion.

The King had good reasons for refusing to allow the new Parliament to meet. His financial resources were just sufficient to
allow him to live without one, and in any case supplies of money
were not likely to be forthcoming. The Commons would, as
before, act as a focus for all opposition and faction. An immediate
and violent attack could be expected against James. The elections
had produced a House of Commons that would obviously be
even more obstinate and extreme than the last.

IV

The importance of the general elections held in August and
September, as compared with those of the spring, was that by
now the candidates were far more clearly divided into two opposing parties. Local interests and family connexions still formed the
basis of most candidatures and contests, but many elections were
now fought in addition on national issues. Since the division on
the Exclusion Bill had established the political adherence of most
of the members, the attitude or record of a candidate sometimes
became more important than his local standing and influence.

---

[1] Sidney, i. 182–3.   [2] Shaftesbury Papers, VI A, 351. Luttrell, i. 33.

Moreover, the Press, which in the previous elections had been of little influence, contributed greatly to the systematic political character of the contests. Finally, in contrast to the previous elections the Court was now organized and ready to challenge the Whig ascendancy.

Opinion was divided as to whether the elections were likely to produce a House more favourable to the King, although some such assumption must have been made when the first Whig Parliament was dissolved. Some Whig gentlemen were reluctant to stand because of the expenditure that would be necessary, and feared that over-frequent parliaments and elections might be used by the Court to discourage its opponents and eventually to produce a compliant House of Commons.[1] On the Court side some were optimistic, and hoped at the very least to reduce the number of their opponents considerably. This time some effort was made to influence the elections. The King personally encouraged courtiers to stand. Many Lord Lieutenants and justices of the peace showed themselves active in the Court interest, and in some cases instructions were issued through them. It was said that the date by which the writs were returnable had been put back, so that there should be time for the removal of mayors and officers, and that some had been in favour of a still longer delay until the creation of new sheriffs. Danby recommended that the commissioners of customs should use their influence in the port towns and that the interest of courtiers in the boroughs should be concerted. In several cases the clergy, both episcopal and parochial, acted as an organized block in support of the Court interest.[2]

There was still a fairly narrow limit to Court organization. Money was no more plentiful than in the spring, and most courtiers could still expect no more encouragement than a verbal recommendation from the King. Like their opponents many of them were deterred from standing by the probable expense, in their case the likelihood of failure adding to their faintheartedness. Lord Longford, who had fought a bitter and costly election in the

---

[1] *The Freeholders' Choice* (1679). Carte, 103, f. 221. HMC, *Ormonde*, N.S., v. 155–6.

[2] Carte, 39, f. 62. Addl. 28042, f. 19. Tanner, 34, f. 148.

spring in Surrey, was reluctant to stand again, and eventually decided not to do so. His Whig opponents made extensive preparations for the contest, bringing freeholders from all over the county only to find that there was no opposition, and so no poll. But although this was an exceptional case, and over most of the country the Tories offered much stouter resistance than formerly, their organization and to some extent their spirit were inadequate. This was seen by Bishop Morley, of Winchester, who wrote that he could not expect a better choice of members; 'the zeal of the ill affected being much more for the undermining, than that of the well-affected for the upholding of the present government both in Church and State.'[1]

Nevertheless, the Court efforts were sufficient to alarm the Whigs and greatly to increase the ill-feeling directed against the Court. The dissolution seemed all of a piece with the return of James, the first important acquittal in the trials for the Plot—that of Wakeman which was generally construed as an attempt to hush up the Plot and disparage the witnesses—and the continued immunity from punishment of Danby and the five Papist peers. As compared with the previous elections these were held in an even more embittered atmosphere. The King was now virtually identified with the most sinister and evil influences at Court, and even moderation was now regarded with suspicion.

For this intensification of bitterness and conflict the Press was largely responsible. At this time, L'Estrange having been forced into temporary exile, it was predominantly Whig. Its influence was very considerable, extending even into the country-side and small towns, where pamphlets and newspapers were received in taverns and coffee-houses which became informal Whig clubs. One important effect was to counter-balance the influence of the clergy from whose sermons many of the ordinary people normally gained much of their information and opinions. Many of the pamphlets were written specifically to give guidance to the voters, and to offset the increased vigour and activity of the Court. The writers stressed the decisive importance of the elections, one proclaiming 'all is at stake', and another that in the crisis there was only

[1] Tanner, 38, f. 72, 29 July 1679. *Domestick Intelligence*, 16.

one way of escaping the present danger, which was 'by a Prudent Choice of Old English Spirits'.[1]

The main concern of the pamphlets was to point out to the electors who were entitled to be returned and who should be rejected. The publication of the *Unanimous Club of Voters* gave publicity to the names of those alleged to have been Danby's pensioners; previous lists, printed in Holland, had had a more restricted circulation. The electors were urged to repeat their actions in the last elections, but if necessary to go even farther. Pensioners should be branded, minors and beggars shunned, dependents rejected. Instead the electors should support men of courage, who would not be hectored but would keep the trust reposed in them. For fear of discouraging possible candidates the electors should reduce the financial charges of a contest as far as possible by their forbearance. But they were to lay their representatives under political obligations, insisting particularly that they should prosecute the Plot, 'how high soever they look', an obvious reference to James. The appearance here of instructions to be laid upon the members, even if expressed in fairly wide and vague terms, was later to be developed in much more specific manner as part of the Whig electioneering technique at its most efficient stage.

Among the advice given by another pamphlet was the recommendation that national issues should be put before local interest. The inclinations and votes of former members should be reviewed. All officials without exception should be rejected; 'an office to a Parliament man is but a softer and safer word for a pension.' Dependents on great men were not to be trusted, since they would use their election to get a 'lift to a good Employ'. In the final piece of advice can be seen the beginnings of the management of elections by party leaders, and the subversion of the local ascendancy of the gentry. Voters were urged: 'Rather take a Stranger if recommended by an unquestionable Hand, than a Neighbour ill affected to your interest. 'Tis not pleasing a Neighbour, because rich and powerful, but saving England that you are to eye.

[1] *England's Great Interest in the Choice of this New Parliament* (1679). *A Seasonable Warning to the Commons of England* (1679).

Neither pay you private obligations at the cost of the Nation.'[1]
This advice was not neglected, but it was only in the larger towns,
and above all the counties, that it could usually be followed. The
changes with political significance were those in places where the
electors were not dominated by any single preponderant interest;
in the smaller boroughs and those with a restricted franchise local
influences still continued to dominate the elections.

Greater prestige was always attached to service in Parliament
for a county. Hence despite the much greater cost of fighting such
an election, often with a poll lasting several days, contests were
very common. In these the extent of Whig successes depended
on how far the influence and power of the Tory partisans, with
the offices of local government in their possession, could be
overwhelmed by popular enthusiasm and determination. In War-
wickshire the majority of the county gentry, led by the Earl of
Denbigh, a strong Tory and a dictatorial Lord Lieutenant, decided
at a county meeting to re-elect the former knights, who were both
supporters of the Court. Despite this the Whigs, led by a few
among the gentry, challenged a poll and offered serious resistance.
They alleged that they were defeated only because of the malpractices of the sheriff, who was accused of having at Denbigh's
instigation polled unqualified voters for the Court candidates, and
of allowing his subordinates to assault and disperse Whig freeholders. Denbigh was affronted that the Whigs should have stood
at all after he had declared himself. During the election he managed to have a summons sent from the Privy Council to Mariet, one
of the Whig candidates, so as to prevent him being present at the
poll. This intrigue miscarried. Mariet's friends at once approached
Shaftesbury, then still Lord President, who was able to declare
with authority that the summons was a trick, and need not be
obeyed. Later, after the purge of the Whigs from the Council,
Denbigh procured Mariet's dismissal from the commission of the
peace.[2]

In Norfolk Lord Yarmouth, the Lord Lieutenant, was as energetic as Denbigh. Aware of rumours that he was about to be

---

[1] *England's Great Interest.*
[2] *CSPD,* 1679/80, 288, 395, 404–5. Addl. 34730, ff. 48, 54.

dismissed and replaced by Townshend, his bitter rival, he was at his own request made an Earl so that the county could see that he was 'borne up', and still in favour despite the disgrace of Danby, his former patron. His authority and energy were enough to carry both the Norwich seats, despite opposition and a wide franchise, but in the county election he failed. In February he had succeeded in a most bitter election, but the Whigs had petitioned success- fully, and the result of a second and even stormier contest was that the representation was shared. Now both sides attempted to win both places. Yarmouth's son got hold of the writ and held it back in order to weary the Whigs with waiting, and then surprise them with a snap poll. When the election was at last held the sheriff sought to obstruct the Whigs by attempting to enforce upon their voters the oath that they had attended church and received the sacrament within the last year. He justified this by claiming that they were mostly 'fanatics', but when Hobart at once pro- tested he was forced to desist—an example of the usefulness to a candidate of attending in person, for in February there had been no check on his misdeeds.[1]

The Essex election saw a notable Whig triumph in a memor- able contest.[2] Here the sheriff was honest, or impartial, but he found that his task of keeping order was almost impossible. The Duke of Albemarle, the Lord Lieutenant, was determined to carry both places and especially to defeat Colonel Mildmay, the able if unpleasant and unscrupulous Whig member. Albemarle appeared at the poll with most of the gentry in support, as well as a regiment of over 200 clergymen. Inevitably scuffles soon broke out. The Tories alleged that the Whig freeholders had spoken disrespectfully of their betters, calling Albemarle a devil and reviling the clergy. For their part the Whigs claimed that the Tories had done all they could to provoke disorders, and reserved their bitterest accusations for the clergy, who they alleged were the worst behaved of all, many being the worse for drink. The result was a triumph for the discipline and endurance of the Whig

---

[1] Addl. 27447, ff. 412, 421, 423.
[2] *Essex Excellency, or, the Gallantry of the Freeholders of that County* (1679). *Eng- lish Intelligencer*, 7 (23 Aug.).

freeholders. The poll lasted from Tuesday to Friday, and this in the middle of the harvest. They had come to the poll without a second candidate, resolving to vote only for Mildmay, but when a colleague was nominated, the young and inexperienced J. L. Honeywood, they were sufficently organized and disciplined to carry his election as well.

This feat of defying the Lord Lieutenant, the gentry, and the clergy could not have been achieved by the freeholders alone, or even with Mildmay at their head. The reason for their successful resistance to official pressure was the presence on the Whig side of members of the aristocracy, who thus redressed the social balance. The appearance of lords Grey and 'Shandish'[1] with strong retinues deterred the Court faction from open disorder, and encouraged the freeholders to remain steadfast. Almost certainly it prevented the Tory magistrates from embarking on prosecutions of their opponents for alleged riot, in which strictly partisan Tory justice would have been administered. When the result was announced Grey seems to have taken charge. He thanked the freeholders for their 'gallant carriage and behaviour'. In particular he praised their forbearance in paying their own election charges, which was certainly calculated to appeal to Mildmay who had resolved to be at no charge.

His hope that this example would be followed was given wide publicity by the Whigs, who also reported other cases. They claimed that at the Surrey election the money originally intended to meet expenses had been given to the poor, and that there was no treating beyond the provision of a meal for those freeholders who had come from a distance. Similarly, in the Kent election part of the money which had been subscribed was given away. At Dunwich not only the freemen and gentry but even the bailiff, recorder, and town clerk bore their own charges; later the members came down in person and gave a dinner, besides contributing £50 to the poor. The electors at Northampton were so worthy that they were said to have refused an offer of fifty hogsheads of ale.[2]

---

[1] Presumably Lord Chandos, still at this time a moderate Whig.
[2] *Domestick Intelligence*, 16, 21, 23, 25.

THE BREAK WITH THE KING

Essex was not the only county election in which Grey was concerned. He led a strong retinue to Brentford to support two Whigs for Middlesex, and there ensued a scuffle with some red-coats on the way.[1] Grey's electioneering activities won for him the title of the Prince Elector. In 1685 a Tory, the Earl of Bath, was to earn the same title, but for very different reasons. Bath exercised electoral influence as Lord Lieutenant, as a great land-owner, and as the head of the most important and influential territorial and family interest in Devon and Cornwall. Grey, on the other hand, was, like many other Whig peers, of greater service to his party as a popular hero than as a territorial magnate. For the Whigs' aristocratic influence, especially in the counties and larger boroughs, often meant popularity rather than a settled interest. Monmouth, whose progresses were to make him the Protestant hero, was not a very important landowner in England. Like Monmouth, his friend, Grey also relied mainly on his attract-ive presence and personality, his graceful bearing, and his easy familiarity with the ordinary people. Tory peers could sneer at the popularity hunting of the Whigs, but it was a valuable elec-toral asset, a deterrent as in Essex to malpractices by the Tories with their preponderance of justices and deputy lieutenants.

This usefulness of the Whig peers was again demonstrated by the Buckinghamshire election. In the spring the Hampdens had been ready to abandon the contest if the poll was to be held at the town of Buckingham, a Court stronghold. In fact it had been at Aylesbury, and the Whigs had been victorious, but now in order to give the Tories an advantage the sheriff transferred the election to Buckingham at only one day's notice. But the Whigs were not easily disheartened, and the presence of the Duke of Buckingham and Lord Paget greatly encouraged them. In a cara-van, with carts carrying those freeholders who had no mounts, they crossed the entire length of the county to a rendezvous at Winslow. They refused to spend the night at Buckingham itself; since the townsmen had sold their votes not a penny was to be spent at such an infamous and venal place. Making an early start, so as to anticipate any further tricks by the sheriff, they poured

---

[1] *Domestick Intelligence*, 19. *Friendly Intelligence*, 1.

into the town. The Court supporters saw that the sheriff's stratagem had failed and were unable to challenge a poll. To cries of
'No Timber Temple! No Traitors son! No Pensioner!' Wharton
and Hampden were once again returned. This result was for some
reason particularly displeasing to the King. When Buckingham
came up to Court he declined to see him, 'and said 'twas because
he had stood up for two men for Bucks who would cut his
throat'.[1]

The Whigs won an equally striking victory in the election for
the county of Southampton. When the freeholders assembled, Sir
Francis Rolle had the greatest measure of support, Edward Noel
a courtier and Lord Lieutenant rather less, with a third candidate
some way behind. Then someone, it is not clear who, introduced
the name of Lord William Russell whose consistent support of
Exclusion and of Shaftesbury had already made him famous. The
official Whig version had it that he 'before was not thought of in
this county', but as a friend of the Marquis of Winchester he was
not unknown, and this connexion was the reason for his success.[2]
It may well be that this was a deep stratagem, for Russell was also
elected for Bedfordshire and decided to sit for that county. Consequently a by-election had to be held in which a second Whig was
elected, which he might not have been on the day of the original
poll. Lord Russell's prestige, combined with his family interest,
made his position in Bedfordshire almost impregnable. Charles
ordered Ailesbury to go down there to make an interest for 'good'
members, but without effect.

Apart from the shires the Whigs placed a great deal of emphasis on their successes in the bigger towns, and especially in
London. The City election was usually regarded as an example
for the country to follow, and perhaps for this reason the Court
decided that this time it should be one of the last elections to
be held. In the spring the Court interest had not been able to
resist the Whigs, but now their use of the lieutenancy enabled
them to organize a challenge even in this stronghold of the
Opposition. They were encouraged to do so by the defeat in the

---

[1] *A Letter from a Freeholder of Buckinghamshire* (1679). Carte, 228, f. 121.
[2] *Domestick Intelligence*, 18. The second Whig was Thomas Jervoice.

shrieval elections of an extreme Whig named Jenks, a man of comparatively humble origin, a friend of the Independents, and associated with the obscure semi-republican groups with which Buckingham had connexions. The Tories, or 'Yorkists' as they were termed by the Whigs, created support by forming clubs, holding meetings, abusing their opponents as fanatics, and claiming for themselves a monopoly of loyalty to the King and Church of England. These efforts ended in a fiasco. Over 5,000 persons qualified to vote attended; of these the Tories could rely on fewer than 500. Whigs claimed that they could have out-polled their opponents several times with Church of England men alone, thus refuting the claim that they endangered the Church. This was a satisfactory victory, all four Whigs who were re-elected had voted for Exclusion, but the situation in the City was still disquieting. If the citizens had shown themselves to be Whigs, the lieutenancy formerly appointed by the Duke of York had shown itself to be dominated by Tories. The Whig pamphleteer lamented: 'O unhappy City! whose Governors of the militia are for the most part Servants to those that you most dreadfully fear.'[1]

The use of the lieutenancy did not prevent the defeat of the Tories in the City, but in many smaller boroughs the Whigs found it impossible to resist official pressure. There was, however, a reserve, on which they relied increasingly. Official pressure might secure the election of a Tory, but the use of the committee of elections and privileges could often be relied upon to have him unseated. In Monmouthshire the arrogance and overbearing attitude of the Lord Lieutenant, the Marquis of Worcester, were resented by the majority of the gentry. They resolved to oppose his son, Lord Herbert, one of the former knights of the shire, who was eventually forced to abandon his candidature, although his father's steward had ordered a court leet to be called, so that 'all my Lord's tenants must appear, and then will be seen what members can be made'. Instead he stood for Monmouth town, a single member borough, where pressure could be exerted more effectively. Not unexpectedly the corporation was in his favour. The

---

[1] Carte, 228, f. 105. *HMC, Ormonde*, N.S., iv. 541. *Hatton Correspondence*, i. 132. *London's Choice of Citizens* (1679).

mayor went to invite Lord Herbert to stand, obviously acting on instructions, and when John Arnold declared that he too intended to stand, rebuked him. He was told by the mayor and recorder that 'he did very ill in opposing the most noble Marquis of Worcester, whom they all owed such respect to; and that they would see the son of that worthy Lord prevail against all opposition'. Faced with Arnold's persistence, for time was to show that he had no respect for Worcester, the mayor adjourned the court and canvassed the corporation. The Tories claimed that Herbert was elected by a comfortable majority, Arnold having the support of only one of the fifteen electors. Nevertheless, when Parliament met Arnold at once petitioned, and not surprisingly the Whig committee declared in his favour, seating him and displacing Herbert.[1]

Official pressure was also encountered at Dover, where the governor had formerly claimed a right of nomination to one place. This claim had been successfully disputed in a by-election in 1673, and again in the spring of 1679. Now the governor had recourse to influence; he dismissed Stokes, one of the Whig candidates, from his post as captain of the trained bands, and treated the freemen. With austere rectitude, or in Papillon's case more likely parsimony, the Whigs declined to do any treating, but there was no danger as a rival dinner was provided on their behalf by some of the inhabitants. In Coventry some Tory aristocrats failed to over-awe the citizens. Fearing that they came to 'put some restraint upon their free choice', the townspeople refused Lords Digby and Coventry admittance to the town, and in the election the former was at the foot of the poll below two Whigs.[2]

The Whigs detested official pressure, and praised those who struggled against it, because it was invariably at the service of their opponents. They were alarmed because sheriffs, and other returning officers in some cases, were selected because they were known to be supporters of the Court. Frauds by returning officers

¹ HMC, 10th Report, iv (Throckmorton), 151–2. The English Currant, or, Advice Domestic and Foreign, 1. True Domestic Intelligence, 21. On the use of the committee of elections and privileges for partisan purposes, see J. R. Jones, 'Restoration Election Petitions', Durham University Journal, March, 1961.
² Domestick Intelligence, 17, 30.

had always been common, but now they had increasing political significance. But the uncertainty of the franchise gave the committee of elections a pretext for interference in boroughs where the prevailing influence was Tory. The franchise was declared, as at Windsor in the first elections of 1679, to be in the inhabitants at large so as to override the influence of the King over the mayor and bailiffs. But the Whigs were not, of course, opposed to influence if it was exercised on their own behalf. The cases of independence which they praised and publicized were those against a dominating Tory influence. As it has been said, there was no village Hampden in Hampden's villages.[1] There were no Whig protests when Lord Lovelace exercised his influence in the Berkshire elections. In those boroughs where they possessed predominant interests, Whig magnates were not willing to tolerate any resistance to their orders.

Apart from their popularity many Whig peers also disposed of considerable territorial influence. The Earl of Bedford's large properties formed the basis for the impregnable interest of his son in Bedfordshire. His second son, Edward, was assured of a seat at Tavistock, where the freeholds had been in Russell hands for over a century. A third son, Robert, sat for the small corporation borough of Camelford. The Marquis of Winchester owned large properties in Yorkshire as well as in Hampshire, and sent specific orders to his steward as to how he should instruct the tenants to vote.[2] In Buckinghamshire, Berkshire, Wiltshire, Westmorland, and the North Riding, the Whartons had extensive estates—the basis for the future career of Thomas Wharton as a great boroughmonger and election manager. Besides his commercial interests Shaftesbury was a leading landowner in Dorset. The Duke of Buckingham still had the wreck of his vast fortunes. A stage lower in the social scale many Whig members owned property which made them virtually certain of election. The Hampdens owned the borough of Wendover. Thomas Thynne, 'Tom of Ten Thousand', the greatest of all Whig plutocrats, was the largest

[1] Carte, 109, ff. 433–4. In the Wendover election of 1673 Hampden threatened squatters with summary eviction unless they voted for his interest.
[2] Bodleian, Fairfax MSS. 33, f. 51; during the first elections of 1679.

proprietor in Wiltshire, for which he served as knight of the shire. Owner of more recently acquired wealth, Sir Robert Clayton with his business partner had a controlling interest at Bletchingly. At Gatton, also in Surrey, where in 1620 there had been only seven houses, Thomas Turgis sat throughout the Restoration period and survived even in 1685. Another borough already rotten, Old Sarum, returned Whigs to all three Exclusion parliaments. The Boscawen family monopolized Truro, a borough with corporation franchise, and Tregoney where much of the property was in their hands. The Eliots had a similar hold in St. Germans.

In addition the Whigs, when it was convenient to do so, did affect popularity. Their supporters among the gentry might demand subservience from their own boroughs, but where the townsmen were trying to free themselves from a Tory patron or interest they could count on Whig assistance. The most blatant example was at New Windsor. In the spring the Court members had been unseated on the ground that the franchise was not restricted, but belonged to the inhabitants at large. This meant that the King, who had previously relied on the mayor, had to alter his tactics. The 'castle interest', which was to become predominant in the next century, was now organized for the first time. All the royal servants were sent to vote, some coming on purpose from Whitehall to do so. The poll was adjourned while the admissibility of their votes was discussed, but as might be expected the mayor accepted them and declared the Tory candidates elected. But once again this return was upset by the Whig committee, and the two Whigs declared to have been elected.[1]

Windsor was a special case; in most boroughs the country gentry were the ones who attempted to dominate the choice of the townspeople. The Stafford election is a striking example of a contest between the gentry of the county, on the one hand, and the inhabitants supported by outside influence, on the other.[2] A county meeting, called to nominate members for the shire election, and attended by a full bench of magistrates, rebuked two gentlemen for introducing strangers and so cutting across the ties of local

---

[1] *Domestick Intelligence*, 17.   [2] Carte, 243, f. 383.

influence and interest. The reasons why these two men had done so show how public opinion could in places still make itself felt, and how strongly it was against the Court. Mr. Chetwind, a moderate Whig, was admonished for giving his support to Sir Thomas Armstrong at Stafford. Armstrong, a stranger, had owed his previous election entirely to Monmouth's recommendation, which was now repeated. Since the spring, when he had been comparatively obscure as a soldier of fortune and Guards officer, he had become notorious as Monmouth's chief agent. He had been disgraced and forbidden the Court. Doubly repugnant to the bulk of the gentry as an intruder and an extreme Whig they decided that he should not be re-elected, and threatened that if he was they would withdraw their customary meetings and all patronage from the town. These threats of a boycott were unavailing; Armstrong was again returned and was also to sit in the Oxford Parliament. In the other case, at Lichfield, Thynne intruded another stranger, Daniel Finch, who was inclined to the Court. Nevertheless, his imposition was almost equally resented by the gentry. The second interesting point is that in order to persuade the townsmen to elect him, Thynne was obliged to undertake that Finch would not vote or act as a courtier in the Commons: a strange promise for one of the tellers against Exclusion to make. A Whig example of local independence against intruders occurred at Stockbridge. After defeating a Tory attempt to bring in strangers, a Whig Protestation was drawn up and publicized.[1]

This Stockbridge Protestation also denounced bribery. On this the Whig attitude was apparently clear, for they had introduced a bill with drastic punishments for corruption during the last session, but in fact it was equivocal. They castigated their opponents for offences which they committed themselves. Thus a Whig paper denounced the mayor of East Looe for swearing twenty-nine poor men as freemen, in a cock-loft, but at Maldon they were themselves guilty of the mass creation of freemen.[2] Accusations were made, concerning these elections, that the Whigs made a speciality of faggot votes, or the creation of bogus forty-shilling

[1] Domestick Intelligence, 17.
[2] True Domestic Intelligence, 25. HMC, 14th Report, ix (Round), 274.

freeholds either by subdividing property to make votes, or more simply by committing perjury at the poll by swearing to the ownership of non-existing property.

The Whigs were hypocritical and practical: their purpose was to eliminate opponents and at the same time gain a reputation for virtue. The Wiltshire Grand Jury levelled complaints against the conduct of officials, accusing the sheriff of having held back the writs. The under-sheriff was alleged to have exploited his office by demanding 10 guineas for the precept for Cricklade.[1] The jury presented as a very great grievance 'debauchery, drunkenness and excess' at elections, and particularly at Great Bedwin and Ludgershall. These places were singled out not because of their wickedness, but because of their choice of members. In the case of the latter the Whigs gave themselves away, for another Whig pamphlet inconsistently exhorted boroughs not to imitate the hypocritical rectitude of Ludgershall, 'whose dry Drunkenness has proved more pernicious to the Public safety than their liquide; and have made a worse choice, Sober, than perhaps they had ever done, stark mad'.[2] But many cases of electoral rectitude on the part of both members and electors were fully reported, and served as an accompaniment in the Whig press to the constant news of Whig electoral victories.

V

The elections confirmed Shaftesbury in his resolution to persist with the policy of Exclusion, and they gave him the means with which to intensify pressure on the King. The Whigs had made important gains, and a high proportion of those who had voted against Exclusion were defeated. Shaftesbury was assured of a commanding majority in the new House. Already he had discovered how illusory was his office of Lord President. Now, after the elections, the return of James and Monmouth's banishment, he began openly 'to undervalue his station, and would affect to be discharged harshly as the way to enhance him elsewhere'.[3] In

---

[1] *Domestick Intelligence*, 11.   [2] *Mild but Searching Expostulatory Letter* (1679).
[3] *HMC, Ormonde*, N.S., iv. 535; Sir Robert Southwell, 20 Aug. 1679.

particular James's return could be exploited. It was received with
popular indignation and it served to increase tension and excitement. In the City a leading Whig, Sir Thomas Player, made an
inflammatory speech in which, declaring that the presence of the
Duke increased the danger to the security of the citizens, he demanded that the watch should be doubled. He forced the Lord
Mayor to deny a report that he had promised to proclaim James
had the King's illness proved fatal. Once again the King and the
Court could be charged with being under James's malign influence.[1]

Monmouth's banishment, on the other hand, although it did
not amount to his disgrace, was a decided check. Monmouth was
depressed at what he recognized was a blow to his pretensions,
but he did not listen to those who advised him to disobey his
father's orders. Although his father was kind, both in his letter
telling him to go and in the leave-taking, his exile could not but
shatter the rumours and the belief that Monmouth's hold on his
father's affections was so strong that it would eventually lead to
his legitimization and acknowledgement as successor. The love
of many of the ordinary people for Monmouth was increased by
what was now represented as his martyrdom. But they would
have preferred him to stay, and it was noticed that the gentry did
not share this Whig enthusiasm. When Monmouth set out for
Holland he was virtually unattended, while at Whitehall the
courtiers now paid more attention to James than to the King.[2]

Shaftesbury, in undervaluing his office and privy councillor-
ship, was overestimating the strength of his position as the leader
and organizer of an Opposition. He knew that he was in no personal danger. There were rumours that he, Buckingham, and
other Whig leaders were to be arrested, and even that the City
was to be disarmed, but Shaftesbury was rightly confident that
Charles would not dare to take such risky action, even if his
brother did recommend it.[3] But in thinking that Parliament was
bound to meet at the appointed time, which would at once put

[1] *Hatton Correspondence*, i. 194–5. *Vindication of Sir Thomas Player* (1679).
[2] Barrillon, 25 Sept. Carte, 232, f. 60. Lord Longford, 26 Sept.
[3] Carte, 228, f. 157.

him in control, he was ignoring the very considerable changes which had occurred in the political situation. Shaftesbury believed that time was on his side, that things must get worse before they could get better, and that eventually the King would have to pay the price he demanded. This was a high one. When he was dismissed from the lord presidency and the Council on 15 October, Shaftesbury replied 'that he knew not that he had ever disserved His Majesty, and that when His Majesty thought so too he should be still ready to attend his commands'.[1] One rumour had it that he demanded a new queen. When Sunderland, in his effort at reinsurance, started negotiations for Shaftesbury's return to office, he found him obdurate.[2] Nothing would satisfy him but the elimination of both the Queen and the Duke. In November, possibly in a reference to this intrigue, Shaftesbury was boasting that he had refused an offer of the Lord Treasurer's staff and the power of nominating the great officers of state. He claimed that he would not accept any such offer unless his repeated demand was met, that all Papists should be abandoned and the Queen and the Duke left to Parliament.[3]

Shaftesbury's belief that he was indispensable, and that his recall could not long be delayed, ignored the fact that the return of James, and the determination now being shown by the King, were rallying to the Court all those who disliked the Whigs, their policy, and its possible results. Courtiers were now no longer afraid that they would be abandoned to the vengeance of the Whigs. Even though they had been worsted in the elections these courtiers, or Tories, were becoming more formidable with time and the encouragement of the King. Although they cannot be described as an organized political party in any sense, the Tories' very existence was a denial of the claim, implied in their former title, that the Opposition represented the 'country'. Instead they were a mere sect, a group of fanatics and factious men like the Covenanters of the south-western counties of Scotland, the Whiggamores.

---

[1] *HMC, Ormonde*, N.S., iv. 545; Southwell, 18 Oct.
[2] Sidney, i. 181.
[3] *HMC, Ormonde*, N.S., iv. 559-60; Southwell, 18 Nov.

Hitherto the Opposition had claimed that its enemies represented only themselves, the corrupt and alien Court. Now this became less plausible. Whether or not the Whigs were a majority (and it is impossible to make any estimate, which in any case would have little or no meaning), they were a faction, that is only a part of the nation. Moreover, the adherence of the King to their enemies led many who had previously regarded them as patriots and stalwarts against Popery to suspect them as factious. The crisis was still far too serious, excitement among the people still too intense, for them to be attacked by judicial means as a faction, but few contemporaries believed that opposition to the King, if not to his ministers, could ever be constitutional. Court propaganda, reminding the nation of the events and consequences of 1641, began to have some effect. Others besides courtiers were coming to suspect that the real if unavowed purpose of the Whigs was the subversion of all royal authority.

The strength of these suspicions, and an ominous sign of the increasing confidence of the Duke of York and his supporters, can be seen in the Meal-tub Plot. This was an attempt by jealous if rash Papists to attack the Whigs with the same technique and weapons of informers, discoveries, forged papers, and double-spies as those employed with such success by Oates and his imitators. In the autumn of 1679 the time seemed to be propitious. The acquittal (in July) of Sir George Wakeman, one of the King's physicians, on a charge of conspiring to poison the King, had been a blow to the credit of Oates and his fellows. The summing up of Scroggs in favour of the prisoner had been interpreted as an official change of attitude to the Plot. Now this impression was reinforced by the dismissal of Shaftesbury, Monmouth's exile, and the eclipse of the independent councillors.

The chief agent in the Papist counter-attack was Mrs. Celier, the celebrated if rather disreputable Papist midwife, and an experienced and accredited political intriguer. The witnesses brought over from the college at St. Omer for the defence of the Jesuits against Oates's perjuries had been lodged, and doubtless rehearsed, at her house. She had assisted an adventurer called Lane in his accusations of sodomy against Buckingham. Her obstetrical practice gave her access to many aristocratic families, and whatever her faults she was, like Oates, a person of some spirit and personality. In the spring she had been employed by James in his negotiations with Shaftesbury, and she now continued in his service. Her greatest achievement was the winning over of Sir Robert Peyton, the hottest of all City Whigs, whom she introduced to James. She built up a network of informers in the City, and showed herself active in their recruitment. In Newgate she found a man suitable for her purpose. This was 'Captain Willoughby', a young adventurer whose main assets were his handsome and confident appearance and his virility. His real name was Thomas Dangerfield, a thoroughly dishonest rogue with an appalling criminal record behind him, eager to swear to anything in order to advance his fortunes and procure his release. What took place between the two is uncertain, since their later accounts naturally differed and neither was in the habit of telling the truth.[1] At any rate a story was concocted for the ruin of the Whigs. Once at liberty 'Willoughby' was introduced by Mrs. Celier to her patroness, the Countess of Powis, another enthusiastic but indiscreet Papist. She was influential as the sister of the Marquis of Worcester, and as wife of one of the unfortunate Papist peers in the Tower was eager to bring about the ruin of those who were demanding his trial and execution. But she had none of the finesse necessary to manage a Plot so successfully as Shaftesbury had done, and does not seem to have any scruples or second thoughts about employing such a disreputable, and potentially disloyal, informer. 'Willoughby' was also taken to see the Earl of Peterborough, an intimate friend of James, who showed himself more cautious although he introduced him to the King and to the Duke of York. 'Willoughby' thus passed from Newgate to Whitehall in a matter almost of hours, which although not so uncommon an achievement at the time did at least give promise of a prosperous future.[2]

---

[1] Dangerfield's own *Narrative* (1679), and his evidence before the Lords and Commons (Addl. 17018, ff. 135, 159-63) are entirely unreliable. M. Petherick, *Restoration Rogues* (1951), 183-263, gives a detailed but far from impartial account of the Meal-tub Plot. Peterborough wrote his version, R. Halstead (pseud.), *Succint Genealogies* (1687), 434-9. See also Morrice, f. 228.

[2] Halstead, 437.

'Willoughby', however, was a poor informer as compared to
Oates, and in particular his methods left much to be desired. After
the fiasco of the Bedingfield letters, which but for his effrontery
might have proved fatal to his career, Oates had been very careful to rely solely upon his prodigious and conveniently selective
memory.[1] 'Willoughby's' reliance on papers was fatal, for once
he had bungled an attempt to plant them on a Whig, Mansell
who was steward to the Duke of Buckingham, his credit was
destroyed and his sham exposed. Indeed, he showed himself so
incompetent that some at the time, and many historians since, have
suspected, or even asserted, that Dangerfield (as he really was)
had been from the very first instructed by the Whigs so as to
trepan or trap their opponents. This is not impossible in a concern
where all those taking part were crooks, but there is no real evidence to show that this was the case. Peterborough did not think
so.[2] But after the failure to plant papers on Mansell, and with the
discovery of more sham evidence in Mrs. Celier's meal-tub,
Dangerfield's unreliability became dangerous to those who had
employed him. He saw that he could not expect them to procure
him either release from Newgate or any further money; at best
he would be doomed to a long stay on the 'common side' of the
jail, which even to an experienced criminal was a dismal prospect. The Whigs on the other side could offer him release,
supplies of money, and future protection. It was not surprising
that he should accept, and his new employers were quick to exploit his account of the organization and purpose of the sham
plot.

The results were very gratifying. Not only were prominent
courtiers involved, but the Tories throughout the country had
been over-eager to believe that his story was true. Like Oates's
revelations in the Popish Plot, the alleged discoveries had been
intended to appeal to the prejudices and assumptions of a section
of the nation, albeit a much narrower one. Dangerfield and his
original employers were producing evidence to prove what all
stout Cavaliers believed, that the 'holy cheat' was again on foot,
and that the Whigs were no better than rebels intent on subverting

[1] Pollock, *The Popish Plot*, 74–75.   [2] Halstead, 438.

the authority of the Crown. The Earl of Yarmouth hailed the news as confirmation of the factious character of his opponents.[1] Much of the detail of the sham plot was as nonsensical as the rubbish contained in the informations of Oates and his imitators. Whoever had compiled the list of conspirators alleged to be plotting against the King, was either sadly ill informed and out of date, or truly catholic in his dislikes; it included not only undoubted Whigs but men like Halifax and Radnor who were by no means out of favour at Court, even if their influence had temporarily diminished.

While the Tories betrayed themselves by their over-eagerness, the Whigs were furiously indignant at the sham plot. At a time when spontaneous excitement against the original Popish Plot was just beginning to subside, popular fears were once again raised to fever pitch. Shaftesbury's position as the great champion and defender of protestantism was confirmed by the fact that he had been the chief target of farcical attempts at assassination as well as of the sham. The King was unable to prevent the Meal-tub Plot being exploited to his own disadvantage. Mansell was reprimanded by the Council for printing his narrative without authorization, but the damage was already done, and no prosecution followed.[2] Charles asked the new Lord Mayor, Sir Robert Clayton, why he had interfered in a matter that was none of his business by examining Dangerfield. Clayton, a Whig but one who was always concerned for his own safety and property, replied that groups of citizens had been waiting in the streets near his house, anxiously expecting news. He had feared that if he had not been able to satisfy their fears for their leaders he would have been De-Witted.[3] Moreover, the sham came at a convenient time for the Whigs. On 17 November, the official birthday of Queen Elizabeth, a great political demonstration was organized. Pope-burnings had been common, but never on this scale. The mammoth procession through London was watched by over 150,000 people, among whom were said to be Charles and, at the risk of his life,

[1] Addl. 27447, f. 436.   [2] *True Domestic Intelligence*, 42.
[3] Morrice, f. 232. Carte, 228, f. 128.

Barrillon the French ambassador.[1] Public opinion was only too receptive, and antipapist sentiment was greatly stimulated by this great popular manifestation, a tribute to the quite unprecedented political showmanship and capacity for organization of Shaftesbury and the Whigs.

Shortly afterwards the populace had another opportunity to demonstrate their political sympathies. On the excuse that he had been named in the sham plot as one of those concerned, Monmouth made a surprise and unauthorized return from exile. He did so without the knowledge of the Prince of Orange, but apparently on the advice of Shaftesbury, lying at the Earl's house before announcing his return in a letter to his father.[2] This unauthorized return was premature and disastrous. In his letters Charles had continued to show him great kindness, and the prospects were that the exile would not be of long duration. Already proposals had been made that he should return to Court permanently. Monmouth's return, and still more his refusal to obey the King's orders to retire forthwith overseas, finally and for ever forfeited for him the King's open favour. Monmouth fortified himself in the people's applause and support, but the rest of his career was to show that these were no substitute for the offices of which he was now stripped, and the favoured position at Court which he now lost. Furthermore, the loss of his official salaries and grants was not unimportant to one who was so extravagant.

The people did not realize the damage they were doing him by the warmth of their welcome. The Court had already been alarmed at the prospect of disorders on 17 November; the welcome to Monmouth was all the more disturbing because it was spontaneous. The City was ablaze with bonfires from one end to the other. More sinister, and an ominous indication of what might have happened in August had the King died, and might still

---

[1] Sir George Sitwell, *The First Whig* (1894), gives an amusing and picturesque account of these monster processions and organized Pope burnings. They were organized by the Green Ribbon Club at the King's Head tavern. For the activities of this club, on which Sitwell's account is totally misleading and worthless, see J. R. Jones, 'The Green Ribbon Club', *Durham University Journal*, Dec. 1956.

[2] Barrillon, 11 Dec. 1679. Sidney, i. 194–5. *Hatton Correspondence*, i. 206. HMC, *Ormonde*, N.S., v. 244, 248–9.

happen in an emergency, the Guards lit bonfires in the streets outside Whitehall to welcome back their former commander.[1]

This continued evidence that popular excitement was still
dangerously high confirmed Charles in his determination not to
allow Parliament to meet. A number of members were already
assembled in anticipation, and were learnt to have agreed on a
course of extreme action from the start.[2] The soundings which
Charles made of Shaftesbury through Warcup's agency showed
that he too was intransigent, and confident that by means of pressure he could ultimately achieve his objectives. Nothing would
be gained by allowing Parliament to meet. As Barrillon observed
on the Meal-tub Plot, popular feelings could be disregarded and
were unimportant in themselves so long as there was no Parliament in session to act as a focus or sounding-board for opposition
and discontent.[3] The King could live for a while without parliamentary supplies, but if a session were begun the consequences
could not be foreseen, and an early dissolution might prove to be
necessary. This would merely still further embitter the atmosphere. Hence Charles was resolved to continue the prorogation,
and emphatic in his refusal of the Whig demands for the assembly
of Parliament, which were soon to become vociferous as a nation-
wide campaign of petitions began.

[1] BM, Portland deposit, 711E, portfolio 1. Newsletter of 29 Nov. Magdalene
College, Pepysian Library, Miscellanies, vii. 478.
[2] Carte, 228, ff. 89, 161.
[3] Barrillon, 7 Dec.

5

THE APPEAL TO THE NATION

I

THE Whigs bitterly criticized the King's refusal to allow the newly elected Parliament to meet. They denounced his decision as immediately dangerous, since it would prevent a thorough investigation of the Meal-tub Plot, and ultimately pernicious in that it appeared to threaten the constitutional position of Parliament. To the Whigs Parliament was the soul of the Commonwealth, which alone could 'apprehend and understand the symptoms of all Diseases which threaten the Body Politic'.[1] Hence, and above all in a time of crisis, meetings should be frequent; to fail to summon it was an infringement of the fundamental rights and liberties of the nation. Therefore when a prorogation until January was announced, the Whig leaders set out systematically to put the maximum pressure on the King by organizing petitions which called for the immediate assembly of the new Parliament.

The petitioning agitation was a sign of the unprecedented efficiency and resolution of Whig organization. It extended to the mass of the people, down even to the lowest classes, the split that already existed since the Exclusion division and the elections among the political nation. In form these petitions were an appeal by the people to the King against the advice, influence, and actions of the evil ministers who were blamed for the return of James, the prorogation, and Monmouth's exile and disgrace. In fact they were an appeal by the Whig leaders to the people, an attempt to bring pressure to bear on the King, a demand that Parliament should be summoned to state the nation's grievances

[1] *Vox Populi* (1681).

and to carry into law those measures which it judged necessary to ensure its security.

In contrast with earlier attempts since the Restoration, these Whig petitions were avowedly popular in character and appeal, and in this they resembled those organized by Pym. The prorogation of the first Whig Parliament in May had been hastened by the news that a petition was being prepared in the City in which the Commons were to be thanked for their proceedings and assured of support.[1] A second, and much more menacing, petition had been organized in June, again in the City, which had attempted to take advantage of the rising of the Covenanters in Scotland. It denounced the royal forces as an illegal standing army. The acts making it treason for English subjects to invade Scotland were quoted in an obvious attempt to deter the Council from sending any English soldiers north to assist in the anticipated civil war. Finally, the demand was made that the Duke of York should be brought to trial and Parliament assembled in order to meet the crisis. It was anticipated that if this petition 'took' in the City, it would then be sent to the grand juries in the provinces, but with the news of Bothwell Brig the whole project lost its point and had to be dropped.[2] Nevertheless, this first attempt was in some ways to be the pattern for the petitions of the autumn.

It was natural that the first petitions should be organized in the City, where the organizers could enjoy the advantages of anonymity and of a magistrature more favourable to them than elsewhere. In addition they could exploit the prestige of the City; if London led the way the counties could be expected to follow. In October an Exeter Whig wrote that many were in despair at the prorogation, and wished that a petition should be organized from London, 'all agree that London should lead the dance'. The object was not merely to demand that Parliament should be allowed to meet in January, but also that it should be permitted to sit until security was obtained for the King's person and the Protestant religion, thus re-emphasizing by implication the need for Exclusion.[3]

---

[1] Browning, ii. 82.   [2] Sidney, *Letters*, 113, 123. Addl. 15643, f. 10.
[3] HMC, *13th Report*, vi (*Fitzherbert*), 21.

The organization of these petitions, which began to get under way in November, was extremely thorough. In many ways it resembled that which had been used with such success in the elections. The whole movement is most important because the Whigs now elaborated and perfected the methods by which they could obtain and mobilize popular support on a scale and with an efficiency hitherto unknown, and indeed not to be equalled during the eighteenth century. The way was led by the Whig peers. On 7 December an address, asking that Parliament should be summoned in January, was presented by nine peers. Seventeen had signed, but the number who accompanied it to Whitehall was restricted so as to keep within the law.[1] There followed a monster petition from London and Westminster, and a score of others from the country. These petitions displayed the strength of the Whigs' popular support, and in addition helped considerably in stirring up the feelings of the people. Like some twentieth-century petitions they were intended as a means of activating the masses, those who had no vote and often no concern with politics. Ordinary people were flattered at being consulted; the arguments which were put forward to induce them to sign must often have persisted in their minds for long afterwards. House-to-house canvassers collected signatures. Tables, pens, ink, and forms were placed in taverns and at the Royal Exchange. Dr. Oates, the saviour of the nation, crossed the river to Southwark to give countenance to the petition being organized there by a City Whig and one of the Whig candidates who had been defeated in the recent elections. Agents were sent into the counties with printed forms for subscription; many of these men had previously been active during elections. They, together with local men, went from parish to parish collecting signatures, and leaders were appointed to present the completed petitions.[2]

Naturally the Tories alleged that many of the Whig petitions were fraudulent, that many names had been forged, many obtained by intimidation, and that they did not represent the sense of the better and more substantial citizens. But the Government

[1] *Domestick Intelligence*, 45.
[2] *Hatton Correspondence*, i. 215. R. North, *Examen* (1740), 542–3.

admitted their importance by the attempts which it made to prevent the agitation and to discourage subscriptions. The proclamation issued to prohibit petitioning was largely ineffective; it was a sign of Court weakness that no concerted attempt could be made to enforce it.[1] Whig pamphleteers asserted the legality of petitioning, and the judges on whose advice the proclamation had been made were attacked for the inadequacy of their legal knowledge and denounced for their subservience to the Crown. But the main reason for the failure to prosecute the organizers was their standing. Prominent Whigs showed themselves active. Often, as might be expected, the local Members of Parliament took part. The Oxfordshire petition was the work of the two Members for Oxford city. The two knights of the shire, with another prominent Whig, recommended the petition to the people of Essex, and presented it to the King, this being the occasion on which Charles received a crushing snub from Colonel Mildmay.[2] In Hertfordshire two borough members, Sir William Cowper and Sir Thomas Byde, signed the petition as an example, recommended it to the freeholders, and gave their advice as to how it should be carried on. When the Tories spread rumours and caused the Wiltshire petition to hang fire, Thomas Thynne went down at once to deny in person that he disapproved of the proceedings. He signed and undertook to present it himself. Only a few Whigs stood aloof, some being intimidated by the proclamation. Others, more far-sighted, feared that the petitions would defeat their own ends, believing with some justice that 'Portsmouth, Lauderdale, Sunderland and the Secret Cabal . . . will use these petitions as a handle to effect their other designs'. Certainly they were right in warning that the effect might be to harden the King's resolution against allowing Parliament to meet. With even greater insight Sacheverel, although an extreme Whig, opposed the petitioning agitation as premature; he believed that

---

[1] Steele, *A Bibliography of Royal Proclamations* (1910), i. 449. Luttrell, i. 28. The proclamation touched off a controversy, Whig pamphlets defending the legality of petitioning; for instance see *A Letter written by a Member of Parliament . . . on reading the* Gazette (1679).

[2] *True News, or, Mercurius Anglicus*, 20. In reply to Charles's rebuke 'I remember '41', Mildmay replied, 'Sire, I also remember '60'.

the King was not yet sufficiently reduced in circumstances for this pressure to be effective.[1]

The King's position was indeed strong enough for him to disregard, but not to suppress, the petitions. He showed his feelings quite openly by the insulting manner in which he received petitions and their presenters. In deliberate contrast he was extremely cordial to those who brought him the counter-petitions organized by the Tories, and commended these abhorrences on the ground that they were official in character. In fact not all the Whig petitions were unofficial, the one from York being signed by the Lord Mayor, the recorder, and his deputy, most of the aldermen, the sheriffs, the town clerk, and the members for the city. But in general the Tories despised the Whig petitions because they were popular, containing the signatures of men of no consequence or standing. In part this contempt was spurious—the Tories at this time could not organize popular support in any way comparable to the backing possessed by the Whigs. However, it represented their belief that government was the King's, that the duty of subjects was to obey him and his commands, and that they had no right to interfere in matters above their comprehension. Tory addresses generally came from officials, from the justices, corporations, or carefully packed grand juries. Nevertheless, the Tories could boast of one important success. The first petition from the City was unofficial, subscribed by so many inhabitants that it was said to have been 100 yards long, though if it was of this size it is far from clear how Charles was able to walk off with it in his hand, as the Whig press reported. Its effect would be greatly increased if an official petition from the City government could also be organized. Several Whig peers put intense pressure on the Lord Mayor, Clayton, to induce him to call a Common Council. He, a Whig but a timid one, was in an unenviable position. The King, afraid of the result, ordered him not to call one, but Clayton demurred on the ground that he was legally bound to convoke it. But when the Common Council did meet the proposed petition was rejected by a narrow majority. The King and the

---

[1] BM, Portland deposit, 711E, portfolio 1. Ashe, 23 Dec. 1679. *HMC, Ormonde*, N.S., iv. 576.

ministers were greatly and naturally elated by this success, and all
the more so because it was directly the result of a new Court
policy.[1]

The majority against petitioning in the Common Council was
obtained by a purge of those common councillors who were not
qualified under the Corporation Act. Several were excluded from
the meeting, others stayed away judging themselves not to be
qualified. This was only a beginning, a general purge was now
initiated of all Whigs from offices, the lieutenancy and militia,
and the commission of the peace. Charles was by now convinced
that compromise was impossible with those who insisted on
Exclusion. They were trying to put pressure on him, so in self-
defence he attempted to eliminate them from all positions of
influence and power. This reflected the change in the political
situation. In May, Shaftesbury had suggested a general inspection
of the commission, which under his direction would have been
used to oust all those known to have been courtiers. Deprived
of the assistance of his friends the King's authority would accordingly have suffered. Now it was the Whigs who were purged.
Composed almost exclusively of Tories, the militia and the
commission of the peace were now to become even more valuable
instruments of royal policy. During the last two months of 1679
the lord lieutenants, and leading Tories like Lord Longford, were
sending in lists of those recommended for ejection. The resolution
was taken to purge all promoters of petitions, but apart from these
there must have been many put out by local rivals for purely
personal reasons. By the early summer of 1680 the purge was
virtually completed.[2]

At the same time an attempt was being made with rather less
success to purge the boroughs. Orders were sent to put the Corporation Act into execution.[3] This had often been neglected, and
dissenters and their sympathizers had gained office and sometimes
a controlling interest. These orders were frequently disobeyed.
Without a revival of the special commissions such as had been

[1] Sidney, i. 248, 255.
[2] HMC, 11th Report, ii (House of Lords), 172 ff. Addl. 25125, f. 81.
[3] Protestant (Domestick) Intelligence, 70, 77.

appointed in the years after 1661, there was no way in which an
unwilling corporation could be compelled to obey, short of actions
of *Quo Warranto*. In fact there was a somewhat hesitant start to
the latter policy, one that was to be elaborated and extended during
the later years of the reign. York had particularly offended the
King by its chilly welcome to James during his journey to Scotland, and by its official support of a Whig petition. The King
asked that the city's charter should be inspected to see if there was
any pretext for its forfeiture, but the action was in fact to be
postponed for some years to come.

These purges still further increased political divisions within
the nation. They embittered those who now found themselves
legally at the mercy of local enemies who filled the Bench in their
place, and could be expected to dispense strictly Tory justice. The
Whigs denounced the activities of the abhorrers as especially
dangerous and detestable. Petitioning was the undoubted right
of the subject; the abhorrers were denying and so attempting to
subvert one of the main liberties of the nation, as well as encouraging the King to refrain from calling Parliament. Meanwhile
the person of the King, and so the safety of the nation, was still
exposed to the plots and assassination projects of the Papists. This
was all the more disquieting since the Plot was no longer being
prosecuted with much energy or success. Charles was still not,
at least in form, regarded as responsible. The Whigs continued to
use the convenient fiction that it was the self-interested advice
of the Duke of York, and the evil ministers afraid of parliamentary
impeachment, that led the King to decide that Parliament should
not meet. Shaftesbury wrote to the independent members of the
Council, advising them to disassociate themselves by resignation
from the illegalities and unpopularity which continued membership would involve. This in itself would provide more pressure
upon the King, and would encourage the Whigs to remain
intransigent by increasing their confidence that in the end the
King would have to accede to their demands. 'You ought to
quit, and that presently, and in a body together; both for your
own sakes, the nation's and the King's service . . . as our affairs
stand we have no hopes of a good composure, but by the weight of

the nation . . . to this end your Lordships going out together at
this time extremely serves.'[1] This advice was supplemented by an
apposite biblical quotation from the book of Esther, which, with
its striking parallels to the Plot, must have been much in men's
minds at this time.

Shaftesbury's appeal was only partly successful. Radnor, who
had succeeded as Lord President, refused to abandon his new
honour and thought himself important enough to stand on his own
feet.[2] Temple, never a Whig, had by now virtually withdrawn
from active politics. Although he did not attend its meetings he
had no intention of making a demonstration out of his resignation.
Essex, although by now again suspicious of the King, remained a
member of the Council, and still held himself apart from the
Whigs. But his brother, Sir Henry Capel, together with Russell,
Cavendish, and Powle, was thoroughly discontented with the
King's actions and intentions, and aware of his own anomalous
position. With their concerted withdrawal the reconstituted Privy
Council, as a body which included both sides, came finally to an
end. Thus the division of the nation into two hostile factions was
virtually complete and irrevocable.

This division was the effect, but it had not been the deliberate
intention, of the King's policy. During the months of prorogation Charles was pursuing self-contradictory aims. On the
one hand, he was trying to gain time in which the people's
excitement would subside and political passions become less
intense. Once the crisis appeared to moderate then support for
Exclusion would almost certainly diminish; only the extremity
of the danger had persuaded many to countenance such a revolutionary measure. But the King's encouragement of his own supporters, now rallying as Tories, and the deliberate humiliations
which he inflicted on the Whigs, kept alive tension and distrust.
Opposition was repressed for the moment, but its causes were not
removed. Royal policy was negative and unconvincing. The
Press was suppressed by proclamation, Whig pamphleteers were

---

[1] Shaftesbury Papers, VI A, 351.
[2] Sidney, i. 237. He refused to resign as 'he did not come in with them, and he
will not go out with them'.

severely punished. In a policy reminiscent of that used by Danby, an attempt was made to allay suspicions by initiating an ambitious and apparently anti-French foreign policy. Envoys were sent to Berlin, Stockholm, and Copenhagen to seek a general alliance on a Protestant basis. At home Charles was extremely careful to govern within the law so as to give the Whigs no new grievances to exploit. For a time this policy appeared to have at least some measure of success. A few Whigs became discouraged by the long prorogations and the evident disfavour of the King. When Charles paid a visit to the City in March he was given an enthusiastic reception, especially by Clayton who might be regarded as a kind of political barometer. In April, Sunderland wrote with confidence, dismissing the Whigs as a spent force, their credit diminishing and unlikely to be able to achieve anything when Parliament finally did meet. He boasted that the measures taken by the King would prevent anyone hurting him.[1]

Sunderland's confidence was slightly spurious. He was trying to convince Henry Sidney and the Prince of Orange that Charles would allow Parliament to meet in the near future. The fact that there was no intention of doing so shows that both Charles and Sunderland realized that the crisis had still not sufficiently moderated to make such a step possible. But in fact the situation was deteriorating still further as the King's illness showed in May.[2] This, although not so serious or of very long duration, caused as much alarm as in the previous August. Both sides made feverish preparations. Whig confidence was if anything increasing; time seemed to be on their side. Shaftesbury was remarkably successful in maintaining an atmosphere of tension and popular excitement throughout the months of the prorogations. If the public were becoming satiated with stories of the Plot (and this was certainly

---

[1] Sidney, i. 301. Prinsterer, v. 392. 6 Apr.

[2] Sidney, ii. 60–61, 63–64. Barrillon, 27 May 1680; he reported that had the illness continued the M.P.'s assembled to hear the announcement of a further prorogation would have refused to disperse, but claimed that the crisis justified their continuation. The Court had followed the course of ordering frequent and short prorogations as part of the attempt to reduce the political temperature; prorogations had been ordered to 26 Jan. 1680, then to 15 Apr., 17 May, 1 July, 22 July, 23 Aug., and then finally 21 Oct. (*CJ* ix. 635–6.)

not the case with the lower classes), Whig organization supplied
much of what was now lacking in spontaneity. Although the
Tories alleged that it was a sham, the attack on a Whig, John
Arnold, was popularly construed as an attempt by the Papists to
revenge the execution of a Jesuit for which he had been responsible.[1] The incident created a great stir, and revived old fears.

The City was still in a receptive mood to believe the news of an
Irish Plot, which Shaftesbury communicated to the Council in
April. Fearing that, as in the case of the Meal-tub Plot, premature
disclosures, and investigation exclusively by the Council, would
rob the evidence of much of its effect, he wisely reserved the
full details until they could be exploited when Parliament met.
Moreover, even if most Englishmen believed implicitly that the
Irish Papists must be planning a rebellion and probably a massacre
like that of 1641, a great deal of organization was necessary so that
the details of the evidence would be clear and consistent. Discontented members of the Irish Council were willing to give their
assistance. A few pioneer informers were sent across to find more
evidence and to recruit new witnesses. Supervised by Shaftesbury's completely unscrupulous agent, Hetherington, they were
active most of the summer, and had no difficulty in securing
reinforcements. By September whole squads of informers, cattle
thieves and renegade priests for the most part, had come over,
their necessities provided for, their fabricated stories prepared,
to be greeted on arrival in London by their exemplar and future
mentor, Titus Oates.[2]

Monmouth was also active during the summer. His friend
Armstrong was busily engaged in the hunt for the Black Box,
with the evidence to prove Monmouth's legitimacy and so his
hereditary right to the succession. These stories of the Black Box,
although not entirely incredible in view of the first and secret
marriage of James shortly after the Restoration, had a considerable
effect on the ignorant and credulous but, as more knowledgeable

[1] Ailesbury, *Memoirs*, 30. Prinsterer, v. 394. Luttrell, i. 41. National Library of
Wales, MSS. 1461c, ff. 154–93 (a MS. account of the Arnolds of Monmouthshire).

[2] Ormonde's correspondence, and copies of the letters which he intercepted, in
the Carte Papers contain a great deal of evidence on the organization and manufacture of this Irish Plot.

Whigs saw, a detrimental effect on the educated.[1] Monmouth's popularity now reached its height, but as always it was greater among the common people than among the gentry. In any case popular adulation could not compensate him for the loss of his offices and his father's consistent severity towards him. Ralph Montagu and those who had advised his return from exile disavowed their action when they saw its results. In order to retain his popularity with the people Monmouth could not make terms with the King without risk. If he regained his lost offices it could only be at the price of losing the support of his political friends. When in January 1680 Charles ordered him once again to leave the country if he was to expect pardon and a restoration to favour, Monmouth answered that he would do so only if Lauderdale and the Duchess of Portsmouth were also sent away.[2] This brave reply did not, however, prevent him from seeking an accommodation in March, but he found the conditions unacceptable. The price of pardon was the revelation of the names of his advisers on certain occasions in the past.[3] To accept on these terms would mean, as was intended by the King, the alienation and abandonment of his former Whig associates, and pardon must have been judged an insufficient reward for a desertion with such consequences. Instead of relying on his father's generosity and favour, and acquiescing in his own political impotence, Monmouth preferred to stick by his friends and assist their cause and his own pretensions.

In the summer of 1680 he made his triumphal tour or progress (since it was modelled on a royal journey) through the west country. Despite the slights of Tory officials he received an almost frantic popular welcome and created a legend which was to have important results in 1685. Charles tried to deter the Earl of Pembroke from giving hospitality and to prohibit Monmouth from starting. The latter refused to recognize a verbal order, and

---

[1] *HMC, Ormonde*, N.S., v. 314. Addl. 28094, f. 71. *CSPD*, 1679/80, 447, 448–51. *A Letter to a Person of Honour concerning the Black Box*, written in May 1680 to undo some of the damage, claimed that the stories about the Box had been invented and circulated by James and his associates to ridicule the belief in Charles's marriage to Monmouth's mother.   [2] Carte, 228, f. 153.
[3] Ibid., 243, f. 444. Sir R. Reading, 9 Mar. 1680.

demanded that it should be put into writing. This, of course, would not be binding on him, but it would commit the ministers. Afraid that they would be held responsible for such an order, knowing that it would expose them to violent personal attacks in Parliament, the attempt at intimidation was abandoned.[1] Similarly, the propaganda put out by the Court and the Tories proved ineffective. Although true, the stories that Monmouth had been brought up as a Papist could not harm his reputation. They were irrelevant by the side of his present activities and sufferings, so called, for the defence of protestantism. When Charles, in an uncharacteristic frame of mind, expressed the belief that Lucy Walter had been a whore to other men, Lord Macclesfield, a companion of his years of exile but now a Whig, did not remember.[2] Despite the damage done by the Black Box agitation Monmouth's pretensions were gaining support. Even some of William's associates were being forced to realize that they must now be taken seriously. When another official approach was made, offering Monmouth the restoration of all his former places on condition that he voluntarily withdrew abroad during the forthcoming parliamentary session, he again refused. Indeed, the private meetings which took place between him and the King during this negotiation went far to convince the Whig leaders that Charles was slowly but inevitably coming round to the idea of Exclusion.[3] Such had been Shaftesbury's success in holding together the Whigs during the prorogations that Monmouth became more confident. Naturally he preferred to play for higher stakes than a mere pardon, and to trust that continued political pressure would eventually enable him to achieve his full pretensions.

II

Events during the summer testified to the decline of the Court interest and the growing strength of the Whigs. Both factions chose to regard the London shrieval elections as a trial of strength.

[1] Carte, 39, f. 168.
[2] H. C. Foxcroft (ed.), *Correspondence of Gilbert Burnet* (1907), 31.
[3] Barrillon, 30 Sept., 31 Oct.

Relying on the pressure which could be exerted by officials, and making all the interest they could, the Court hoped to be able to block the election of two particularly obnoxious Whig candidates, Henry Cornish and Slingsby Bethell, a reputed republican. The first election was invalidated because they were not qualified under the Corporation Act, which merely infuriated the City Whigs still further against the recorder, Jeffreys, and the common serjeant. The Court managers found that they could not perform what they had promised; in the second poll, which was conducted with great bitterness, the Whigs had a majority of more than two to one. Not surprisingly, after this incident, negotiations for a loan from the City broke down, and Papillon was said to have frustrated a further attempt to obtain a loan from the East India Company.[1]

The confidence with which Shaftesbury looked forward to the session, and the strength which he believed he retained despite the prorogations, were strikingly demonstrated by the attempts to indict the Duke of York as a Papist recusant, and the Duchess of Portsmouth as a common nuisance.[2] These attempts have generally been dismissed as abortive because the indictments were suppressed at the instigation of Lord Chief Justice Scroggs. Admittedly, the Whigs were furious at his conduct, and were to make it the basis for an impeachment, but in fact the attacks on James and the Duchess entirely fulfilled their purpose. This bold move convinced waverers that the Whig leaders would not have gone to this extreme had they not been assured of victory in the forthcoming session. But the Whig leaders had nothing to lose. They had already alienated James to such an extent that they could expect nothing but vengeance from him. If he did come to the throne their attempts to force through Exclusion would, as a pamphlet predicted, 'be judged expiable by no less than the blood of those worthy Patriots'.

The reasons adduced for the presentment of James were calculated

[1] Barrillon, 29 July, 16, 30 Sept., 17 Oct. *CSPD*, 1679/80, 557, 558, 564. Luttrell, i. 49. J. Cartwright, *Sacharissa* (1893), 282; Sunderland later claimed that he had not wanted to intervene but had been misled by the lord mayor and recorder.

[2] Shaftesbury Papers, VI B, 420-2. Luttrell, i. 49. BM, Sloane MSS. 2496, f. 55.

to make good propaganda in favour of Exclusion.[1] Being a
Papist he was accused of encouraging the Plot and protecting the
plotters. With his influence on the King, and above all in the
appointment of officers, he was an immediate danger to the nation.
As long as he remained heir to the throne there could be no
security for the nation: 'Queen Mary having proved the wisest
Laws to be of little force, to keep out Popery and tyranny under
a Popish prince'. In law there was no reason why James should not
be prosecuted, his conversion being in itself criminal.

The attack on the Duchess of Portsmouth had a more immediate
purpose—her intimidation. This was achieved by the rather
lurid articles prepared against her.[2] In addition to the general
accusation of working in the French interest, and thus promoting
the designs of Popery and arbitrary government, serious crimes
were alleged which included a tentative charge of having attempted to poison the King. The implications of this were fright-
ening. Should Charles die (and he had been seriously ill again in
May) nothing could save her from a hideous death, either at the
hands of the Whigs or as a scapegoat abandoned by the Court.
Alarmed by the attack, she chose to try to ensure her position
by starting negotiations with the Whigs and promising her
support and personal influence in favour of Exclusion.

The support of the Duchess of Portsmouth was all the more
important because of her close connexion with Sunderland. His
former confidence, if it had ever been genuine, had now disappeared. As before, acting according to his political maxims, he
sought to insure himself with each section. In the first place he
again began to propagate the interest of the Prince of Orange.
Together with his friends he repeatedly, but unsuccessfully,
advised William to come over for the approaching session. In
doing so his real purpose was not so much to protect William's
interests as to further and perpetuate his own influence. He would
naturally act as William's principal adviser; together they would
dominate the King. As always Sunderland's advice was self-

---

[1] The attempt provides a good example of co-ordinated Whig action; the
grand jury was packed, the court room full of leading Whigs.
[2] Carte, 72, ff. 520-1.

interested; he used Monmouth's popularity to try to alarm William and bring him to accept his policy.[1] William was rightly wary. He was troubled at the crisis which made England of no possible use as an ally against France, but he could see no obvious or easy solution, whereas the risks to himself were all too plain. He knew that as a foreigner, unfamiliar with English politics and institutions, he would be at a permanent disadvantage, dependent on unreliable advisers. Whatever happened he would quite probably ruin his reputation with one side or the other, and possibly with both.

Cold, cautious, and detached, William was far too astute and reserved to play anybody else's game. The death of Ossory had deprived him of the one man whom he trusted; with good reason he was suspicious of his other self-appointed advisers. By his absence from England, and by his care to maintain connexions with each group, William avoided committing himself, and so saved himself from the indiscretions and blunders which were to be fatal to Monmouth. Throughout the crisis William's attitude was correct. Early in 1679 he expressed the hope that Danby, then in hiding, would not compromise him by seeking refuge in the United Provinces, although he generously added that he would not refuse asylum to one to whom he owed such obligations should Danby actually come.[2] Later in the same year William entertained Monmouth at The Hague. Although the two men must have regarded each other as potential rivals, and their interests clearly conflicted, William showed his guest every kindness.[3] The reason was that, as Charles's letters made plain, Monmouth still retained his father's favour. But when Monmouth returned to England without permission William was quick to disavow any responsibility.[4] In addition he maintained a continuous correspondence with his father-in-law in the summer of 1680, assuring him of support against Monmouth's pretensions, which

[1] Sidney, ii. 77–78; on 28 June Sunderland urged Sidney to tell William to come over. Kenyon, 50–51.
[2] Carte, 70, f. 423. William to Ossory, 16 Apr. 1679, copy by Carte.
[3] Sidney, i. 193 n.
[4] Carte, 70, f. 423. William to Ossory, 15 Dec. 1679, copy by Carte. 228, f. 140.

at least it was easy to do. When Exclusion was under way William wrote effusively, but still equivocally, to the loyal but obtuse Jenkins, and he also wrote regularly to his wife's uncle, Lord Rochester.[1]

William's attitude was one of deliberate personal inactivity. He believed that Charles was at heart a Papist, and he could not see how James could ever succeed to the throne since the over-whelming majority of the nation was in favour of Exclusion.[2] He was not, however, prepared to intervene in favour of its passage; any influence exerted in favour was deliberately indirect, by means of subordinates and friends who could if necessary be disavowed. Still less was he going to allow himself to be used to buttress up the personal position of Sunderland. The latter was forced by this failure to rely on the support of his own associates, who assembled at Althorp in June. All, including Halifax, appeared to be agreed on the policy which should be followed. Limitations or expedients were to be offered in place of Exclusion, an alliance with the United Provinces was to inaugurate an anti-French policy for which it was hoped enough money could be obtained to fit out a fleet. Some effort was made by personal negotiation to win support for this scheme from prominent Whigs. But the chances of success were not sufficiently great for Sunderland to rely entirely on this policy—and later events were to show how unrealistic it was. He had never entirely severed relations with the Whigs; now he resumed negotiations with them.[3]

Sunderland found that the Whigs were still determined to secure Exclusion; they rejected all idea of limitations and thought that proposals of foreign alliances were hardly relevant. The price of accommodation with them was the promise of assistance towards the passing of an Exclusion Act. The assistance which Sunderland, and to a lesser extent the Duchess of Portsmouth, could offer would be of the very greatest importance to the

[1] Sidney, ii. 126–7, an effusive letter from William to Jenkins, 22 Nov. 1680, which Dalrymple (of course) printed.
[2] Temple, *Memoirs* (1700), 388. Sidney, i. 130, 7 Sept. 1679.
[3] Barrillon, 17, 31 Oct. 1680. Kenyon, 47–48.

Whigs. They had won such successes at the elections that, as before, they could expect to dominate the proceedings of the new House of Commons. But this was not enough. Shaftesbury had used his majority to force himself upon the King for a time, but his dismissal and the dissolution had shown that he and his policies were unacceptable to the King. If Exclusion was to pass he must gain the support, or at least the neutrality, of the King. Unless this was secured the bill would have little or no chance of passing the House of Lords, where the bishops and royal dependents could be relied upon to turn the balance against it. Sunderland and the Duchess were important because they could supplement the parliamentary pressure exerted by the Whigs with personal persuasion and Court intrigue. When Sunderland promised that he could obtain the King's consent, or at least complaisance, it would seem that nothing could impede the passage of Exclusion. If this promise was fulfilled then courtiers like Arlington, waverers such as Radnor, and many of the less important dependents would desert James and support the bill in order to follow the King's wishes.

During the last few weeks before the session was due to begin Sunderland became convinced that Charles would eventually desert his brother. James's unpopularity had not diminished in any way. As had been demonstrated by the attempt at his indictment, the Whigs retained their confidence. Sunderland believed that Charles realized he could never agree with Parliament so long as he stood by his brother, and that when hard pressed he would abandon him. He was not alone in this belief. James himself doubted his brother's resolution. Barrillon reported that in his opinion Charles, for all his protests to the contrary, would give way. The only alternative to an agreement with Parliament, which must necessarily involve the sacrifice of James, would be a renewed approach to France. The Duchess of Portsmouth, not a very sound political observer, agreed with Sunderland. But even courtiers and Tories like Hyde and the Lord Chancellor also feared that James would be abandoned. Accordingly, but without entirely committing himself to this one course of action, Sunderland now devoted most of his energies to negotiations with the

Whig leaders. At the same time the Duchess of Portsmouth started meeting Monmouth in private.[1]

These negotiations reflected the change in the political situation as the session approached. Whig strength and confidence were becoming stronger every day. In the negotiations after the Althorp meeting in June, Sunderland and his associates had tried to persuade individual Whigs to support the ministerial policy of limitations and an anti-French alliance. Now Sunderland was reduced to offering his assistance to the Whigs to carry out their policy. From the Whig view there was, however, one serious defect in the proposals which were made by Sunderland. With considerable justification the Whig leaders were suspected by the rank and file of being intent on self-advancement. The latter could remember the series of desertions in the Cavalier Parliament, and those which had followed the reconstruction of the Privy Council the previous year. Indeed, members of one section were intriguing for office at this time. Therefore any concession by the ministers must be an open one, freely declared, and preferably before the start of the session. If Shaftesbury and the other leaders made any secret and private bargain with Sunderland and the Court it might well be repudiated by their followers, as had happened with the agreement made by Holles before the start of the previous Parliament. But Sunderland was totally unable to offer any important or public concession before Parliament met.[2]

As a minister entirely dependent on the King's favour he knew how unpopular he was, not only in the country but also with his fellow courtiers. His continuance in office depended upon his following the King's wishes, or (and this was very much more difficult during the crisis) interpreting the King's intentions. Sunderland's conduct was based on his belief that Charles wished

[1] Barrillon, 19 Sept.; 24, 31 Oct.; 4, 11 Nov. Prinsterer, v. 422. Sidney to William, 7 Oct. *HMC, Ormonde*, N.S., v. 454. Longford, 16 Oct. 1680. Kenyon, 51–53, 56–57. It should be added that, as he rightly emphasizes (61), Sunderland and Portsmouth were on bad terms at this time although they were working on the same tack, separately.

[2] Barrillon, 19, 30 Sept.; 28 Nov. Barrillon was renewing his contacts with members of the Opposition because of the uncertainty of the situation at the start of the session.

to be forced into consenting to Exclusion.[1] Although he was generally assumed to have decided to abandon his former insistence on James's right of succession, he could not for form's sake appear to give his assent willingly or readily. So Sunderland could not give any definite assurances to Shaftesbury at the beginning of the session. In order to retain the royal favour he was obliged to wait until parliamentary pressure was such that the King could plausibly plead that he could not resist it. But even before the session showed how intense this pressure would be, Sunderland appears to have come to an understanding with the Whigs and to have begun to hint to the King that James must be abandoned.

III

Whig organization showed itself even more efficient in the new House of Commons than in the previous session. Shaftesbury had now reached the height of his power as a party leader. The chief minister and the chief mistress had promised their support and held out the prospect of the King's agreement. Danby was trying to come to terms.[2] Popular excitement and support showed no signs of lessening.

The House was full from the first day.[3] An abundance of grievances offered opportunities for taking the offensive, but some advised a cautious start so as first to obtain a guaranteed length for the session. On the other hand, Barrillon believed that the new, ignorant, and aggressive provincial members would dominate the proceedings, and that the nominal Whig leaders would have to ascertain their opinions and then try to follow them.[4] This did not prove to be the case. Of the several groups among the Whigs probably the most influential, and certainly the most vocal,

[1] HMC, Ormonde, N.S., v. 454. Kenyon, 58–59. Even Charles's attitude and speeches at the council meetings on 13, 15 Oct. were not absolutely conclusive.
[2] Addl. 28053, ff. 203, 205. 28042, f. 32.
[3] Letters had been sent to members, requesting their presence, although such letters had been violently attacked when they had been dispatched by the Court in 1675. Carte 39, ff. 192–3.
[4] Barrillon, 7 Oct.

during this session consisted of men who had defected to the Court during the last session and voted against Exclusion. By the start of the session of 1680 many of them, disillusioned with the King, returned to the Whig ranks and soon achieved prominence as advocates of Exclusion and of the rejection of all other proposals.

All the Whig groups were at least united in their insistence on Exclusion and the tactics to be used to achieve it. These were very similar to those employed in the previous Parliament. On the second day Dangerfield was heard at the bar of the House, and even after all the time that had elapsed his story of the sham plot still aroused some resentment. His evidence was followed by a debate which showed how complete was the ascendancy of the Whigs. At this early stage the first moves were made for the reintroduction of Exclusion. Capel, a former privy councillor who had voted against Exclusion, and only a few weeks before had put forward a scheme for a compromise, led the way. In a long speech he attacked Popery, which he blamed for all the grievances of the subject, and connected the danger with the strength of France. He concluded with a motion 'to consider of the prevention of Popery, and a Popish Successor'. Winnington, another who had voted against Exclusion, retailed the long list of grievances, the dissolution, the sham Meal-tub Plot, the proclamation against petitioning, the Tory abhorrences, the suppression of the indictment against James, the judicial action against Whig pamphleteers, and the attack on Arnold. He, too, concluded that there was no security against Popery except by preventing a Popish successor, and the fact that the House proceeded to vote *nem. con.* that it would act 'effectually to suppress Popery; and prevent a Popish Successor' showed how weak were the Tories.[1]

On 27 October Dangerfield gave in his evidence against the Duke of York in writing. The ensuing debate, which began with Tory attempts to throw doubts on his trustworthiness, was diverted and ended with resolutions in favour of the legality of petitioning and against abhorrers. Subsequently a debate was initiated on this subject, engendering great bitterness and ending

[1] Grey, vii. 360-2, 362-5. *CJ* ix. 640.

with the expulsion of two Tory members.[1] A similar tactical ascendancy was established in the committee of privileges, and by declaring Tory members unseated the Whigs strengthened still further their hold on the House. The Whig policy was to hurry on the introduction of another Exclusion Bill with as little delay as possible. Exactly the same procedure was followed as in the last session. Treby once again made a report from Coleman's letters, Russell moved for the repetition of the motion that the Duke's being a Papist had encouraged the Plot, and Booth the declaration that should the King's death be accomplished it would be revenged upon the Papists. The Whigs refused even to go into Grand Committee to discuss expedients which would not affect the succession, they rejected any and every possible alternative to a new Exclusion Bill. Titus expressed the Whig view when he declared: 'was there any place left for Moderation or Expedient I would run into it. . . . But for whom do we urge this Moderation? Is it for one to expect Moderation again? . . . this Bill proposed is the most ready way to secure ourselves.'[2] When Secretary Jenkins attempted to delay the second reading his arguments were contemptuously swept aside.[3] The only delay came from the great Protestant anniversary of 5 November, now more significant than ever, on which even the good work was suspended.

In the debate on the second reading the Tories spoke more effectively than before. They had clearly rehearsed their tactics, and the speeches displayed considerable coherence and coordination in an attempt to embarrass and divide the Whigs by insisting that the intended successor should be named in the bill. Sir William Hickman asked that the succession should go to the 'next right Heir'. A second Tory, Musgrave, insisted that the committee drafting the bill should name the successor. Garroway, a moderate, was for a general instruction that no Protestant should be excluded, or it might appear that a Commonwealth

[1] Grey, vii. 372, 385–91. *CJ* ix. 642–3. The two Tories were Sir Francis Wythens and Sir Robert Cann.

[2] Idem, 400–1, 2 Nov.

[3] Idem, 418–20, 4 Nov. Jenkins, the main Court spokesman, was easily flustered by Whig interruptions and out-manœuvred on procedural matters.

was to be established. Finch argued that the Duke's children should succeed as if their father were dead, while Sir Robert Howard thought that a saving clause in favour of Protestant successors would be sufficient. The Whigs were not to be drawn. On the ground that the King's life would continue to be in imminent danger until the bill had passed, Birch opposed giving instructions to the committee; the bill should stand on its own bottom. Sir John Knight asked rhetorically: 'will you deprive the King by naming a Successor, as if you would suppose the King should not have an Heir of his own?'[1]

This vagueness, and silence on the real issue, covered Whig uncertainty and disunion. The Tory speeches forced them to concede that instructions should be given to the committee that the Bill of Exclusion was to apply only to the person of James. Subsequently the Whigs were obliged to retreat still farther, and in the change which was made the essentially negative character of Exclusion again appears. Although they were united on the necessity for the bill, there was still no general or explicit agreement on who was to succeed. Its primary object was to defend the liberty and religion of the nation from the menace of the Duke of York and his associates. Now, however, the position was becoming more complicated. Since the previous year Monmouth's interest had greatly increased; his hopes were centred on keeping the succession open while the bill was being passed.[2] As the popular hero of much of the nation he was at an advantage to William, who was little more than a name to most people and was in fact distrusted by many as being of absolutist tendencies. Should an emergency occur, such as the death of the King—which would inevitably be attributed to the Papists—as the claimant on the spot he might be able to seize power before William could act.

In their attitude to Monmouth the Whigs were uncertain and divided. His personal friends were busily canvassing his rights.

[1] Grey, vii. 427-8, 429-30.
[2] Barrillon, 21 Nov. If Exclusion passed measures of security would have to be taken, for instance concerning the army and the militia, and in these Monmouth would have found opportunities to secure himself and advance his pretensions.

Shaftesbury appears to have flattered him, but without committing himself. Others regarded him purely as a tool to be used,
but with no intention of ever putting him on the throne. To have
named him in the bill would have caused serious divisions which
the Tories would have been quick to exploit. The Tory arguments
indeed led to what almost appeared as a repudiation of Monmouth's pretensions. On 8 November Russell virtually answered
the Tory demands to name a successor by moving a proviso, that
'nothing in this Act shall tend to disable any person to succeed
other than the Duke of York . . . but that the Crown shall descend
to such person, during the life of the Duke of York, as should
inherit the same, in case the Duke were dead'.[1] This clause was not
such a guarantee of Mary's rights as might at first sight appear.
It could be regarded as a purely tactical move, which was calculated
to facilitate the passage of the bill, but could later be amended—
for instance in Monmouth's favour—at some time in the future
when the Whigs had consolidated their position.[2] Nevertheless,
this clause deprived the Tories of one of their chief arguments.

In an attempt to provide the Tories with effective debating
alternatives to Exclusion a message was delivered on 9 November
to the House from the King. In this Charles once again promised
to give his consent to all remedies presented to him, provided that
they did not alter the succession. Tory ineffectiveness was seen in
the failure to develop this theme effectively. Neither they nor the
King were sincere in expressing advance acceptance of limitations
to be imposed on a Popish King, but they failed to use them as a
means to baffle the Whigs or regain the initiative. Whig speakers
monopolized the debate, the *Answer* drafted in reply was a party
manifesto attacking the royal ministers. The debate on the third
reading of the bill showed even more clearly that the Tories were
on the defensive, that they had no new arguments against it.[3]
The tide was running strongly in favour of the Whigs and
Exclusion. The Tory speakers concentrated on the barren argument, disregarded in the previous Parliament, that the bill was

---

[1] Grey, vii. 431–2.
[2] Halifax appreciated this point; Prinsterer, v. 454, Van Leeuwen to William,
7/17 Dec.   [3] Grey, vii. 433, 446–59.

unjust to James. Whigs effectively demolished this plea for, as
Trenchard said, the religion and liberty of the nation were of
more importance than the rights of one man: 'when a thing is
pro bono publico we ever step over private Rights.'

Far from it being the new, obscure, and ignorant members who
pressed most vigorously for Exclusion, disregarding the advice
of older and more moderate leaders, veteran Whig speakers were
joined by former opponents of the bill. The most forthright advocates of the bill were the two lawyers, Sir William Jones and
Sir Francis Winnington, who sat next to each other and worked
in close association. The former was admittedly a new member,
but he was an old Whig and had an immense reputation for his
legal ability and knowledge. A former Attorney-General, he had
drafted the Habeas Corpus (Amendment) Act in 1679, and was
said to have been promised the lord chancellorship by the Whig
leaders as the reward for his adherence to Exclusion. Notoriously
timid by nature, his support convinced many that success must
be certain. Rarely can a new member have been given such respect
by the House. On the day he made his maiden speech he was
appointed chairman of a committee, and his speech was the leading
one made in favour of the bill. After an introductory piece of
hypocrisy—a reference of esteem for James—he argued that the
bill, so far from being unjust, was a favour to him. There was no
question of James being punished, as some more hot-headed
Whigs demanded, but simply of protecting religion. He enlarged
on the legal argument that there was no alternative course, since
James's succession would automatically annul any attainder. In
one version the speech ended with a fine peroration: 'Let us
disable him! let us exclude him from the Crown! 'Tis Lawful, 'tis
absolutely necessary, without it 'tis impossible to be safe! I per-
ceive no gentleman hath confidence to deny the legality of fact,
or excuse the Black Crimes that appear before us.'[1]

The other principal Whig speakers, Winnington and Capel,
were equally confident. Both had voted against the bill in the last
Parliament, and their reversal of attitude showed how strong was
the trend towards Exclusion. Winnington was no longer equivocal

[1] BM, Birch MSS. 4159, f. 79. Temple, *Works*, i. 351.

as in the past. He denied that James had a *jure divino* right to the succession; on the contrary, Parliament had often diverted and altered it. There was no question of injuring the Duke, but of preventing a future mischief; posterity must be protected from Popery and slavery. Capel's speech is all the more interesting because it revealed the political evolution of other moderates besides himself. Not only had he, as an independent councillor, voted against the first Exclusion Bill, but only two months before this speech he had put forward a scheme for a compromise. Now, however, he spoke for the bill, and rebutted the main Tory argument that Exclusion would mean bloodshed; the succession of a Popish King would inevitably produce confusion and blood. He carefully explained his position: 'in the two last Parliaments I did so argue for moderation that many of my friends told me I had deserted the true interest of my King and country. . . . I am of opinion that this is a case in which there is no room for moderation, if by moderation be meant the making of any other law for the security of our Religion.'[1] Many others shared this view. Sir Robert Howard, Sir Edward Dering, William Harbord, Lord Cavendish, and Henry Sidney, none of whom could have been regarded previously as Whigs, were now in favour of the bill. The Tories were on the defensive and were almost disorganized. When the third reading was moved they at first attempted to challenge a division, but on seeing how weak they were decided instead to withdraw from the House.[2]

The Exclusion Bill received its third reading in the House of Commons on 11 November, but no move was made to carry it up to the Lords until four days later. Apparently this interval was used in an attempt to effect a compromise. This was of the very greatest significance; the delay was tantamount to an admission that Sunderland's earlier promises could not be fulfilled.

[1] *The Faithful Register* (1689), 28.
[2] Grey, viii. 8, 153–4, 158, 279. Ailesbury, *Memoirs*, 48–49. Addl. 28875, f. 146.

IV

From the beginning of the session events began to go wrong badly for Sunderland. His calculations were completely upset by the King's attitude. Instead of abandoning his brother, Charles showed himself unexpectedly but firmly opposed to Exclusion, and he did not attempt to conceal his deep resentment of the Whig proceedings in the House of Commons. In desperation Sunderland renewed his appeals to William to come over, ostensibly to protect his interests from the competition of Monmouth, but in reality to reinforce Sunderland in his attempts to persuade the King to give way.[1] William was unresponsive, the only assistance forthcoming from the United Provinces, a letter which Sidney procured from the States-General, proved ineffective, and was in fact repudiated by William when it became clear that it had failed.[2] It is not surprising that Sunderland, faced with ruin, began to gamble on a large scale and with disastrous results, while the Duchess of Portsmouth spent much of the time weeping in her rooms. After he had committed himself Sunderland found that his influence virtually disappeared. In offering limitations the King was admittedly insincere, but not in the sense which Sunderland had foretold. This was not the prelude to the abandonment of his brother, but a propaganda gesture, designed to rally opposition to the Whigs by exposing their intransigence and unreasonableness.

The King's declared attitude made the defeat of Exclusion certain. James, and even the notoriously stupid Conway, were convinced that if Charles remained 'right' there would be a large majority of peers against the bill.[3] The principal Court speaker in the debate, Halifax, was generally admitted to have eclipsed Shaftesbury. Later generations of historians, accustomed to great parliamentary duels of oratory, have explained the defeat of

[1] Sidney, ii. 120, 122–3. Prinsterer, v. 435–6. Sunderland to William, 1 Nov. Kenyon, 62–63.

[2] Published as *An Intimation of the Deputies of the States-General in a late Discourse with Mr. Sidney* (1680).

[3] *HMC, Ormonde*, N.S., v. 485–6. Conway to Ormonde, 9 Nov. Addl. 17017, f. 169.

Exclusion in the Lords as the result of Halifax's eloquence and influence. But the decisive factor in producing the defeat of the bill was Charles's own personal presence at the debate, as he stood by the fire, making no attempt to hide his feelings.[1] The bill was rejected, with emphasis since it was on the first reading, by 63 to 30, only Manchester, Suffolk, and the easily intimidated Anglesey following Sunderland and voting with the Whigs. This failure discredited Sunderland with every section. He was naturally in deep disgrace at Court, being later deprived of his secretaryship.[2] The King's behaviour made him useless to the Whigs, since his own personal vote in the Lords counted for little against the Court majority. The session was now certain to be barren so far as the Whigs were concerned, and some even began to prepare for new elections. All that could be done was to prepare for the reintroduction of the bill by the intimidation of opponents and by showing the King that their determination had not been lessened in any way.

Although it was Charles who was in reality responsible for the defeat of the bill, the blame fell principally on Halifax. The fiction was still preserved that evil ministers, not the King, were responsible, and as a renegade Halifax's conduct was judged to be particularly reprehensible. Sunderland's analysis of Halifax's reasons for opposing the bill is extremely revealing.[3] He believed

---

[1] Barrillon, 28 Nov. E. S. de Beer, 'The House of Lords in the Parliament of 1680', *Bulletin of the Institute of Historical Research*, xx. 31–37.

[2] Barrillon, 20 Feb. 1681. Sidney, ii. 169. Sunderland was not dismissed until 24 Jan., a delay which it is difficult to explain. Kenyon (69) argues that it was designed to perpetuate a split in the Whig ranks between those in favour of Monmouth's pretensions and the Williamites, and that to have dismissed him earlier would have re-united the Whigs. This seems to be an over-elaborate thesis. Those actively pushing Monmouth's pretensions were only a small group, and they had already had to admit defeat on 8 Nov., at least for the time being. Shaftesbury and the mass of the party were primarily concerned to pass Exclusion, and only after that had been accomplished would they consider the succession. Those pushing William's claims were also a minority, principally composed of recent recruits to the cause of Exclusion—Godolphin, Temple, Sunderland himself. The other reason which Kenyon suggests, that Sunderland's dismissal would lead to an intensification of attacks on the other ministers, seems to ignore the cataract of attacks on ministers which marked the last weeks of the session.

[3] Sidney, ii. 125, 127. Temple, *Works*, i. 354.

that as a rival he was following the same political maxims as himself. At Althorp in June both men had agreed that limitations
were to be preferred to Exclusion. Subsequently Sunderland had
evolved towards a belief that the bill would pass, and that it was
not entirely repugnant to the King. Halifax did not agree, but
equally he did not show that he disagreed until Sunderland had
unmasked himself at Council in favour of Exclusion. This had
been unexpected; Sunderland seems to have thought that the
forcefulness with which Halifax had argued for sending James
away again showed that he too was coming round to the Exclusionist point of view. But once Halifax had revealed his real
attitude the explanation was clear to Sunderland and to many
others besides. His purpose was to ruin his competitor and to place
himself in the position of sole minister to the King.

Halifax naturally came under intense Whig attacks. His unpopularity could hardly have been greater. Halifax had disregarded the warnings of the consequences of opposing Exclusion,
he was blamed for the attitude of the King. The viciousness of the
attacks made against him was a demonstration of the intransigence of the Whigs, and also of the increasing prominence and
influence of the more extreme leaders. No evidence could be
produced worthy of serious consideration, but as the antagonist
of Exclusion he must by definition be an enemy to 'King and
kingdom'. Arguments based on 'common fame' were enough for
most Whigs, and malice supplied what was lacking in evidence.
The attack was led by the entirely unscrupulous Montagu, who
with Colt, Winnington, Harbord, and Vernon went to the most
extravagant lengths in their speeches, the last declaring: 'I would
rather have his head than any Popish Lord's in the Tower.' The
venom of these attacks produced a certain amount of revulsion in
Halifax's favour. Although they did not go so far as to defend
his conduct some moderate Whigs deplored the deficiencies of
the attacks. Birch and Cavendish spoke in favour of an adjournment until there was more satisfactory evidence. Temple and
Godolphin, both of whom were in disgrace at Court for their
support of Exclusion, feared that to push the attack to extremes
would widen the gulf between the King and Parliament, and put

an end to the prospect of a successful issue to the session. But for
the extreme Whigs all chance of any favourable issue that session
had vanished with the defeat of Exclusion. They had no interest
except to prepare the way for its re-introduction, and were entirely
unscrupulous in the methods they had to use. They could hardly
expect that Charles would take any notice of the address for the
removal of Halifax, but it might intimidate him, as Sunderland
and the Duchess of Portsmouth had been coerced into a change
of policy during the summer.[1]

The split between moderates and extremists over the address
against Halifax was not permanent. All were united in their
continued insistence on Exclusion and in the necessity of depriving
their opponents of all power and influence for evil. The debates
on the proclamation which had been issued the previous year,
declaring petitions to be illegal, aroused particularly intense feeling. The House examined the Attorney-General and ended by
voting an impeachment against Lord Chief Justice North.
Following a petition from the City, complaining of his conduct
as recorder, an address was voted asking the King for the removal
of Jeffreys. This Charles found to be expedient; Jeffreys was
replaced by George Treby, an able lawyer but hitherto an extreme
Whig.

The other attacks had no such success, indeed they were really
propaganda gestures. It could not be expected that, unless he was
to reverse his whole line of policy, Charles would take any notice
of the attacks on Halifax, Clarendon, Feversham, Seymour, Hyde,
the Marquis of Worcester, Scroggs, and other judges, and even
minor Tories like Thompson the high-flying Bristol clergyman.
The bills introduced during the remainder of the session were also
intended primarily as demonstrations to satisfy sections of the
Whig partisans. One was for the relief of the subject from arbitrary
and excessive fines—from which the Whigs were to suffer very
severely in the near future.[2] To retain the support of the dissenters
a bill was introduced for the union of the King's Protestant

---

[1] In fact Halifax was unmoved, both by the attacks in the Commons and by the
threats which preceded them. Sidney, ii. 127–9. Grey, viii. 21–31. CJ ix. 655, 660.
[2] Grey, viii. 226–9.

subjects and their relief from all penal laws. They were to gain still further, and their usefulness as political allies was to be increased, by the repeal of the Corporation Act.[1]

Only in one respect did the Whigs achieve a real success. Although he was old, repulsive, and personally insignificant, the conviction and execution of Lord Stafford was not unimportant. The success of the impeachment gave the Whigs some compensation for the defeats of the session. The case which the managers made out does not sound convincing today, but it had considerable effect at the time.[2] Many of the peers who voted for Stafford's guilt were far from being Whigs—several had voted against Exclusion, but it is doubtful whether they would have done so had Charles not declared himself against the bill. This vote against an unpopular and Papist peer was an easy way to rid themselves of the odium of having voted for the right of the Duke of York. More important still, Stafford's conviction enhanced the credit of Oates and the other witnesses who were beginning to relapse into obscurity—rather than discredit—so long had it been since they had claimed a victim. The King was furious at this revival of their credit and importance, but his own attitude was weak too. Saying that he would not have hanged a dog on the evidence which the witnesses had produced, he asked Anglesey why he had voted for Stafford's guilt: the timid peer had enough courage to reply that he had done so for the same reason that Charles had accepted the verdict and agreed to execution.[3]

Stafford's impeachment prepared the way for the disclosures of a new plot which Shaftesbury had been getting ready for some time. But although the witnesses were fully rehearsed the details of this Irish Plot were to be reserved until a new session began. Without a prorogation or dissolution Exclusion could not be reintroduced. A stalemate ensued. The Whigs showed themselves to be united in their insistence on Exclusion. All suggestions for

[1] Grey, viii. 214–18. *CJ* ix. 700.

[2] *State Trials*, vii. 1294–1559. The trial occupied virtually the entire attention of the Commons from 30 Nov. to 7 Dec.

[3] Morrice MSS., *Chronological Account of Eminent Persons*, iii, under the year 1659.

compromise were rejected, limitations were judged to be 'not only insufficient but dangerous'. They disregarded messages from the King in which he again promised to consider any measures which preserved the succession.[1] Debates on almost any subject invariably ended in a discussion of the succession, with Whig speakers advocating Exclusion. When a request was received for a consideration of the condition of Tangier, then under Moorish attack, and for supply to defend it, a rancorous debate followed in which Tangier was mentioned only incidentally. Russell declared that it was madness to talk about the plight of a town in Africa when all three kingdoms were sinking. Titus expressed the same view, but somewhat tortuously, 'to talk of Tangier now, is like Nero, when Rome was on fire, to fiddle'. Most other Whig speakers preferred to discuss the necessity for Exclusion rather than the business of the day.[2] A speech from Temple, that if Tangier had to be abandoned it would probably fall into French hands, received no consideration. Temple had little or no influence, standing as he did outside party, and with his mind chiefly concerned with foreign affairs. The Whigs were relatively uninterested in foreign politics, and with their memories of the talk of Protestant alliances in 1670 and 1678 they rightly suspected the negotiations with the Dutch and their allies to be a sham and a trap. Under no circumstances would they vote supplies of money unless Exclusion was accepted.

The Whigs were not satisfied with repeating their insistence on Exclusion. Besides the propaganda gestures for the comfort of their supporters, there was an important task before them if they were to facilitate the future passage of Exclusion. By this time it was no longer possible to ignore the existence of the Tories. The evil ministers were attacked by name, as were more humble partisans of the Court who achieved notoriety for some reason. The Whigs were forced to realize that there were, in addition, many who supported the King and the ministers in their hostility to Exclusion. The Whigs could no longer pretend that their enemies represented only the Court, or that they consisted predominantly of Papists and those Popishly affected. The proposal for an Act

[1] *CJ* ix. 679, 15 Dec.; 699, 4 Jan. 1681.   [2] Grey, viii. 4–20.

of Association virtually admitted these facts. It was intended, not as a substitute for Exclusion, but to make it effective in operation. It differed very significantly from the suggested association put forward by Essex. He intended such an act as a means of guaranteeing limitations, to ensure that they would be enforced under James. The Whig association would have been much more specific. Only in form did it resemble its famous predecessor, the association concluded in deceptively similar circumstances at the time of the murder plots against Elizabeth, and it differed in emphasis from the act passed after the Revolution. These other associations were genuinely national in character, intended to prevent the success of a small traitorous minority. In contrast the Whig association had as its real purpose their own installation in permanent power, by giving them the means to crush all opposition by judicial means. The fact that such an association should be considered necessary showed that although the Exclusion Bill had the unanimous support of the Whigs in the Commons, it was certain to encounter serious opposition in the country as a whole.[1]

Negligible and ineffective in the Commons, the Tories formed a considerable section of the nation. Resolved to stand by James's interests, they could no longer be ignored. The Whigs, of course, had no sense of a party system, they saw the Tories not merely as political opponents to be deprived of parliamentary representation and influence in the royal councils, but also as actual or potential traitors who must be crushed out of existence by the machinery of the law. In fact the Tories relied very considerably on royal, official, and clerical support, and it could be expected that once deprived of this their strength would largely and soon disappear. But action would still have to be taken against those who persisted in supporting James after the Exclusion Bill passed. Under its provisions all who maintained, advocated, or advanced his claims would be prosecuted as traitors. For a time the attractive proposition of confiscating all lands held by recusants, so as to

[1] Grey, viii. 153–4, 163–7. Association was originally suggested by Cavendish, amplified by Winnington, and reviewed critically by Jones. The Whigs were in a difficulty; an association was to reinforce an Exclusion Bill which, of course, was not yet passed, but Jones saw that it was not, could not, and must not be regarded as a substitute for Exclusion.

extinguish the Papist minority and deprive James of support, was considered. The association was intended to provide additional means to crush all opposition to Exclusion, during the remainder of Charles's reign as well as during the reign of his Protestant successor. In addition the Whigs put forward further demands to increase the security which Exclusion would bring. The magistracy should be purged and Whigs should be appointed as lord lieutenants, deputies, justices, and to offices in the forts and the navy. To Charles this meant that to consent to Exclusion would now involve not only the abandonment of his brother, but also a wide proscription of his own supporters and the virtual annihilation of his monarchical authority.

V

Until the session was terminated, either by a prorogation, or if necessary by a dissolution, Exclusion could not be reintroduced. But, on the other hand, Charles was in need of money, and the Whigs were determined not to grant any supply unless Exclusion passed. In these circumstances of stalemate both sides, some Whigs as well as the King, began to look to France for support.

We know now that French support was eventually given to Charles—with decisive effect—but Louis did not automatically support his brother monarch. In his reports Barrillon provided arguments to justify subsidizing the Whigs as well as for assisting the King.[1] During these years Louis was preparing for the absorption of a further part of the Spanish Netherlands as well as continuing his policy of the *réunions* in Alsace. In order to prevent any interference with his plans the French Government was systematically intervening in the domestic politics of all western European countries. Like all French diplomats at this time, Barrillon feared a revival of the Triple Alliance. Consequently the diplomatic

[1] Barrillon, 29 Aug. 1680. In making the suggestion that Monmouth might be supported and the Court undermined Barrillon was possibly motivated by the diplomatic defeat and personal humiliation inflicted upon him by Charles and Sunderland in January (Kenyon, 40–41). In his dispatch of 4 Nov. he acknowledged instructions to support Charles if he asked for aid.

activity of the English ministers in the summer of 1680 caused
him some disquiet. Temple, Sunderland, and Sidney hoped to
gain credit at home by their negotiations for a Protestant and anti-
French alliance. The rival ambassadors, the Dutch, Spanish, and
Imperial, were active distributing money to assist its conclusion.[1]
The situation was reminiscent of 1678. If, as then, Barrillon could
ensure a disputatious and bitter session, he could frustrate any
positive foreign policy and show the allies how little reliance
could be placed on England.

Having failed to prevent an alliance Barrillon was concerned to
neutralize its effect. He made a shrewd counter-attack by revealing
and publishing a secret clause which provided for mutual help
against rebellious subjects.[2] Yet he, and Louis, took the alliance
far more seriously than was really necessary, and the fact that
they did so shows how fully they shared the universal distrust of
Charles. Barrillon thought that as a last resort he might attempt to
unite his subjects by going to war against France, and that such a
war would be popular. For all his sneers at the confidence and
self-importance of Englishmen who believed that English intervention would deter Louis from foreign adventures, Barrillon
saw that it might well impede French expansion. English neutrality
must be secured if a general European war was to be avoided.
As a last resort Charles could be betrayed in the same fashion as
Danby, by a revelation of his engagements with France, presumably a reference to the secret Treaty of Dover. The results of
such a machiavellian move would, as Barrillon saw, have been
incalculable. He did not underestimate the probable effects when
he suggested that it would ensure Charles's utter ruin, and the
probable establishment of a republic. This, as in the 1650's,
would not necessarily be against French interests, and in any case
it would reduce England to a position in which she could not
intervene on the Continent.[3]

Such an extreme step was not necessary, but Barrillon found
that it was worth while preserving his contacts with those Whigs

---

[1] Barrillon, 28 Mar., 26 Aug. 1680.
[2] Idem, 19 Aug. 1680. The clause was in the recently concluded treaty with
Spain.   [3] Idem, 3 June 1680.

who had previously acted as his agents. The chief ones were still Montagu and Harbord, who had betrayed Danby and had remained in touch ever since—principally to press for payment of the money which they had been promised. Montagu, although rightly suspected by many of being mercenary and dishonest, acquired great influence during the session of 1680 as the most extreme and outspoken opponent of the Court. Harbord could also prove useful. In the spring of 1680 he made Barrillon a remarkable offer. As part of the projected anti-French alliance an envoy was to be sent to the Swiss, who were still important as a source of recruits. Expecting that he had enough influence to secure the job, Harbord offered for a consideration to work in the interests of Louis in conjunction with the French ambassador there.[1]

These two men were entirely unscrupulous and devoted to the advancement of their own interests. Nevertheless, their influence with the more intransigent section of the Whigs was considerable, and their value as French agents all the greater since they could be used to gain others, some directly by bribes, others without knowing that they were being used. Montagu undertook to manage Monmouth in the interests of France. There was some plausibility in this claim, but none whatsoever in his further assertion that he could also influence Shaftesbury. The latter was never at any time manageable by anyone, and detested Montagu, not only as a rogue but as a potential rival. Some of Barrillon's other contacts were of declining importance, and not unnaturally as a foreigner he was often wrong in his estimates both of persons and of political developments.[2] Buckingham, who still on occasion saw Barrillon and made no secret of his dislike of Shaftesbury, was by now a pathetic, sick figure, still retaining some popularity but sunk under the malicious prosecutions engineered by Danby. Algernon Sidney was generally distrusted. Powle's moderation had long since forfeited him all credit.

---

[1] Idem, 4 Apr. 1680.
[2] Idem, 22 July 1680: 'Memoire de ceux à qui on peut faire des gratifications', in which he gave a list of his contacts with an evaluation of their character and value.

More important, Barrillon's constant use of the word 'Presbyterian' as if it was still synonymous with a party, and as if politics still retained a predominantly religious character, was a sign that even the acutest foreign observer could not keep pace with the changes in English politics. He placed a great deal of emphasis on the Presbyterians, going so far as to hire the support of two of the leading ministers in order to influence their coreligionists. In doing so Barrillon appears to have been misled by the fact that many of his original contacts were members of the Holles group which had by now lost its leaders and most of its importance, although Baber remained an accomplished and accredited backstairs intriguer.

Barrillon was equating the Whigs with their nearest continental equivalent, the Louvestein or republican party in the United Provinces. The Holles group had in fact been very similar in composition and objectives, but there was less resemblance in the case of the Whigs. Apart from the crooks and opportunists the Whigs were fundamentally anti-French, whereas Holles had been francophile. Although they were for the moment concerned exclusively with the succession, they hated France and Louis, partly for reasons of religion, because of her increasing rivalry as a commercial, colonial, and naval power, and as the most highly developed and influential of absolute monarchies. But despite the ultimate incompatibility of their interests there were good reasons for Barrillon to play with the Whigs during 1680. Even after his alarm at the projected European alliance had been shown to be exaggerated, his contacts proved to be of value. A new danger appeared. Finding that the alliance was disregarded by the Whigs, Sunderland and his associates began to work for William's interests in England as well as in Europe.[1] Like them Barrillon believed at first that Charles would have to abandon his brother. He feared that Exclusion would pass in such a way that the beneficiary would be William, and therefore he asked Louis whether French influence should not be given to Monmouth.

Louis was not prepared to do so, although he was later to consider the legitimization of his own bastards. But Barrillon could

[1] Barrillon, 21 Nov. Kenyon, 50–51, 52.

do much to increase distrust of William. Like the Dutch republicans many Whigs feared that William possessed absolutist ambitions, in England as well as in the United Provinces. Hampden, for instance, one of those who had received French bribes, openly stated that he feared an alliance with the Dutch would lead to William's intervention in English politics with an army.[1] On a lower level (in his report Barrillon was almost apologetic for the madness of English life) he spread a rumour that William habitually hunted on Sundays so as to discredit him with all sabbatarians.[2]

The failure of Exclusion in the Lords robbed the Whigs of their value in French eyes. Although Barrillon was still not absolutely convinced that Charles would stand by his brother, there was now no prospect of national unity and little chance of English intervention on the Continent. Disappointed of their hopes of French assistance, Montagu and his associates now turned to another line of policy. If it could be secured, a personal settlement with the King and the Court would be preferable to the uncertain receipt of clandestine payments from France. Montagu had always aspired to office, even at times dreaming of becoming Lord Treasurer. Consequently the ministers hated him far more than any other opponent. Most Whigs wanted to reduce the royal prerogative and hold ministers responsible for their actions. That was bad enough, but Montagu was far more immediately dangerous, he schemed to supplant them in office. Montagu and his associates were essentially frondeurs, courtiers who were in disfavour; their opposition was to the persons, not the principles, of the ministers. Ready at any time to sell themselves, the situation at the end of 1680 seemed to be opportune for a deal with the Court. Under their leadership the House of Commons was so intransigent as to ensure that the deadlock would continue indefinitely. They were working in close partnership with a more respectable section of the Whigs—the lawyers led by Jones—and could expect that the King would reward them handsomely for bringing over these men to the Court. Above all the defection of

[1] Cartwright, *Sacharissa*, 264. Countess of Sunderland to Henry Sidney, 20 June 1680.   [2] Barrillon, 30 Sept. 1680.

these two groups would split, and might well destroy, the Whig party both at Westminster and in the country.

The one thing in common between these two groups, between Montagu and Jones, was their dislike of Shaftesbury, a dislike which he entirely reciprocated. Previously he had no rivals, for Buckingham was far too indolent to be a party leader. In the House of Commons the Whig leadership had been vested in men like Hampden, Russell, and Sacheverel who had willingly accepted a subordinate position as Shaftesbury's lieutenants. The new leaders who emerged during the session of 1680 attempted not only to break away from Shaftesbury's domination but also to detach his associates from him. Jones, only too conscious of his own great legal reputation, openly disparaged Shaftesbury. Montagu tried to win over Monmouth by making him definite promises. By consistent extremism an impression was made on the ordinary Whig members, who must have been at a loss to know what to do after the defeat of Exclusion in the Lords.

The first show of independence had been the deliberate omission from the Exclusion Bill of the clause guaranteeing the legitimate succession. This attempt had failed, but Monmouth's pretensions could always be advanced again later. The second example produced a temporary split among the Whigs. Jones and Montagu initiated venomous attacks on Halifax without informing Shaftesbury or seeking his approval.[1] In fact he strongly disapproved, although he hated Halifax, because he judged the attacks to be mistimed and mismanaged. Many Whigs agreed with him, some going so far as to deprecate in debate the transparent malice of attacks and accusations founded on nothing better than 'common fame'. Many Whigs abstained in the division, but nevertheless Montagu and his associates carried with them the mass of the party, and repeated the tactic in further venomous attacks on other ministers. In any case the split concerned methods, not objectives; both groups, those who followed, and those who suspected, Montagu, remained united in their insistence upon Exclusion. But the third example of independent action by Montagu and his associates proved to be far more serious in two senses. It damaged,

[1] Barrillon, 2 Dec. Sidney, ii. 127–9. Grey, viii. 21–31, 41–51.

and might have ruined their reputation, and it threatened to produce a permanent and disastrous split among the Whigs which
would have destroyed the party.

During December Montagu and his associates began to negotiate
secretly with the King.[1] Although the details of this intrigue
remained secret, its existence soon became known. In the first
place the King was offered supply on a generous scale in return
for Exclusion. With their close association with Monmouth
they were bound to insist on this, but had the negotiations
continued for any length of time it is doubtful whether Montagu
would have persisted with this condition before entering office.
Office was in fact the primary aim of many of the Whigs concerned: Montagu hoped to become Secretary of State in place of
the loyal but inept Jenkins, and he also wished to acquire a mar-
quisate. Harbord aspired to the treasurership of the Navy, a post
in which there were endless possibilities for embezzlement. Silas
Titus expected to be the other Secretary, while with still less
justification Thomas Thynne also considered himself suitable for
preferment. The lawyers were not to be forgotten; Jones was to be
appointed Lord Chief Justice of the Common Pleas, while Winnington was to be satisfied with the post of Attorney-General.
The self-interest of those concerned is obvious, and even if specious
arguments could be produced, that as ministers they would be
guardians of liberties and religion, this scheme if successful would
inevitably have been regarded as a betrayal by the Whig rank and
file.

This intrigue had very little chance of success. The fact that
Sunderland was taking a leading part in an effort to save himself
from final disgrace and loss of influence was in itself enough to
doom it to failure. It was based on his entirely mistaken belief that
Charles could still be persuaded to abandon his hostility to Exclusion. Secondly, there was no reason for the other ministers to
welcome the adherence of men like Montagu and Harbord,
even if they agreed to drop their insistence on Exclusion. For one
thing they were known to be more than ordinarily dishonest.
Although their defection would split the Whigs and weaken

[1] Barrillon, 13, 16 Jan. 1681.

Shaftesbury it would be at the price of granting offices which would make them into formidable rivals at Court. But in any case the intrigue could not succeed once its existence became known, and it is to be suspected that the leakages were deliberate. The reaction of the Whig rank and file was explosive. Their long experience, from the defection of Sir Richard Temple to the desertion of their leaders which had followed the new Privy Council in 1679, had made them suspicious of their leaders and distrustful of their motives. In addition Shaftesbury was acutely afraid that those who negotiated with the Court would become the dupes of the King, even if their intentions were honest. Any acceptance of office, without a firm guarantee of Exclusion by the King, would inevitably lead the Whigs into a trap such as the reconstituted Privy Council had proved.

There were few who would have given Montagu and his friends the benefit of the doubt, but by clever tactics they managed to save themselves when news of the intrigue came out. With splendid effrontery they anticipated attacks.[1] Harbord and Winnington themselves moved against members accepting places from the Crown, the former insinuating that the whole business was a sham designed by the Court to discredit the Whig leaders. Titus referred lightly to the rumours that he was to be a minister, and repeated that the design was to raise jealousies among the Whigs. A motion was passed, without a division, that no member should accept office or the promise of one without leave of the House, and that all offenders should be expelled. The intrigue was frustrated, but there was also now less chance of any substantial section of the Whigs being detached. Disappointed, Montagu and his friends had now no alternative but to continue to put pressure on the King in common with Shaftesbury and the rest of the Whigs, and in order to prove their honesty of purpose they once again became the most extreme opponents of the Court in debate.

The King does not seem to have expected anything from the intrigues with Montagu. He was by now convinced that the Whigs must be crushed, and he thought that now time was on

[1] *HMC, Ormonde*, N.S., v. 541–2. Grey, viii. 222–5. *CJ* ix. 695–6.

his side. His decision to prorogue, and then to dissolve, Parliament, and to call the new one to Oxford, was made before he was assured of financial support from France, and in any case the amount which Barrillon was authorized to offer was comparatively niggardly. On 10 January the Commons had about 15 minutes notice of the prorogation. The votes which they hurriedly passed were a logical continuation of all their proceedings since the defeat of Exclusion.[1] They denounced the minister responsible for advising the prorogation, not only as a betrayer of the King and the Protestant religion, but in addition as a pensioner of France and a promoter of the French interest—which was a sign of their political insight even if there was as yet no actual agreement. The other motions were in character very reminiscent of those passed under similar circumstances in 1629. They were pure propaganda. The House voted that the Papists had been responsible for the great fire in 1666, and that the persecution of the dissenters upon the penal laws was a grievance, a weakening of the Protestant religion and an encouragement to Popery. An indication of the growth of his interest, it was declared that Monmouth had been removed from his offices by means of the influence of the Duke of York, and that application should be made to the King for his reinstatement.

These votes were an appeal to the people against the conduct of affairs, and in the next few weeks the Whigs were again to demonstrate their effective organization and mobilization of popular support, first in petitions for the reassembly of Parliament, and then after the dissolution in the elections.

[1] Grey, viii. 289–90. CJ ix. 703–4.

6

THE OXFORD PARLIAMENT

I

THE dissolution of the second Exclusion Parliament infuriated the Whigs. When the prorogation was announced they had some hope of an early session which would have allowed the re-introduction of the Exclusion Bill. The decision to dissolve, together with the purge of the surviving independent privy councillors and the order that the new Parliament should meet at Oxford, not Westminster, was an irrefutable and final indication that the Whigs must in future count on the determined and constant opposition of the King.

Previously they had believed, or affected to believe, that he was in the hands of his ministers. Using this convenient fiction that the King was not a free agent, the Whigs had argued—as had Pym—that all the arbitrary and illegal actions of the Government were attributable to the ministers, not to Charles. This theory, which does not seem very convincing to the historian, was not so baseless as to be mere pretence or hypocrisy, and it had not been entirely destroyed by Charles's avowed hostility to Exclusion and his attitude to the bill during the debate in the Lords. On the other side, there was the general distrust of Charles, amounting almost to scorn for his indolence and undependability. So shrewd an observer as Barillon believed that there was still a possibility of Charles changing his mind and coming to terms with the Whigs.[1] Sunderland and the Duchess of Portsmouth, although with decreasing confidence, continued to maintain that he might still be brought round to agree to Exclusion.[2] Speaking after the

[1] Barillon, 2 Dec. 1680, 13 Feb. 1681. He believed that only the promise of French support would absolutely ensure a decision against Exclusion.

[2] Idem, 5, 26 Dec. 1680; 6, 16 Jan. Later the Duchess decided to go to France (Barillon, 23 Jan.). Kenyon, 69.

defeat of Exclusion in the Lords, Shaftesbury appealed to Charles
to rid himself of the ministers and courtiers whom he favoured
and the principles of government and religion with which they
were associated.[1] In the Commons attempts were made to
distinguish between parts of the King's speeches composed by
the ministers, and those stemming from his own 'good nature'
which gave hope of a change.

The dissolution exposed these theories as pitiful illusions. It now
became clear that the only way of achieving Exclusion lay in
maintaining such pressure on the King as to compel him to capitu-
late. This did not seem to be impossible. With little formal
organization Shaftesbury had been successful in holding together
his supporters, and maintaining their spirit and confidence
throughout the months of prorogation in 1679 and 1680. The
defeat of Exclusion in the Lords had had remarkably little effect.
Faced now with another general election, and the combined
hostility of the King, the Church, and the Tories, most Whigs
remained intransigent, insisting on Exclusion, opposed to all compromise, and considerably more bitter against their opponents.

The number of secessions was extremely small and not of any
great significance. The motives of those who defected were hardly
based on principle, but rather on a belief that in opposing the King
the Whigs were bound to be defeated, and later punished. In fact
during the session of 1680 the current had run the other way,
those whose moderation had taken them over to the Court had
been outnumbered by the accession of former opponents of
Exclusion.[2] But the extreme courses followed after the defeat of
Exclusion did alienate some Whigs both in Parliament and the
country, although not so many as were later to claim an early
repentance in order to escape the Tory proscription. In November
an anonymous correspondent wrote to a member that a 'multi-
tude' had been lost by some of the votes of the House.[3] He
instanced the attacks on Halifax, without any proof of his fault,

[1] This speech was printed and had a wide circulation: *A Speech made by a Peer
of the Realm* (1680).

[2] One of the few members openly to declare against Exclusion was Sir Robert
Markham; Grey, vii. 448; viii. 266.   [3] *CSPD*, 1680/1, 92–94.

the contrast between the great concern felt for such a person as the pamphleteer Harris and the neglect of Tangier. The writer argued that votes passed in turbulent debates or rushed through thin houses could not be taken as representing the voice of the nation. The conclusion clearly betrays the Tory views of the writer; after prosecuting the Papists for attempting to alter the government in church and state the Whigs were now trying to do the same.

This view was repeated, with varying degrees of exaggeration and abuse, by the Tory pamphleteers who were now challenging the Whig predominance in propaganda. More authentic evidence of a real reaction against Whig extremism comes from an ex-clusionist member who wrote two years later that in the session of 1680 he had been young and innocent, believing that his colleagues were really actuated by zeal against Popery, but that he had soon seen through them and, having had a bellyful, had deliberately refused election to the Oxford Parliament.[1] The most notable Whig to begin to trim was none other than Sacheverel. In the first Exclusion Parliament, as in the last decade of the Cavalier Parliament, he had consistently been the foremost and bravest spokesman of the extreme section of the Opposition to the Court. The first man to bring up the question of the succession, he had naturally become the most ardent of exclusionists. In the first few weeks of the session of 1680 he spoke as warmly as ever before. He answered Temple in his old style, when the latter pleaded for a union between King and people in view of the threatening situation on the Continent. Sacheverel replied that disorders at home must first be remedied before any consideration could be given with safety to foreign affairs. With the defeat of Exclusion in the Lords his attitude changed; he spoke only twice during the remainder of the session, and did not again mention the succession. From the beginning of December he became silent, and did not speak at Oxford. His trimming was deliberate; when he was later prosecuted for alleged riot he pleaded in mitigation the fact that he had behaved moderately in the last session, which proved that he had previously erred 'out of error of judgement' rather than from 'malice and design'. Yet he had not changed his

[1] Bodleian, Firth MSS. c. 3. Lionel Duckett, 30 July 1683.

real views, for when the Revolution once again made it safe he resumed his career as the spokesman of the most extreme wing of the Whigs.[1]

Sacheverel was exceptionally prudent and far-sighted, as he had showed earlier in deploring the petitions as premature; most Whigs still believed that they were bound to succeed in the end. Consequently the number of secessions was small, and the short length of the Oxford session masked their effect. Certainly the elections did not reveal any dramatic weakening of the Whig position.

The general election of 1681 is by far the most interesting of the three elections of the Exclusion crisis. By this time the country was more sharply divided into rival factions than at any time since 1642. All known, or suspected, Whigs had been purged from the lieutenancy and magistracy; official pressure could be used directly in favour of Tories. Charles had made his views plain. Yet it cannot be said that this was the most bitterly fought of the three elections, in fact there were fewer contests than in the autumn of 1679. In many parts of the country Tories chose to abstain, an admission of lack of popular support. There were even some revolts and assertions of independence in small, closed boroughs which had previously followed the instructions of their Tory patrons. These facts, as much as the actual results, were a sign that Shaftesbury's hold on the nation, or at least on the machinery of representation, remained as strong as ever.

II

The Whig press and pamphlets played an important part in Shaftesbury's achievements in this election. During the months of prorogation in 1679 and 1680 they had been silenced by the proclamation against the Press, and its strict enforcement by the judges. But from the beginning of the new session in October 1680 publication was resumed under the protection of the House of Commons. Its output became considerable. Reports of debates were printed. Violent attacks were made on the ministers and the

[1] Grey, vii. 375; viii. 100. Morrice, f. 439.

Duke of York. Coleman's letters were reprinted, with inflammatory and inaccurate comments on James. After the dissolution
many pamphlets were published to give specific guidance to the
voters, and it is worth while examining them as an expression
of popular Whig sentiment and opinion. All were agreed on the
importance of the election; Burleigh was quoted that England
could not be undone except by means of a Parliament. The appeal
of the pamphlets was made as wide as possible, the Whigs being
particularly concerned to refute the Tory claim that their support
came from dissenters, old rebels, and the lower classes.

One writer significantly dedicated his work to the citizens of
London, 'the chief Refuge of the People, the curb or Bridle to
the unjust illegal Ambition of all arbitrary and evil men'.[1] He
expressed the hope that its choice would be as good as in the
previous parliamentary and sheriffs' elections, and that its example
would be followed by the provinces. His first concern was to
show that liberty was in danger, for the constitution—the best
in the world—was threatened. Already abroad, in France and
Spain, and nearer home in Scotland, parliaments had become
disused through the 'cunning and address' of princes, the 'servility
and folly' of the nobility and gentry, the 'suppleness, treachery and
fawning' of the clergy, and the 'ignorance and stupidity' of the
common people. Its enemies were to be found both at home and
abroad, the Papist party in England and Louis XIV who, it was
said, 'shakes his fasces over us'.

Moreover, if liberty was in peril so too was property, a strong
additional argument in the seventeenth century. Here again the
writer skilfully appealed to each section of society. He attacked
the clergy not only for their *jure divino* preaching but also for
their alleged belief that all property depended on the pleasure of
the King. Under an absolute government there could be no
security for property. The common people were informed of the
conditions of life under an absolute King and Popery in France,
no good English beef, wooden shoes, excessive Gabelles, nobles
riding down the crops of the peasantry—all arguments that were
to be repeated endlessly in the next hundred years. The gentry

[1] *An Address to the Honourable City of London* (1681).

were warned that heavy taxes were as likely to crush them as the common people. A different argument was used to convince the nobility. Absolutism would mean a standing army, and as experience had shown during Oliver's time, soldiers would make no distinction between the house of a nobleman and that of a farmer. Without parliamentary sessions the value of the privilege of peers would become negligible. All classes, therefore, were exhorted to choose men of wisdom, courage, and integrity. They were to shun all who could be suspected of wishing to sell their duty—inevitably Esau was invoked at this stage—friends of the Lords in the Tower, pensioners, and all who tried to buy their election. The writer recommended instead the election of those who had served faithfully in the past, and those who were of good repute. An interesting qualification was added to the selection of the latter. If men were to be stout patriots and staunch Protestants they must be independent and incorruptible. Therefore it would be well if they were in possession, or at least reversion, of good estates. As a reinforcement of their spiritual interest the ownership of former abbey lands would be particularly effective.

This advice was repeated by other writers, some of whose pamphlets merely repeated the advice given at the last election, others attacking their opponents with shrill abuse. Voters were warned to avoid the return of 'undoing Legislators'. Members must be men of good conscience, not to be intimidated, who were resolved to stand by the power and privileges of Parliament and to search into the Plot and bring to justice all evil councillors. Repeatedly great stress was laid on the example of London, for choosing as members and city officers men 'that make Integrity their Principle, Conscience their Guide, and the known Laws of the Land their Rule'.[1]

The result of the London election heartened the Whigs and fully confirmed the previous Whig successes in elections for city offices.[2] As before, an attempt was made by the Tories to organize

[1] *The Certain Way to save England, not only now but in Future Ages by a Prudent Choice of Members* (1681).
[2] *True Protestant Mercury*, 12. *A True Narrative* (1681)

opposition to the four exclusionist members. Ministers and Tory propagandists claimed that the most substantial City merchants disliked the Whigs and were fearful of the consequences of their extremism and popularity. This claim had been given substance by the dismal failure of the Whigs in the elections for offices within the Levant Company. But in a parliamentary election, as Barrillon pointed out in minimizing the result and its consequences, the franchise was too wide for the influence of the better off to be decisive.

Whig strength lay with the smaller tradesmen and merchants and, it was alleged, with the mean, with those who were not qualified to vote but did so with the connivance of the Whig sheriffs. Moreover, the organization and militancy of the London Whigs were exceptionally effective. Their leaders had at once taken action when the prorogation had been announced on 10 January. Pleading that this meant an immediate increase in tension they demanded the calling of a Common Council, and when this met two days later persuaded it to petition for the meeting of Parliament on 20 January, and to ask the King that the latter should be allowed to sit until Exclusion was passed. When instead a dissolution was announced, the Whigs responded quickly with a petition from the Grand Jury at the Guildhall, asking that measures of security should be taken in the City. When the King ordered the Common Council to see that the Corporation Act should be put into execution, the Whig majority carried a resolution that the letter should not be officially read. With such organization and confidence the City Whigs easily defeated their opponents. Sheldon was again the chief Tory candidate, but even his supporters numbered only a hundred, far too few to be able to challenge a poll without humiliating results. The former Whig members were unanimously returned.

The Tories similarly found in many other places that Whig strength was too formidable for a poll to be challenged. In Worcestershire a party led by lords Coventry and Windsor spent over £500 but were still unable to organize enough resistance to give any hope of defeating Thomas Foley and Bridges Nanfan. These two peers found it equally impossible to block the election of two other Whigs in Worcester city.[1] The Yorkshire Tories, despite their claim that they were supported by almost all the gentry, could not defeat Fairfax and Clifford. At first the Whigs were alarmed by a report that the Duke of York, then in Scotland, would come south to intervene in the north country elections, but he did not do so and in fact wrote that he heard many gentlemen were so discouraged that they did not intend to stand.[2] This was common. At Westminster, where the poll at the previous election had lasted for eight days, the proceedings were over in three and a half hours.[3] A Tory who demanded a poll desisted when he had only twenty votes recorded. In Kent, where the last two county elections had been strongly contested by a Tory interest, there was now no opposition. Sir Thomas Peyton, a staunch royalist and one of the greatest landowners in the county, did try to gather support for a Tory candidate, but finding the task hopeless he did not put in an appearance, as expected, with a 'train of myrmidons'. Instead, the Whigs sat down to dinner at Tenterden, congratulated Dering on his return, and thanked him for his past services.[4] At Lyme, where the former members were re-elected without opposition, a 'voluntary' treat was given.[5] Many letters were sent to members assuring them of re-election without any need for their presence. These were given wide publicity by the Whig press, but there was no particular political significance in them. Some were sent to Tories as well as Whigs. Most of the letters came from remote places, and the fact that the elections were held in the middle of a particularly severe winter is the most likely explanation.

There were some particularly fierce contests. At Derby an attempt was made to oppose Vernon, who had replaced Sacheverel as one of the most extreme Whig leaders.[6] In Norfolk the Whigs again carried the county election, the fourth in two years, but the Tories won both seats at Norwich by a comfortable margin. In Oxford both sides made full use of all means at their disposal.

---

[1] J. W. Ebsworth (ed.), *Bagford Ballads* (1876–8), ii. 1000. *Smith's Protestant Intelligence*, 9.   [2] Addl. 28053, f. 228. *Smith's Protestant Intelligence*, 1.
[3] Ibid., 5.   [4] *True Protestant Mercury*, 22.
[5] *Protestant (Domestick) Intelligence*, 103.   [6] *Smith's Protestant Intelligence*, 3.

All who had any dependence on the colleges were warned that if they voted for the old Whig members they would forfeit their jobs or custom. Realizing that they could not hope to carry both places, the Tories concentrated their opposition on the senior member, Whorwood, a rather cross-grained country gentleman, although the other candidate was anything but acceptable, being the brother of the officer responsible for the crushing of the Cavalier rising of 1655 and a protector of the dissenters, and having refused to attend the service of penance on St. Scholastica's day. As an alderman, Wright was almost certain to succeed. The Tory candidate attempted to secure his own return by the mass creation of freemen, but unfortunately for him they turned against their creator and voted for the Whigs. The city, of course, was Whig, but in order to outface the University outside help was necessary. This was provided by Buckingham and Lovelace, who on their arrival were greeted with a torchlight procession through the streets. The poll was fairly boisterous, but the Whig victory was clear cut. Both their candidates were returned to the accompaniment of traditional city slogans, 'No universities, No scholars, No clergy, No Bishops'.[1]

Whig defeats were usually explained as the result of frauds by returning officers. In Cambridgeshire it was alleged that the sheriff had again favoured the Tories and encouraged his supporters to assault the Whigs. At Bristol the riotous behaviour of the Tories was alleged to have been a deliberate policy on the part of the newly formed Bristol Artillery Company.[2] Brawling also broke out at Southwark, as might be expected when both sides employed watermen as their attendants.[3] Here even the presence of Oates was not enough to gain the day for the Whigs, but at Colchester he was responsible for a most decisive victory. Previously there had been one Whig and one Tory member. In the previous election a second Whig candidate, Captain Reynolds, had finished at the foot of the poll, and since then his interest had

[1] *Smith's Protestant Intelligence*, 4. Anthony Wood, *Life and Times* (1891–1900), ii. 516.
[2] *Smith's Protestant Intelligence*, 15, 19, 20. *Protestant (Domestick) Intelligence*, 104, 105.   [3] *True Protestant Mercury*, 15. Carte, 222, f. 248.

if anything declined. He had been put out of the militia as a Whig. The Tories made a formidable appearance on the day of the poll, their candidate, Sir Walter Clarges, being supported by the Lord Lieutenant, the Duke of Albemarle, the Earl of Oxford, most of the county magistrates, and many of the clergy. As returning officer the mayor was ready to do all that he could to favour the Tory interest. Oates was a match for this combination. Coming down only on the night before the election his presence, his insinuations that Clarges was a papist, and the peers who supported him popishly affected, so influenced the electors that the Whigs took both places.[1]

The pattern of these elections, and the tactics employed in them, were very much the same as in the previous ones. Whig peers appeared in support of candidates—Buckingham with Monmouth at Southwark and with Lovelace at Oxford, Stamford at Leicester, Pembroke in Wiltshire, and Cornwallis in Suffolk. In Dorset Thomas Freke, a friend of Shaftesbury, acted as the Whig manager. Candidates and their agents consulted him. If they satisfied him Freke was ready, after making careful inquiries, to spend money in treating the electors, and offered to go from one election to another with a group of Whig gentlemen. Shaftesbury sent down recommendatory letters, but not with universal success. In Shaftesbury borough his letter on behalf of a Whig who had resolved not to spend money could not prevail against the lavish treating of a rival. Across the Wiltshire boundary at Downton, Shaftesbury advised the electors against the return of one of their former members, but he was disregarded.[2] Equally unsuccessful was an attempted intervention at Christchurch, which Clarendon regarded as his own borough. He was affronted when Shaftesbury and Huntingdon sent down letters in favour of two extreme Whigs, and feared defeat when he learnt that the writ had got into the hands of another Whig, the Marquis of Winchester. Nevertheless, the two Tory members were re-elected. In Oxfordshire Shaftesbury's intervention was of a different character, but again

[1] *Protestant (Domestick) Intelligence*, 99. *The Manner of the Election of . . . Sir Harbottle Grimston and Captain Reynolds* (1681). Carte, 222, f. 256.
[2] W. A. Day (ed.), *The Pythouse Papers* (1879), 89, 95.

it miscarried—which emphasizes how decisive a part was played by purely local factors. The two former knights of the shire were seeking re-election, and as they had both served faithfully in the last session Shaftesbury thought they deserved to sit again. However, a third candidate presented himself, although he too was a Whig, if anything a more extreme one. In order to avoid a poll Shaftesbury wrote to Locke, asking him to try to persuade this third candidate to stand down so as to settle the matter amicably. This proved to be impossible, and on the day of election a poll was demanded and fought out between three Whigs.[1]

This letter, which dealt mainly with arrangements for the Whig leaders to stay at Balliol during the parliamentary session, is a rare survivor of the correspondence between Locke and Shaftesbury. The link between the two men must have been an intimate one, but in default of further evidence any estimate of Locke's part in Whig political organization and activities must be pure conjecture. It is not improbable that Locke destroyed his papers as soon as repressive action began against the Whigs. There is, however, among the Shaftesbury Papers a draft of instructions to be delivered to newly elected Members of Parliament. Although this is a copy, it bears an annotation that the original was drafted by Locke himself.[2] Such addresses of instructions were the feature of these elections of 1681. Their presentation was a demonstration of the efficiency of Whig political organization and electoral skill. Addresses to members had been known before, but never on the scale or with the significance of these Whig instructions.

At this time, after the defeat of Exclusion and faced by a new challenge from the King and the Tories, it was more important than ever for the Whigs to maintain their claim to represent the nation at large. The Whig leaders had always been careful to preserve a good understanding with the people. The House of Commons had published its votes in 1679 and 1680, and had approved the printing of the informations of Bedlow, Dugdale,

---

[1] Bodleian, Locke MSS. c. 7, f. 76.
[2] Shaftesbury Papers, VI B, 399. This ascription is not noted in the transcript printed by Christie, Life of the First Earl of Shaftesbury (1871), ii, appendix vii.

Dangerfield, and others. Whig pamphleteers published accounts of debates, which correspond so closely with later collections that they must have been obtained from members.[1] No action was taken. In a literal sense correspondence between members and the people they represented was desirable. One Whig suggested that a cause of the crisis was the severance of the personal link between members and their constituents. He recommended a revival of the practice, once common but which was dying out at this time, of regular letters from Westminster. He urged every knight of the shire to write each week to the sheriff, borough members to the mayor, communicating all resolves and bills.[2]

The addresses of instructions to the newly elected members were intended to represent the people in a more direct manner. The petitions organized a year before had been in form demands by the people that their representatives should be allowed to meet. The addresses of 1681 were intended as popular demands that Parliament should be allowed to sit until it had enacted those measures which the people judged to be necessary. They were a reinforcement of the Whig Members in Parliament, a demonstration that the people were not to be moved from their insistence on Exclusion. In form they were an appeal by the people, but since they were in no sense spontaneous they represented in fact an appeal to the people.

III

The first example of Whig supporters offering instructions to their members was a premature attempt at the Middlesex election in the spring of 1679.[3] A group of freeholders who dined together drew up three resolutions and sent them to the newly elected members. They asked that the members should further the union of all Protestants, the effective prosecution of the Plot, and make Habeas Corpus more effective. The result was far from encouraging. The senior knight, Sir William Roberts, although he was later to be a staunch enough Whig, went to consult the King and gave an

---

[1] *Debates in the House of Commons at Oxford* (1681), published by R. Baldwin.
[2] Carte, 66, ff. 605-8.   [3] Idem, 228, f. 147.

extremely negative answer, 'that he was for the Church of
England and the prerogative, and he thought he had none of their
votes who opposed those things'. The second knight, the firebrand
Sir Robert Peyton, was vague and non-committal.

By 1681 Whig electoral organization had become extremely
efficient. During the two elections of 1679 it had been comparatively rudimentary; its development was largely due to the
agitation at the end of the year in the petitioning movement.
There are obvious resemblances between the petitions and the
addresses at the elections to the Oxford Parliament. For instance,
the Suffolk address was the work of a Whig attorney, Thomas
Percivall, who had been employed previously on both electoral
and petitioning activities in East Anglia.[1] The Shaftesbury Papers
include a draft for a petition, although one dating from early
1681 when a start was made to demand that Parliament should
not be called to Oxford, and a draft of instructions for members.[2]
In both cases the name of the shire is left blank, and it is clear that
these were intended as models to be followed in the shires.

Of course, this organization did not appear on the surface.
Attempting to preserve an impression of spontaneity the Whig
press was intentionally vague as to the origin of the addresses.
The report of the Westminster election stated only that a paper
was handed about in the crowd until it came into the hands of
Thomas Owen, a Whig of some prominence who had declined
to stand. He asked what he should do with it, and being urged by
the crowd to read its contents found that it was an address. He
then asked the people what he should do, they replying with
shouts that he should present it to the members, which he did with
great applause.[3]

The copy of the draft instructions in the Shaftesbury Papers
concentrated on essentials, and as far as these were concerned obviously served as a model for the addresses presented at county
and borough elections all over the country. There was, however,

---

[1] *CSPD*, 1680/1, 533; 1683 (1 Jan. to 30 June), 350.
[2] Shaftesbury Papers, VI B, 392, 399.
[3] *A Faithful Account of . . . the Election of Sir William Poultney and Sir William Waller* (1681).

one significant exception. Locke mentioned the need for defence against Popery, but he included no positive religious demand, for the union of all Protestants or for religious changes in ritual or discipline. Otherwise the variations in the addresses were in matters of lesser importance, often reflecting local interests. Locke's draft began by justifying its presentation; the preamble stated that it contained 'some particulars so manifestly and in-disputably necessary that we cannot omit to give you our Instruc-tions and Directions beforehand in them'. These, of course, began with Exclusion, of all Papist successors in general and the Duke of York by name. Secondly, it demanded that what it called, with understatement, an 'adjustment' should be made to the preroga-tive so as to ensure annual Parliaments, 'for without the certainty of Parliaments meeting in due Distance of Time from each other, and there sitting so long as shall be necessary . . . our laws, Liberties, Lives and Estates should become in short time at the will of the Prince'. It also desired that there should be freedom from mercenary soldiers, and concluded by asking that no money should be granted until the people and their liberties were secured.

These last words, that no money should be voted until an Exclusion Bill had been passed, were often repeated verbatim by the addresses actually presented. Exclusion was the common demand, but as in the case of the Whig members in the last session it was expressed in general terms. Most addresses named the Duke, although a few merely talked of Papist successors in general. Significantly they did not mention who was then to succeed. It was left to an ambiguously worded Chester address to ask, 'that you will use your endeavours for a Protestant succession in the Right Line'.[1] Other safeguards were demanded against arbitrary government besides Exclusion. The Sussex address asked for the establishment of a Protestant Association, others that all bills introduced in the previous session should be revived.[2] The in-structions, given as they were 'by the people' to their representa-tives, naturally sought to enhance the prestige of Parliament and to increase its independence and effectiveness. The Essex address

[1] *National Library of Wales*, Wynnstay MSS. c. 37. This address was presented to William Williams.   [2] *Smith's Protestant Intelligence*, 12.

followed Locke closely in asking for endeavours to be made to secure frequent parliaments, and also a guaranteed length of session.[1]

Concern was often expressed that elections should be made free and independent. Faced as they were by the pressure of a magistracy purged of all Whigs, and often put at a disadvantage by the frauds of returning officers, the Whigs were genuinely anxious to preserve some freedom of choice in elections. The Tories naturally alleged that the Whigs were hypocrites, guilty of the electoral crimes against which they preached, but the Whigs did seriously advocate electoral reforms and regulation. They had introduced a bill in 1679, and many further proposals had been made—for the ballot, nomination of candidates by the freeholders, and a residential qualification for all borough candidates. Elective returning officers or alternatively the exercise of their duties by the freeholders themselves had been suggested. Less drastic suggestions had been made to place limits on treating, to prevent arbitrary adjournments of the poll, and to make illegal all pre-engagements of voters and letters of recommendation from the King, the great officers of state, and all peers.[2] These propositions were echoed in some of the addresses. The Yorkshire and Taunton addresses asked for a law to prevent election 'excesses and Exorbitances'.[3] Surrey demanded the passing of a bill, apparently to be identified with the one introduced in 1679, for both the regulation of elections and the frequent holding of parliaments.[4]

Other subjects which were given prominence included the assertion of what was described as 'our (almost lost) Right of petitioning', the punishment of all abhorrers, sham-plotters and pensioners, and the utmost prosecution of the Plot.[5] As might be expected, several addresses associated with this last demand a call for the union of all Protestants. In Leicestershire, where one of the

---

[1] *Protestant (Domestick) Intelligence*, 100.

[2] *The Bill for Regulating Abuses* (1679). *A Safe and Easy Way to obtain Free and Peaceable Elections* (1680). Carte, 80, f. 827.

[3] *Smith's Protestant Intelligence*, 6, 10, 14. *Protestant (Domestick) Intelligence*, 105. BM, Stowe MSS. 746, f. 16.   [4] *Protestant (Domestick) Intelligence*, 100.

[5] Ibid., 97; Chichester.

knights was a prominent sympathizer with the dissenters, the address gave thanks for 'your zealous promoting the Happy Union of all the good Protestants in the land; not only by good and wholesome laws to that end, but by repealing those which were destructive to it'.[1] Religious demands, not mentioned by Locke, were very common. Many specifically requested the repeal of the statute 35 Queen Elizabeth.[2] Several, including the City, which had just refused to put its provisions into effective execution, demanded the repeal of the Corporation Act. The Surrey address advised the passing of a bill for the suppression of pluralities, non-residence, and scandalous ministers. Taunton asked for legislation against all profaneness and debauchery.

Additional demands were often the result of local interests and grievances. The Monmouthshire Grand Jury, which sent its foreman to thank the two members, presented as a great grievance the Court of the Marches at Ludlow, describing it as a nuisance, useless, and of very great expense. Echoing the arguments used in the Commons, it denounced the garrison at Chepstow as a terror to the county and a receptacle for Popery.[3] The Berkshire address wanted an inquiry into the abuses alleged to exist in the courts in Westminster Hall. Several mentioned the protection of 'our Properties' as well as the defence of religion and liberties. More specifically, Winchelsea wanted a voluntary register of freeholds and houses, a legal reform which is frequently encountered as a demand at this period. It showed its maritime interest by asking that care should be taken of the navy.[4]

The constitutional importance of these addresses can be, and has been, exaggerated. Their purpose was not so much to subordinate Members of Parliament to the people, a doctrine which nearly all Whigs would have abhorred as levelling, but to preserve Whig unity in the immediate future. As the preamble to the Sussex address said: 'though we have no intention to limit or circumscribe the Power we have laid in you, yet we must desire . . . that you would please as our Representatives, to have an

---

[1] *Smith's Protestant Intelligence*, 10.
[2] Bedfordshire, Berkshire, and Middlesex; *Smith's Protestant Intelligence*, 6, 10, 14.   [3] *True Protestant Mercury*, 23.   [4] Ibid., 26.

especial regard to these particulars following.'[1] The real intention
of these addresses was to encourage Whig members to remain
steadfast to Exclusion and all the other measures regarded as
essential, with an implied suggestion that re-election would at
least become more difficult and expensive if they did not. The
Whig organizers and leaders used popular support in this way for
their own purposes, but there was no question of their allowing
policy to be determined by the freeholders or people. The fact
that the Tories imitated the Whigs in organizing addresses is in
itself proof that they were regarded in the main as popular
demonstrations of great propaganda value, for the idea that the
electors should dictate to members would not for a moment be
accepted by the Tories, who had strenuously but vainly opposed
the printing of votes as an appeal to the people.

At Maldon the Tories succeeded in stifling a Whig address,
and substituting one of their own.[2] The members were asked to
prosecute the Plot, a safe demand, for even the Tories still affected
to believe in its existence, or, with the exception of L'Estrange,
did not dare to deny that there had been one. But they were also
asked to preserve the King's prerogative—'having still respect to
the rights and liberties of the subject'—and the Church of England
in all its essentials. A more extreme and specifically Tory address
was presented at Bristol, where after a stormy and riotous election
the mayor returned himself and another Tory.[3] In Cheshire the
Tories were deliberately provocative. Although they were unable
to organize sufficient support to take the Whigs to a poll, the
Tories prepared and tried to present an address of their own in
order to annoy and infuriate their opponents. Admittedly it began
by asking for the prosecution of the Plot, but it went on to demand
the execution of the 'wholesome laws' enacted against the dissenters, who were described as having killed the best of Kings
under a pretence of holiness and zeal for liberty of conscience.
A further point was almost equally unacceptable; in contrast to

[1] Smith's Protestant Intelligence, 12.
[2] Loyal Protestant, 3. The publication of this Tory news-sheet shows how the
Tories were imitating, with some success, Whig political methods.
[3] Ibid., 4; 19 Mar. But the True Protestant Mercury, 24, denied its existence.

the almost universal Whig demand that members should not vote money until Exclusion had passed, the Tories asked the members 'cheerfully' to vote the King supply. Not unnaturally the Whigs prevented the presentation of this address, and in his speech of acceptance of the Whig address Henry Booth reaffirmed his Whig sentiments and principles.[1]

Speeches of acceptance by the newly elected members were common, many of them receiving a full report in the Whig press. Booth's was also printed as a pamphlet. It deserved its wide publicity, for it was a clear statement of general Whig principles as well of immediate polemical value. Booth, who was to prove himself the staunchest of all Whigs, declared that his purpose was to promote the Protestant religion and the interests of the King as well as of the people. He disclaimed any intention of impairing the royal prerogative: 'for this is my principle . . . that the King's prerogative when rightly used, is for the Good and Benefit of the People; and the Liberties and Properties of the People are for the support of the Crown and the King's Prerogative.'[2] This was the 'blessed harmony' which was supposed to have existed in the reign of Elizabeth; its absence at the present was not the fault of the Whigs but entirely the responsibility of the 'restless councillors' of the King who were concerned only to further their own ends. A great deal of the speech was devoted to answering the slanders of his opponents in the county, and allegations made against the Whigs in general. The fact that Booth considered this to be necessary was an admission that the Whigs had lost their former monopoly of propaganda and that their enemies were taking the initiative. He contrasted the Cavalier Parliament, which he alleged had largely consisted of members who sold their country for private advantage, with the two earlier Whig parliaments, which could hardly be matched for riches—significantly placed first— integrity, learning, and experience. He concluded his speech with a promise of faithful service in the forthcoming session, he would remember on whose errand he was sent, and swore that neither rewards, threats, hopes, nor fears would prevail upon him to desert his duty.

[1] Ibid., 21.   [2] *The Speech of the Hon. Henry Booth* (1681).

IV

In addition to the instructions offered to the members at the elections Whig pamphlets also urged their supporters to continue to insist on Exclusion and to obtain it by continuing to exert intense pressure on the King. Outwardly at least there was no sign of weakness, but only increased bitterness against Tory opponents and the ministers. Yet, as in Booth's speech, there were some indications that the Whigs were now on the defensive. The most clearly reasoned pamphlet contained a justification of Parliament, a statement of its constitutional importance as an essential part of government.[1] Old arguments were repeated, quotations of the obsolete statutes of the fourteenth century for annual parliaments, arguments from Coke that Parliament should not be dissolved while any petitions remained undiscussed, and that the King was obliged to redress the grievances of the subject. Many Whigs anticipated a short session at Oxford, and although some believed that the King was on the point of capitulation, others were prepared for an early prorogation or even a dissolution and fresh elections. But there was one means by which an early end to the session could be prevented; this was by the immediate exploitation of the case of Fitzharris.

This case is yet another mystery of the period which, like the death of Godfrey, has never been satisfactorily explained.[2] Fitz-

[1] *Vox Populi* (1681).

[2] Barrillon, 17 Mar., 7 Apr., 1681. Addl. 32520, ff. 190, 191. Petherick, *Restoration Rogues*, 264–324, gives a long account of the Fitzharris affair from a strongly anti-Whig standpoint. The chronology of the case was as follows. Fitzharris was arrested at the end of February and sent to Newgate. Here he was examined by the Whig sheriffs, Cornish and Bethel, but in order to prevent their coming to any arrangement with the prisoner he was removed to the Tower, and all access forbidden, before the meeting of the Oxford Parliament. There, in order to get him back into their hands as well as to ensure against an early dissolution or prorogation, the Commons voted his impeachment. The Lords refused to accept this impeachment, partly on the grounds that an indictment at common law had already been issued against him. With the dissolution Fitzharris was doomed; the Court had good reason to silence him, and his wild attempts to accuse Danby and the Queen, as well as the Duke of York, of having been responsible for Godfrey's murder failed to postpone his trial, condemnation, and execution. It is hoped to examine this case at a later date, using unpublished material.

harris, a ne'er-do-well member of an Irish Catholic family of some past distinction, had tried to retrieve his fortunes by engaging in political intrigue. An amateur at this game he was soon in trouble, being seized by the redoubtable Protestant magistrate, the priest-hunting Sir William Waller, and found to be in possession of a pseudo-Whig libel, *The True Englishman*. At first the Whigs were indignant, the whole affair was reminiscent of the sham Meal-tub Plot, and they suspected Fitzharris of having planned to plant this libel, written in the most immoderate language, on some of their members. They believed that it had been intended to break at Oxford, where with the Guards in attendance it would be easy for the ministers to order the arrest of the Whig leaders. Whether this was so or not there is no doubt that Fitzharris had been in the service of the Court, and that he had received encouragement although the exact nature of his employment is uncertain. Having failed miserably to do anything, Fitzharris was useless to the Court, but now the Whigs saw their opportunity to make political capital out of the case.

In return for a promise of protection Fitzharris, like Danger-field, might be induced to give evidence in a way that would implicate the Duke of York and other ministers. Indeed, he was only too willing to do so, and accused Danby of being responsible for the murder of Godfrey. Moreover, in contrast to the Meal-tub Plot, this opportunity could be used to bring the informer before Parliament while popular excitement was still at its height. Investigation of the case could be placed in the hands of a com-mittee of the House of Commons composed exclusively of Whigs. The King would be deterred from ordering a prorogation or dissolution since such action would be construed as deliberate suppression of evidence. Therefore the Whigs hoped to be able to ensure a certain length of session and to incriminate their chief opponents. Once again the Court would be forced on the defensive from the very start of the session.

If the maximum political capital was to be made out of the case, and control over his disclosures placed in the hands of the Whigs, it was essential that Fitzharris should be impeached in Parliament rather than tried in the King's courts of law. The Whigs were intent on exploiting his revelations, the Court was determined to silence him by putting Fitzharris to death, and by all means to prevent a long drawn-out propaganda impeachment with the prisoner working in concert with the managers for the prosecution.

This case is perhaps the best example during this period of how both sides were—for quite genuine as well as purely interested reasons—using judicial processes for their own advantage. The Whigs feared that in a court of law the judges, acting as they always did in political cases under the influence or on the orders of the King and his ministers, would stifle any evidence which Fitzharris possessed. The Court—even if, as is unlikely, they had nothing to hide—knew that the Whigs would try to suborn the prisoner and tamper with his evidence, diverting it to their own purposes. Therefore Fitzharris was removed from Newgate to the Tower, where all access to him could be strictly controlled. In the Lords the Tory majority of Court peers refused to accept an impeachment. With this the unfortunate adventurer lost all importance. His Whig counsel was arrested; Waller, who did not want to give evidence, was forced to appear and to help to convict the prisoner. With the failure of the efforts to prevent the trial and to procure an acquittal, Fitzharris lost all value to the Whigs, and their attempts to make him into a martyr had little success. Moreover, the determination with which he was harried to death showed clearly that the King was preparing to take action against the Whigs. The Attorney-General passed over the Westminster Grand Jury, which had been packed by the sheriffs to include a number of Whig Members of Parliament. The judges decided that the voting of an impeachment was not a bar to proceedings, and in doing so showed that they were confident of royal protection from future parliamentary attacks.[1]

Assured of French subsidies, there was no need for the King to have called the Oxford Parliament at all.[2] Even before the conclusion of a secret agreement with France, he had decided on an early dissolution unless the Commons proved to be more conciliatory than in the past. The Whigs were now at his mercy. Had the session been at Westminster they might have dared to

[1] Carte, 222, f. 294. *State Trials*, viii. 223-330.   [2] Barrillon, 24, 27 Mar.

defy an early dissolution by transferring their proceedings to Guildhall on some pretext that they were in danger from the Papists. At Oxford they were separated from their allies in the City, and surrounded by the Guards.

The King's policy was designed to allow the Whigs to discredit themselves by their intransigence, and thus to justify future repression by the King. In his speech at the start of the session Charles emphasized the contrast between his own conduct and that of the Whigs, and stressed his own respect for the law.[1] He complained of 'strange unsuitable returns' made to his past propositions, and again renewed his promise that he would consider all expedients for the security of the liberties and religion of the people provided that they did not alter the succession. The constitutionalism of his case resembled the arguments put forward by Charles I and Hyde in the months before the civil war. Charles identified his interest with that of the nation; unless the liberties of his subjects were secure the Crown was not safe. Merit was claimed for calling another Parliament so soon, despite the ill behaviour of the last. A promise that he would observe the law himself was accompanied by a warning that the Whigs must do likewise.

The Whigs could not accept this apparently conciliatory attitude of the King as genuine. It was not accompanied by concessions, and the renewed opposition to Exclusion made his speech obnoxious to them. As in the last session the Whigs regarded all mention of expedients with suspicion as a trap. Moreover, after new elections the Whigs, in insisting on Exclusion as the only effectual means of security, now claimed with increased confidence that they represented the people and their wishes. The very first motion of the new session was for the printing of votes, in itself an almost unprecedented action, and one that would be deplored as demagogic by later generations of Whigs. When Secretary Jenkins described the motion as an appeal to the people, this was in itself a recommendation to the Whigs. Tory arguments in favour of expedients were met with assertions that the Whig policy of Exclusion was what the people wanted.

[1] Grey, viii. 291. *CJ* ix. 705.

As Sir William Cowper said, 'the weight of England is the People, and the world will find, that they will sink Popery at last'.[1]

Significantly, Whig members used the instructions presented at the elections in order to justify their insistence on Exclusion and disregard of the King's injunction not to attempt any alteration of the succession. In moving the introduction of the bill Clayton declared, 'we can discharge our trust no better, than to observe the directions of those that sent us hither', and explained that he had an address for Exclusion from the City. Pulteney, ancestor of a great Whig line, but not a particularly important member, declared that 'by express directions of those I represent I am enjoined to adhere to the Bill of Exclusion'.[2] This was the opinion of most of the Whigs, speaker after speaker declared that there could be no security without Exclusion. It was for the Court to offer expedients so that the Commons could judge them. At last, after an attempt at delay, a definite scheme was put forward by Littleton; previously the Tories had talked of expedients in general without elaborating the details. This was the proposal for a Regency under which James was to be left only the title of King and was even to be banished.[3] The Whigs found it easy to expose the weaknesses and fallacies of the proposal. Jones contended with all his legal authority that if James were to succeed to the title of King all incapacities laid upon him would be nullified; it was not enough to strip him of all his royal powers. Both he and Vaughan asserted that to maintain a Regency would require a far larger army than in the case of Exclusion. Carew posed the question of what would happen if James refused to accept the restrictions laid upon him, and asked whether those who resisted him in order to maintain the law would then be traitors.[4] Only one member, Meres—whose twists and turns had been more numerous than those of any other—spoke in favour of the scheme as an alternative to Exclusion.

Some of the real reasons for the outright rejection of the scheme

---

[1] Grey, viii. 292–3. The printing was moved by Hotham.
[2] Ibid., viii. 309, 316–17.   [3] In a very long speech, Grey, viii. 317–20.
[4] Ibid., viii. 315–16, 320–2.

for a Regency were not voiced in the debate. Many Whigs might
have accepted it, but were afraid that if they did so openly they
would lose all credit with the people. Even more important was
the fact that the suggested Regency would not favour Monmouth.
Temple had prophesied failure for this reason, and had believed
that if William was named as the probable Regent the scheme
would be rejected and he would forfeit all his credit.[1] He would
be compromised, and everyone would believe that he was working in the interests of his father-in-law.

Only if Monmouth was specified as Regent would the Whigs
have given the expedient serious consideration.[2] By now his
pretensions were at last receiving serious support, as had been
shown by the votes passed in his favour at the end of the previous
session. In the bill of 1680 a proviso had been inserted to safeguard
Mary's interests, but at Oxford the question of who was to succeed was to be left open. Previously, Shaftesbury and most of the
Whigs had not been committed to the support of Monmouth.
They had exploited his great popularity, but they had been able
to gain it by no more than half promises and vague, imprecise
assurances. It was not until the Oxford Parliament that Shaftesbury committed himself to the support of Monmouth's claims to
the succession, and even then there is no evidence that they were
accepted by the majority of Whigs. This in itself was a weakness
which would inevitably have destroyed the Whig party. In the
early stages of the crisis all its members could be united on the
necessity for excluding James, but the fact that in two years no
decision had been taken on who was to succeed shows how
essentially negative were the factors which bound the Whigs
together.

Shaftesbury still apparently believed that eventually the King
must give way. Following his maxim that things must become
worse before they could be better, he had maintained pressure on
the King, and shown unremitting hostility to the ministers. But
as before his policy was based on miscalculations. Charles was not
to be intimidated; whereas most men grow timid with age, he

[1] Sidney, ii. 177–8.
[2] Prinsterer, v. 492. Conway to William, 29 Mar. 1681.

—as he told Shaftesbury—rather grew more determined.[1] Moreover, the Whigs showed excessive rigidity in the tactic which they
followed. These might satisfy their faithful followers who, for
instance, were horrified at the details of the Irish Plot, but Whig
propaganda was becoming monotonously repetitive and stale.
Whig pamphlets continued to expound the danger from the
Papists and the Duke of York, the need to secure Parliament and
the liberties of the nation from evil ministers. But by now their
Tory rivals were exploiting with equal or even greater success the
deep and widespread fear that Whig intransigence would lead to
violence and another civil war. A reaction began in favour of the
King, which his own calculated policy did much to assist. Its
extent must not be exaggerated, for the elections had shown how
strong was the Whig hold in the country, but Shaftesbury was
now no longer in such a commanding position as to make it
unsafe for the King to rule without a Parliament.

Although few Whigs had expected a long session, they were
surprised by the sudden dissolution which cut short their parliamentary campaign. Years later Lord Grey, a most doubtful
informant, claimed that Shaftesbury had attempted to organize
resistance, that he had called on members of both Houses to
remain in session in defiance of the dissolution.[2] This is unlikely.
Had the session been at Westminster a retreat into the City might
have been practicable. Many historians have made a great deal of
the armed retainers who accompanied Whig members and peers
to Oxford, but they were intended for defence, not aggression.
Even though the city was strongly Whig, there was no question
of an attack being launched against the disciplined and vastly
superior strength of the regiments of Guards.

Indeed, there appeared at the time to be no reason for such
drastic reaction as an insurrection. For some time the Whigs did
not realize that the dissolution was more than a check, that it was
in fact a decisive defeat which ensured their ruin. In the following
months they—and Tories as well—confidently expected another
Parliament, and many at once began to make preparations for

[1] Barrillon, 7 Apr.
[2] Lord Grey, *Secret History of the Rye House Plot*, 21–22.

new elections.[1] They did not believe that it was necessary to abate their demands. The loyal addresses which poured in after the dissolution, which thanked the King for his Declaration justifying the action, were discounted as of no importance.[2] Whig pamphlets compared them with the addresses which had assured Richard Cromwell of the support of the people, and had subsequently proved to be worthless. They were attacked as an usurpation of constitutional rights belonging to Parliament, and an attempt to discredit the institution in the eyes of the King. The reflections made against the conduct of the previous two Whig Houses of Commons were construed as an attempt to fetter freedom of debate, and the right to withhold as well as to grant supply. Whigs complained, with arguments which they were in no position to use, that these 'loyal' addresses added to heats and animosities, and created parties and divisions among the people. The supporters and subscribers were disparaged as a combination of the 'engineers'—the clergy and officials—with the scum of the people.

More convincingly it was easy for the Whigs to show that many addresses came from places which had returned Whig members during the elections. Indeed, the Bedfordshire address went so far as to admit that they did not expect to be able to carry the next election for anyone recommended by the King.[3] But although the Whigs could with some plausibility explain away these addresses, they were still a sign of increased Tory efficiency. Moreover, in their reflections on the conduct of the previous Whig parliaments, the subscribers showed that they were confident of the King's protection in the future against the kind of treatment which the abhorrers had suffered during the session of 1680.

There were a certain number of desertions to the Court, but these too could be explained away. Macclesfield made his peace with the King, only to return later to association with the

---

[1] Barrillon, 14 Apr.; 22, 25, 29 Dec. 1681. Carte, 222, f. 286. *CSPD*, 1680/1, 473.

[2] The addresses were printed in the *London Gazette*, and sparked off another pamphlet controversy. See, for instance, the Whig *An Impartial Account of the Nature and Tendency of the Late Addresses* (1681).

[3] In fact the Tories were to carry both places in 1685.

Whigs.[1] When Townshend, the original leader and still the nominal chief of the Whigs in Norfolk, went over to the Court his interest at once collapsed.[2] Those who had previously been regarded as his connexions and dependents repudiated his move, and rallied round Sir John Hobart, an intransigent Whig. However, without a Parliament it was not clear at the time, nor is there evidence now, how considerable was the number of desertions. On the other hand, it is clear that the hard core of the Whigs remained intact, intransigent, and determined if now less hopeful. But without a Parliament they were crippled, even though no one could foresee that there would not be another for four years.

The position of the Whigs deteriorated steadily, but they were not by any means powerless, and in 1681 they were able to defend themselves successfully. They could still rely on a measure of popular support and they continued to control the City. Yet their popularity was a wasting asset, ineffective without elections, and events were to prove that the Whig position in the City was not impregnable. Once again determined use of the royal prerogative was to prove decisive. The Tories had for long described the Whigs as a faction. Now after the dissolution of the Oxford Parliament they could be treated as such in what were, in the very real sense of the words, the King's courts.

[1] Carte, 222, ff. 290, 292. In 1682 he helped to organize Monmouth's visit to the north-west.

[2] Addl. 27448, ff. 96, 114. Manuscripts in possession of Mr. R. W. Ketton-Cremer, William Windham, 21 Dec. 1681; Sir John Hobart, 31 Dec. 1681, 22 Mar. 1683.

7

THE DECLINE AND COLLAPSE OF THE
FIRST WHIGS

I

As the Fitzharris case showed, both Whigs and Tories, Charles and Shaftesbury, recognized the political character of legal cases and verdicts, and were prepared to use the courts of justice as a political arena. At the lowest level they wanted to see friends acquitted and enemies convicted and punished, not only from reasons of personal animosity but also because they regarded opponents as the enemies of law and the constitution. To blame the Tories for the excesses of unjust judges, or the Whigs for the flagrant packing of juries, is to misunderstand the contemporary attitude to the law.[1] The weakness of the state, the dependence of so much upon the life of the King, the insecurity of property, the lack of effective means by which either plotting or ordinary crime could be detected or repressed, produced legal procedure in which the odds against the prisoner were heavy. This was particularly the case in the trials of those charged with treason. Tories believed that as the Whigs were a dangerous faction they must be tried and punished if rebellion were to be avoided. This was precisely the attitude which the Whigs had themselves adopted towards the Papists involved in the original Plot; they knew that they were guilty and therefore set out to prove that this was so. In the modern sense no political trials of the period were fair or equitable; judges, jury, counsel, and the public all prejudged the issue according to their political beliefs.

[1] For the general state of the law at this period, see A. F. Havighurst, 'The Judiciary and Politics in the Reign of Charles II', *Law Quarterly Review*, lxvi, Jan. and Apr. 1950. Pollock, *The Popish Plot*, 288–303.

Nevertheless, although the conduct of judges, juries, and witnesses may seem to be purely partisan and opportunist, it was only in the case of the last that this was usually so. Many of those concerned may have been actuated by purely mercenary motives, but fundamental constitutional, legal, and political issues were also involved. Long before the crisis developed, Lord Chief Justice Scroggs expressed the view that it was his duty to uphold the prerogatives of the King and his interests.[1] During the trials for the Popish Plot he tried to follow the King's intentions; when he learnt that Charles did not credit the Plot, or favour Shaftesbury, his attitude towards those accused by Oates and his fellows at once changed.[2] This, rather than the Whig allegations of massive bribes, is the explanation for the acquittal of Wakeman in the summer of 1679. When Tory witnesses, who were all committing perjury, failed to persuade a partisan Whig jury, ministers complained that the King could not obtain justice in his own courts.[3] Of course there was nothing at all new in this, the Tory views were a continued expression of the view summarized by Bacon, that judges should be lions under the throne. Nor was the Whig attitude in any sense revolutionary or an innovation; they not merely complained against the injustice of the judges, but claimed that in the past they had been, and still ought to be, independent of the Crown. Moreover, their stress on the importance of juries was more than mere opportunism. Juries were representative in the same sense as was Parliament, the two were regarded as of equal antiquity as institutions safeguarding the liberties of the nation.[4]

Partisan feelings led both sides to ascribe the worst and lowest motives to each other's behaviour. To the ministers and the Tories, London jurymen were perjured rogues who on instructions would ignore the plainest evidence in order to save traitors from their deserved punishment. One Tory claimed that he could tell that a jury was knavish and fanatical by the cut of their hair.[5]

[1] Carte, 79, f. 77.
[2] R. North, *Lives of the Norths* (1890), i. 196; the anecdote may be exaggerated as it is told, but it contains more than an element of truth.
[3] *CSPD*, 1680/1, 500. Barrillon, 30 Oct. 1681.
[4] This was asserted, for instance, by *The Englishman's Right* (1680).
[5] Carte, 72, ff. 524–5.

The Whigs responded with accusations that the judges were bought, either by the Court and the hope of promotion, or in Wakeman's case by the money of the Portuguese ambassador. Whigs believed the witnesses implicitly when they were swearing against Papists; when they turned on their former paymasters their evidence was thought to have lost all value. Similarly, the Tories, who had poured contempt on the Irish witnesses with their wild stories of an imminent Papist rebellion, gave them credence when they turned and began to accuse Shaftesbury.

Whig anger against the judges rested on two accounts. First they were blamed for what were regarded as their partisan directions to juries and their conduct of trials. The Whigs attributed this behaviour to dependence on the Crown for tenure and promotion, with subservience to ministers and to James. The Whig charges had some justification.[1] But although Whigs protested bitterly when Scroggs treated Oates with the contempt which he deserved, there had been silence when the same judge had browbeaten and vilified Papist prisoners. Whig grievances and complaints against excessive punishments lose much of their effect when one recalls the unsavoury attempt to question the mitigation of the sentence passed on Stafford.

Although less dramatic in effect than partiality in court the extra-judicial opinions of judges were regarded as equally subversive of popular liberties. Whigs compared the proclamation against petitioning with the notorious opinions which had been delivered in the reign of Charles I and later reversed by the Long Parliament. In the interest of preserving the fundamental laws and the religion of the nation unjust judges must be punished. Whig pamphlets repeated how Alfred had had a short way with them, hanging no fewer than thirty in a year.[2] Winnington quoted the fate of Tresilian and Belnap, who had infringed and attempted to subvert Magna Carta. They had been

---

[1] These charges were printed at the time in *Report of the Committee of the House of Commons on the Proceedings of Judges* (1680).

[2] A crude, and wildly unhistorical, version of legal history can be found in the self-explanatory *The Triumphs of Justice over Unjust Judges* (1681).

hanged, and equally vigorous action was necessary if the constitution was to be preserved and the fountains of justice to run
clear.

Naturally the Whigs wished to get rid of Scroggs and his
fellows, either by impeachment or more practicably by intimidation. But their hostility to the judges was not merely opportunist
and partisan. Just as they hoped to be able to guarantee the complete independence of Parliament, so they intended to place the
judiciary permanently on an independent tenure. In the Commons
Hampden moved that judges should hold their commissions *quam
diu se bene gesserint*, although it is to be presumed that unpleasant-
ness to Dr. Oates would have been enough to justify dismissal.[1]
Nevertheless, even if the Whigs were concerned primarily to
further their own interests and immediate policy they were at
least putting forward a principle that would eventually become a
guarantee of equal justice.

The Whig attitude to juries rested similarly on two levels, the
immediate need for defence against the judges, and long-term
concern for the protection of liberties and property. Faced after
the summer of 1679 with almost invariable hostility from the
judiciary, the Whigs exalted the importance of juries as the only
means of defending the innocent against condemnation by corrupt
judges. In the Commons Winnington went so far as to declare:
'the two great pillars of our government are Parliament and
Juries. It is these that give the title of freeborn Englishmen.'[2]
This again was a theme which had been developed long before
the Exclusion crisis, but now it was further elaborated. Whig
writers asserted the antiquity of juries as proof of their place in the
constitution, tracing them back as far as the days of the ancient
Britons. More practically the Whigs made additional use of juries,
as well as packing them in order to produce favourable verdicts.
The London grand jury which threw out a bill against College,
the Protestant joiner who was subsequently convicted at Oxford
by a Tory jury, asked the bench to present a petition to the King
complaining that Papist priests in Newgate were responsible for
sham plots against Protestants. A 'loyal' address from Norwich

[1] Grey, viii. 187. 18 Dec. 1680.   [2] Carte, 72, ff. 508–9.

was presented by the Middlesex grand jury as a libel in an effort to discourage the movement.

The Whigs were most vulnerable, and totally unjustified in their conduct, in their unscrupulous use of witnesses. It is unlikely that they actually instigated the original informers, but once they appeared Oates and his imitators were given every encouragement—financial, moral, and political. Whig peers attended trials to give them countenance, subscriptions were raised for their maintenance. Many had disreputable records, nearly all had been in prison at one time or another, but none was turned away or disbelieved. As spontaneous excitement caused by the original discoveries began to die away, more organization became necessary. The mobilization of evidence, it can almost be said its manufacture, reached its highest development in the Irish Plot, revealed at the end of 1680. But despite the very bitter antagonism which had existed ever since the massacres of 1641 against all Irish Papists, this so-called Plot failed in its purpose. Shaftesbury expected that its exploitation would produce the ruin of Ormonde, the Lord Lieutenant, but it fell far short. Essex refused to believe in its authenticity.[1] The witnesses succeeded in gaining the conviction of the most celebrated, and noble, of all the Catholic martyrs of the reign, but if this execution of Archbishop Plunkett was gratifying to religious bigotry and hatred, it had little political value.[2]

The execution of Plunkett even caused a revulsion among many moderates. In any case the public were becoming satiated. The witnesses who came over from Ireland were despised bog-trotters and thoroughly contemptible in their characters. With much justification the Tories could sneer at them as men 'who would die for their Religion, yet hated the bloody counsells of the Jesuits for bringing in of their religion'.[3] Whig pamphleteers in their replies had to exercise considerable ingenuity in explaining that these Papist witnesses should be believed. As Papists, it was argued, they believed that they would be damned if they swore

[1] H. C. Foxcroft (ed.), *Some Unpublished Letters of Gilbert Burnet* (1907), 22.

[2] *State Trials*, viii. 447–500. See also A. Curtayne, *The Trial of Oliver Plunkett* (1953); written in order to help promote his eventual canonization this book not unnaturally takes a severe view of the Whigs.

[3] Carte, 243, f. 456. Sir R. Reading.

against co-religionists, whereas—and this argument was to prove
convenient when the Irish witnesses changed sides—they would
cheerfully swear to anything against Protestants without fear of
the consequences.[1]

The Whigs soon discovered how unreliable these Irish witnesses were. They, the most despicable element, were the first to
desert.[2] The readiness with which they were prepared to give
evidence recommended them to the ministers, who were equally
unscrupulous in their exploitation of perjury. The Irish led the
way, but they were soon followed by most of the others, including
such veterans as Turberville and Dugdale. The original Plot was
now almost played out, the subscriptions raised for their maintenance were falling off. In their eagerness to turn to better paymasters, and to what now seemed to be the winning side, the only
way in which the informers could retrieve their fortunes was by
manufacturing evidence against the Whigs. They concentrated
first on the most culpable and vulnerable of the Whig managers,
Shaftesbury's agent Hetherington. He had enlisted the witnesses
in Ireland and brought them over and instructed them in their
perjuries against Plunkett. Now, when he was arrested on a charge
of high treason, his accusers were his former protégés, John and
Dennis Macnamarra, Smith, Dennis, and Ivey. These men also
tried to persuade other informers to join them, some were even
more ingenious, offering their services to the Court and at the same
time telling the Whigs that attempts were being made to suborn
them. One or two succeeded in getting money from both Whigs
and the Court.

The first of the Whig victims, College the 'Protestant joiner',
fell to Dugdale, Turberville, and Smith, all of whom had recently
sworn with effect against Stafford. College's case was a foretaste
of what was to come.[3] The Whigs packed a London grand jury

[1] No Protestant Plot, third part, 116. As the title suggests, the Whig pamphleteers
were now on the defensive.
[2] CSPD, 1680/1, 418; information of Lawrence Mowbray, one of the most
despicable Whig witnesses, taken in Aug. 1681 by Justice Wolstenholme, one of
the few remaining Whigs in the commission of the peace.
[3] State Trials, viii. 563–717. Bodleian, Rawlinson MSS. D, 384, f. 69. He was
charged, on very doubtful evidence by former Whig perjurers, with having

which naturally threw out the bill against him. The case was then transferred to Oxford, where a carefully selected Tory jury, with savage and constant encouragement from the judges, made short work of him. This success enhanced the credit of the witnesses, and opened the way for an attack on Shaftesbury himself.

The arrest and indictment of Shaftesbury were intended to be decisive. His popularity had waned since the dissolution of the Oxford Parliament, and after his arrest many Whigs began to minimize his importance and disavow any connexion with him. Few showed any pity towards the old man in his danger. Buckingham, who had always resented Shaftesbury's leadership, commented that this was the first case of which he knew in which a man was betrayed by his own witnesses, and that Shaftesbury had ruined the Whigs through his imprudence.[1] The appearance of this rift between Shaftesbury and some of his former supporters encouraged the ministers to press the accusations, and to make use of the contemptible witnesses against him. They believed that once he was eliminated the rest of the Whigs would submit; prosecutions might be launched against some of the more obnoxious, but although there were rumours of the impending arrest of Monmouth and Essex, a general proscription does not seem to have been intended.

The ministers both feared and hated Shaftesbury, and in their determination not to spare him personal animus undoubtedly played a large part. Halifax and Seymour had for long been on the worst possible terms with him. Hyde, who was acting as the representative of the Duke of York, fully shared his hostility to the Whigs and their leader. Charles, who now believed that his life and throne had really been in danger—from the Whigs not the Papists—was eager to have Shaftesbury's head. He overruled the opposition of a small minority among the councillors, although later, when the prosecution had failed, he put the blame on his ministers for having misled him.[2] It was proposed to appoint Ormonde as Lord Steward to preside over the trial by

planned violence during the Oxford session—the origin of the legend that a rising had been planned.

[1] Barrillon, 14 July, 4 Sept. 1681.　　　　　　　[2] Idem, 3 Nov., 8 Dec.

Shaftesbury's peers,[1] and his attitude was certain to be one of implacable hostility to the prisoner. He detested Shaftesbury as the enemy of the King, as well as having some private accounts to settle. Shaftesbury had rejected his conciliatory approach in 1679. Instead he had tried to secure Ormonde's dismissal and later to fabricate a charge against him of high treason, instigating Irish witnesses to swear that he had been concerned in the alleged Irish Plot. With Ormonde as Steward and the other thirty peers selected from among his bitterest enemies there would be little chance of an acquittal.

Old, seriously ill, and isolated in the Tower, Shaftesbury lost his customary resolution. His wife and Locke informed him that all his friends were deserting him in the hour of his need. This report seemed to be borne out when Shaftesbury began to organize his defence. He wrote to Lord Huntingdon asking him to attend at the hearing before the grand jury so as to give countenance to the defence and the jury. Huntingdon had done so recently, when with several other peers he had attended the hearing of the case against College in the City. Now, however, he excused himself on the ground of bad health, a clear indication of Shaftesbury's waning interest.[2] Convinced that he would be condemned, and knowing that execution would then be inevitable, Shaftesbury in desperation made a tentative approach for a pardon.[3] Among the courtiers the only man with whom he remained on good terms was Arlington, his old colleague in the Cabal, who habitually and for profit acted as a go-between. Arlington was asked to sound the King, to ask whether submission or exile, even to a plantation with a pledge not to return, would secure a pardon.

When Charles was cautiously approached he firmly insisted on seeing Shaftesbury's letter to Arlington. The latter, financially dependent on his offices, dared not refuse. The surrender of this letter could have had dangerous results. The King had no intention of pardoning Shaftesbury, and the ministers were determined to

[1] Barrillon, 8 Sept.
[2] Shaftesbury Papers, VI B, 400; Huntingdon to Stringer.
[3] Morrice, f. 319. Bodleian, Clarendon State Papers, 88, f. 5, 'A Paper given to my Lord Chamberlain by Mr Shepheard from Earl of Shaftesbury, 7ber 28th 1681'.

secure his condemnation. But news of the letter became known, and this offer of submission could be construed as an admission of guilt, which would prejudice the case even before a Whig grand jury, and might wreck Shaftesbury's interest in the country.

There was no need for Shaftesbury to have been so despondent. If Locke believed that all was lost, many other Whigs were still determined to save their leader from the scaffold. Charlton, Shaftesbury's chief confidant—an important although shadowy figure— was furious when informed by Arlington of the approach. Like many other contemporaries he could see that the confidence of the King and the ministers was extremely ill-founded. Although he would be tried before a special court of his peers, Shaftesbury had first to appear before a grand jury selected from a panel nominated by the Whig sheriffs of Middlesex. Obviously they would choose only known and resolute Whig jurors.

All chance of the return of a true bill virtually vanished when the Lord Mayor and the sheriffs prevented any alterations being made in the panel. In October Secretary Jenkins complained that only two out of the forty-nine jurors returned by the Whig under-sheriff were churchmen. With Tory exaggeration he described the rest as 'desperate sectaries, most of them Fifth Monarchy men'.[1] To prevent an ignoramus, and Shaftesbury's discharge, consultations were held between Halifax, Hyde, and Pemberton, who was to be the judge at the proceedings. They considered several proposals, to provide a jury from Southwark, or to try Shaftesbury in the court of the King's Verge, to put further pressure on the sheriffs, or to transfer the case to Westminster where the jury would be nominated by the bailiff.[2] All proved to be impracticable; Shaftesbury now derived the full advantages of his City residence in Aldersgate.

Shaftesbury's case was virtually settled long before the hearing. On 18 October a Whig grand jury returned ignoramus to the bill presented against Rous, a minor City Whig accused of high treason.[3] By their fury the King and the ministers betrayed the

[1] CSPD, 1680/1, 500.
[2] HMC, Ormonde, N.S., vi. 226. Tanner, 36, f. 173. BM, Stowe MSS. 144, f. 19.
[3] CSPD, 1680/1, 525. Bodleian, Rawlinson MSS. D, 384, f. 74.

certainty of failure. The only hope of gaining a true bill, the exertion of influence on the jurors by the Lord Chief Justice, did not promise much. The jurors were all Whigs, but many of them were men of standing and substantial fortune. Such men could not easily be intimidated, some possessed legal knowledge, and four of them had sat in the Exclusion parliaments.[1] From the beginning of the proceedings they showed themselves resolute and independent. The occasion was made a party demonstration. Outside a large mob gathered to intimidate the witnesses and celebrate the expected discharge of their leader. In the court itself Whig magnates attended to stiffen the jurors and prevent undue browbeating by the judges.

The Whig jurymen knew well enough that if they returned a true bill against Shaftesbury he would certainly be condemned by his peers, and that execution would then inevitably follow. But their concern was not limited to returning ignoramus to the bill. The lesson of College had been appreciated. He had been cleared by a City jury only to be condemned when the case was transferred to Oxford. The Whigs were afraid that Shaftesbury would fall a victim to the same manœuvre, and therefore they set out to discredit the witnesses. They disregarded the judges, who maintained that it was not for a grand jury to go into the detailed proofs, nor to hear evidence disparaging the witnesses. But although the judges refused leave for affidavits of subornation to be produced and examined against them, they were unable to prevent the jurors making a searching examination of their stories.[2] This had already been done in the hearing of Rous's case, when the jury had questioned the witnesses whether they had heard any treasonable words spoken outside London. Apparently caught by surprise, and unwilling to commit themselves to statements without prearrangement and collusion, they had been afraid to go

[1] PRO, State Papers, 29/417, ff. 112–13; list of the members of the grand jury, with comments.

[2] State Trials, viii. 808, 811. Although the witnesses were allowed to sit in court listening to each other, and despite attempts by the Lord Chief Justice to come to the rescue, they were soon faltering under the pertinent questions of the jury. Attempts to interrupt or silence Sir Samuel Bernardiston, the foreman, proved entirely ineffective.

beyond what they had deposed in their informations. Any im-
promptu stories would certainly have been subject to intense and
searching examination later. This course was repeated in Shaftesbury's case, and the jury were determined to destroy the credit
of the prosecution witnesses so that they could not be used again
against any Whig. Shaftesbury's friends had made the most
intensive preparations, particularly as to the character of the witnesses, some of the informers who remained loyal to the Whigs
providing plenty of evidence of attempted subornation.

Although the jury were not able to produce this evidence of the
bad characters of the witnesses, they were able to tear the prosecution case to shreds. The witnesses were forced to admit that a
considerable period had elapsed between the alleged speaking of
treasonable words by Shaftesbury and the date on which the informations had been sworn. To make matters worse some of these
men, before they had gone over to the Court, had during this
time subscribed a Whig petition to the Common Council complaining that constant efforts had been made to suborn them.[1]
Their only excuse was that they had signed this petition without
reading its contents. Under the searching questions put by the
foreman of the jury, Sir Samuel Bernardiston, they began to wilt.
Judicial interventions were an admission of failure, and did not
induce the jury to alter their policy. Not only was an ignoramus
verdict certain, but the jury succeeded in putting a stop to the
judicial attack on the Whigs. Until a new set of perjured witnesses came forward, and the juries in the City could be packed
by sheriffs working in the Court interest, it would be futile to
initiate prosecutions against the Whig leaders.

The Whigs were justified in showing so much vigilance, skill,
and thoroughness in Shaftesbury's case. Dugdale, a former Whig
witness who had been bought up by the Court but had not been
employed in the case against Shaftesbury, offered to come forward fully expecting that as in the case of College a second trial
would be held. Soon after this, John Booth, who had given evidence and was now back in the familiar surroundings of a prison,
wrote that if he was set at liberty he was sure a second bill could

[1] *State Trials*, viii. 809, 816.

be found if the case was transferred to Oxford.[1] The reaction to the ignoramus made this impracticable. To their chagrin the ministers found that by their obduracy in continuing the prosecution they had revived Shaftesbury's popularity and brought the Whig leaders together. His release, commemorated by a famous medal, was a Whig triumph, but one that was essentially defensive and therefore negative. Shaftesbury's life was saved, and a general proscription prevented—or at least postponed. But most Whigs, if not Shaftesbury himself with his confidence increased by his release, were now being forced to realize that the position of their party was becoming steadily weaker, and would continue to deteriorate unless a Parliament was called.

II

Earlier in the year most Whigs, and many Tories, expected the summoning of a new Parliament. They based this belief on two factors: the personal intervention of the Prince of Orange and, secondly, the danger of a general European war as the result of French aggression in the Low Countries. After being urged for so long William at last came over, but his visit in July 1681 proved to be completely abortive both for him and for the Whigs.

As always in his interventions in English politics, William had two main objects in visiting England: first to protect and further the interests of his wife and himself, and, secondly, to enlist English support for a continental coalition against French aggression and expansion. He saw that the dissensions between the Court and the Whigs made English intervention abroad impracticable, but although he had consistently advocated a union and an understanding between King and Parliament he had never been able to show how it could be brought about. His belief that Exclusion was inevitable had come close to compromising him in the eyes of the Court. Before the Oxford Parliament the Dutch ambassador, Van Leuwen, had openly supported the Exclusion Bill.[2]

[1] *CSPD*, 1680/1, 600. 1682, 163.
[2] Barrillon, 30 Jan. 1681.

William himself appeared to be recommending acceptance of the
Whig demands. But he had characteristically not committed himself. Van Leuwen could be disavowed all the more easily because
he was ambassador from the States, not from William. When
Hyde, probably for reasons of his own, assumed that William was
advising the King to agree to Exclusion, he received an angry and
explicit denial.[1]

When William arrived he found that the difficulties in the way
of an agreement between the King and a new Parliament would
be almost insuperable. At a meeting of the Privy Council the
ministers gave him their version of what had happened in the late
sessions of Parliament.[2] When they pressed him, whether he
would have advised accepting such Whig demands as putting the
militia and the forts into their hands, William had to admit that
he could not have done so. Moreover, he found that the Whigs
were still intransigent, and would not make any settlement with
the King except upon their own terms. As they had shown since
the beginning of the crisis, the Whig leaders were relatively uninterested in continental politics. Still absorbed in the struggle to
secure Exclusion, they would welcome a European war since it
would further their own ends. Either the King would have to
call a Parliament, and ask for supplies in order to assist his allies,
or by remaining inactive he would expose himself to charges
that he was in the pay of France. The question of checking
the advance of France, which was William's primary concern,
they considered as comparatively irrelevant, although Whig
pamphleteers were always ready to exploit popular hatred and
fear of Louis XIV. Moreover, they were equally quick to exploit
William himself for their own purposes, and he found that his
attempt to effect a compromise was threatening to turn the King
against him. Shaftesbury being at that time in the Tower, William consulted Essex, Russell, and Jones, but he found that they
were not to be moved from their insistence on Exclusion.[3] He
was invited to a Whig dinner in the City, which was to be made

[1] Prinsterer, v. 484, 493.
[2] Barrillon, 7 Aug. 1681. He, naturally, kept extremely alert during the visit.
[3] Ibid.; H. C. Foxcroft, *Life and Letters of Sir George Savile* (1898), i. 307-8.

the occasion for a great party demonstration. Having unwisely accepted, probably without realizing the full implications, the peremptory orders which he received from Charles not to go made William realize his danger. He was soon sorry that he had ever come over, and convinced that he could gain nothing from England.

A compromise between the King and the Whigs, a union against French aggression, was, of course, out of the question. In addition to Whig intransigence, the King's secret undertakings with France prevented him from coming to any agreement with William. They also prevented him from calling a Parliament, as Halifax was advising, and appealing to the patriotism of the members. Halifax's influence was again beginning to decline now that the crisis had begun to moderate. No longer indispensable, Halifax, as in 1679, was eclipsed by party men, particularly by Hyde, the representative of the absent Duke of York. Whereas Halifax wanted a compromise between moderates on both sides, and an end to party warfare, Hyde and his associates stiffened the resolution of the King against calling a Parliament and offered strong opposition to the suggestion of any terms short of capitulation to the Whigs. In September 1681 a proposal was made to bring about a general pacification by means of an act of indemnity to mark an end to the Popish Plot and to quieten the fears then current that the accusation against Shaftesbury would be the prelude to a wide proscription of the Whigs. The Whig negotiators declared that they would give undertakings not to reintroduce Exclusion and to abandon the impeachments of the ministers. The fact that an act of indemnity would require the calling of a Parliament made the negotiation futile. Later, in December 1681, negotiations were renewed, but although Halifax favoured a compromise settlement, once again there could be no chance of success since Charles had promised Louis that he would not summon a Parliament.[1]

Having failed to come to a general settlement with the Court, several Whigs now attempted to come to terms individually. They too met with indifferent success. The King had no need to

[1] HMC, Ormonde, N.S., vi. 165, 274.

buy off their opposition. Thomas Thynne, for instance, was hardly worth any consideration when he approached the Court. But for a short while it did seem that he might be worth more to the Whigs dead than alive. When he was assassinated, on the orders of a Swede—Count Konigsmarck—who wanted his wife, the Whigs tried to make him into a martyr, another Arnold or Godfrey. They also suggested that the intended victim had been Monmouth, who shortly before the murder had also been riding in the coach. Prompt action by the Government prevented any such political exploitation. The assassins were arrested, tried, and executed. Konigsmarck, who certainly did not lack courage, brazened the affair out, and complaints were stifled since he was cleared by a jury of Whigs.[1]

Lord Townshend was a more considerable person than Thynne, but he found that even submission to the King did not bring him all the benefits he had expected. When he went over to the Court, at the cost of alienating all his old Norfolk associates, he was rewarded with a viscountcy. But fearing that this promotion in the peerage would be followed by a restoration to his old political influence and office of Lord Lieutenant, the Norfolk Tories entered a caveat against him.[2] By now Charles was the effective leader of the Tory interest, and he could not afford to antagonize those who had been faithful to him by showing favour to men who had opposed him and them. When, in May 1682, Monmouth attempted to secure reconciliation with his father, he made it a condition that he should not have to submit to the Duke of York.[3] Naturally, this offer was rejected; once the danger of a general European war had diminished, Charles had no reason to show Whigs either mercy or favour. Past experiences still vivid in his mind, he had no thought of calling a new Parliament, and without one the Whigs were impotent.

[1] Ibid., 208. *CSPD*, 1680/1, 515. E. C. Godley, *The Trial of Count Konigsmarck* (1929).
[2] Tanner, 36, f. 228, Bishop of Norwich to Sancroft, 8 Feb. 1682.
[3] Carte, 216, ff. 47, 53; 232, ff. 103, 105.

III

Having dissolved the Oxford Parliament, and finding himself under no obligation to call another, Charles was now at last really King of England. But so long as the Whigs retained their control over the City government he was still not King in London. Since the very beginning of the crisis the City had been the loyal and most important ally of the majority in the House of Commons. The ignoramus verdict in Shaftesbury's case was its greatest, but also its last, service to the Whig cause. In his fury at being baulked of Shaftesbury's condemnation, Charles showed determination to wrest control over the City from the Whigs by all possible means, and, in addition, to subvert the independence of the City once and for all time.

This independence of the City embodied principles of government diametrically opposed to those represented by the King, the Court, and ministers with absolutist leanings. With its own trainbands and treasury, an elective Lord Mayor and sheriffs, and representative institutions with a fairly wide franchise, London was virtually a republic, an Amsterdam on the Thames. Moreover, it was also the stronghold of militant protestantism, believing itself to be particularly vulnerable to the assaults of the Papists —who were by 1678 believed to have caused the great fire of 1666. City mercantile interests disliked the financial policy of the King, and were worried by his policy of friendship with France. Therefore, as earlier in the century, the opponents of the Court received the support of the dominant interests in the City. Besides its four members, who all voted for Exclusion, several citizens sat for provincial counties and boroughs.[1] The City also provided more direct assistance for the Whigs; it led the way with petitions and instructions to its members, the Common Council encouraged provincial boroughs to defy the King by its refusal to put into execution the provisions of the Corporation Act.

---

[1] Clayton owned the pocket borough of Bletchingley, Thomas Turgis owned Gatton, both in Surrey. Ward represented Pontefract, Papillon sat for Dover, Bernardiston for Suffolk, Edward Boscawen for his family seat of Truro. Evesham provides an example of a borough coming under the direct control of Londoners of local origin, two of whom, Rushout and Rudge, sat in 1681. Both were Whigs.

After the dissolution of the Oxford Parliament the Whigs attempted to use the Common Council as a substitute for the House of Commons and as an instrument to put pressure on the King. This attempt, by means of a petition in the name of the Council, the mayor, and the aldermen, was ill received by Charles. He made a deliberate contrast between the kindness he showed a 'loyal' Southwark address, and the rebuke which he gave the City, taking the opportunity to lecture its representatives on their function. He told them that he had expected to find that the petition dealt with particular City matters. Instead it concerned matters of state, 'things which do in no sort appertain to you, but are quite out of your sphere'. He denounced the petition as a usurpation and encroachment on the prerogative; the representatives were told, 'you are not Common Council of the Nation'.[1]

This harsher note demonstrated a change of attitude on the part of the King. He and his ministers had always been very keenly aware of the importance of the City. Although at times afraid that it would give the Whigs physical as well as political support, they knew that open interference with the rights of the City was impracticable so long as the King was obliged to allow Parliament to meet. The Court confined itself to giving indirect support to the 'loyal' or Tory group, with very little success. In 1680 the King came up from Newmarket to countenance the Tories in their attempt to win the shrieval elections. Later in the same year Charles made his one important retreat when he agreed to the dismissal of Jeffreys and the appointment of the Whig Treby as Recorder. Only in the case of the militia did Charles possess direct influence in the affairs of the City, and as in the case of the armed forces of the nation, this he was determined to retain and exercise. Early in 1681 he prevented a Whig being appointed leader of the Artillery Company,[2] and in May all known or suspected Whigs were purged from the lieutenancy—something that had been done over a year before in other parts of the country.

After the dissolution of the Oxford Parliament an attack on the

---

[1] Charles's harsh answer to the Whig petition, and his welcome of the Tory addresses, were published as propaganda; *The Answers Commanded by His Majesty* (1681).   [2] W. D. Cooper (ed.), *Letters to and from Henry Savile* (1857), 183.

Whig hold in the City became practicable. But in order to destroy their control a long and bitter struggle was necessary. In the City the Whigs could still depend upon a large measure of popular support. Moreover, this could be effectively mobilized for party purposes and in defence of the rights of the City, whereas elsewhere there was no constitutional machinery which could be used in defence of municipal rights against the Crown. In the provincial boroughs Whig office-holders were systematically excluded even before the wholesale forfeitures and surrenders of the charters. In contrast the City could defend itself, but a successful action would be decisive. Not only would a successful action of *Quo Warranto* against the City charter permanently, completely, and constitutionally subordinate the government of the City, but it would also be calculated to encourage the surrender of the remaining provincial charters. But the *Quo Warranto* was only one side of the attack. Since the action would be contested the proceedings were certain to be long drawn out. Therefore, in addition, the King intervened to give the Tories support, and the Whigs were weakening to such an extent that even before the forfeiture of the charter enabled the King to remodel the corporation, the Tories had already seized effective control.

The struggle was at first evenly contested. In May 1681 the Tories mustered 77 votes in the Common Council against the Whig majority of 91 who supported the petition to the King.[1] The size of the minority was noted with some surprise; it showed that the more substantial citizens were deserting the Whigs, either to abstain from politics altogether or in some cases to join the Tory interest. But the Whigs retained their popular support, and their organization was still superior to that of the Tories. Both sides made intensive preparations for the 1681 election of sheriffs; success for the 'loyal' faction would have ensured Shaftesbury's condemnation, and the Whigs realized this. By their organization and enthusiasm they managed to gain a large majority. But with the election of Sir John Moore as Lord Mayor the Tories gained their first important victory.

[1] *CSPD*, 1680/1, 275–6. Barrillon, 26 May 1681. *True and Brief Relation of the Proceedings of the Common Council* (1681).

The Whig success in the shrieval elections gave this election added importance. Charles was determined to procure Moore's election by all possible means. If a Whig came at the top of the poll some pretext of irregularity was to be used to justify a refusal of confirmation. The Court interest was mobilized for the election. Charles returned from Newmarket in order to overawe the Whigs. Orders were sent to tradesmen to attend and vote for Moore on pain of losing all royal patronage, and 'loyal' clubs showed intense activity. Nevertheless, Moore was elected only as a result of a split in the Whig vote. All attempts to concentrate on one common Whig candidate failed. This split reflected the division between the more extreme and popular wing and the more prominent leaders in the City. The former, as always suspicious of their leaders, feared that Sir John Shorter, although a dissenter in sympathies, would prove amenable to royal pressure since the King owed him a considerable sum of money. In any case, for the Whigs to have been able to prevent Moore's eventual nomination the two Whig candidates would have had to be at the top of the poll, since the Tories claimed that the King could refer the first two names to the Court of Aldermen for one to be selected as mayor, and royal pressure would inevitably have produced the choice of Moore.[1]

Subsequent minor elections showed that in the autumn of 1681 and the following spring the two rival factions were evenly matched.[2] The Whigs succeeded in the election for the office of coroner, defeating an attempt at direct nomination by the Tory mayor. When the Tories discovered that the Whig elected was not qualified under the Corporation Act the Common Council overruled opposition and accepted a certificate that he had recently received the Sacrament. In an election to fill a vacancy as alderman for Bishopsgate ward the Whigs showed themselves over-confident, and a Tory was elected. But in the elections to the Common Council the Whigs retained their majority, though they lost some places. When the Tories obtained the invalidation of the election of some Whigs for a City ward the second election

[1] Luttrell, i. 129. CSPD, 1680/1, 457, 474–5, 479–80.
[2] Ibid., 680. Luttrell, i. 111, 127, 155.

returned the same persons, who had in the interval qualified themselves.

But throughout this period the Tories were gaining in strength and confidence. Tory clubs were formed. Members of the nobility such as Halifax and Ormonde condescended to dine with the club of loyal apprentices. A mob of Tory law students and hired water-men smashed the windows of the King's Head and assaulted the watch. Within the Court of Aldermen and Common Council the Tory group, known as the 'royal club', waged a constant struggle with the Whig majority, using tactics with the flavour of modern municipal politics. For instance in April 1682 a Whig alderman submitted his resignation, ostensibly on grounds of ill health but in reality to make way for a Whig who was intended to be a candidate at the next shrieval elections. His letter of resignation was sprung on the Tories at a thinly attended Court, but the latter, seeing that if the question was put the manœuvre would succeed, left *en bloc*, so that there was no quorum. On the next Court-day they rallied their supporters, so that the Whigs in their turn now faced defeat; if the question was put a Tory would be put in to fill the vacancy. Therefore they produced another letter from the Whig alderman, withdrawing his resignation on the plea that he had received untold benefit from the country air.[1]

Despite the organization of clubs and their pamphleteering activity, the Tories avowedly relied on official countenance rather than popular support. They despised the ordinary supporters of the Whigs as the 'rascality and meanest of the people', whereas the Tories were claimed to be 'the substantiallest and ablest citizens'.[2] Tory pressure and propaganda were in fact doing much to produce this position. Fearing that recourse to extreme methods would lead to disorders and social and economic upheavals, men like Clayton, the former Whig Lord Mayor, attempted to disassociate themselves from a reputedly violent party. Once again severe repressive action was reducing the number of those who regularly attended conventicles. But the main reason why the

[1] Luttrell, i. 212. Carte, 232, ff. 99–100. Morrice, ff. 351, 353. Ailesbury, *Memoirs*, 64–65.   [2] Carte, 216, f. 195. Longford, 3 Oct. 1682.

Tories despised Whig popularity was the fact that—as was made evident by the elections of 1681—they possessed far less support themselves. In the decisive contests of 1682 the Tories, by the tactics which they employed, recognized that the Whig majority in the Common Hall was impregnable, and placed their reliance on the advantage of having a Tory as Lord Mayor.

At the Bridgehouse feast in May 1682 Moore formally drank to Dudley North, an avowed Tory, and by doing so claimed to have nominated him as one of the sheriffs for the coming year.[1] The Tories claimed that in nominating North the mayor was merely exercising an established right and custom. This, of course, the Whigs denied in the pamphlet war which followed. The Tories asserted that this form of nomination filled one place, leaving only one vacancy to be filled by election. The Whigs replied by stating that this right had not been exercised since 1674, and that in any case it did not bind the Common Hall. Frequently, they argued, a nomination had been made and disregarded, or the nominee had withdrawn. This had been the Whig attitude in 1680 when Clayton, one of their own party, had drunk to a man named Hockenhull.[2] A heated dispute had taken place although Hockenhull was obscure and of no political importance. The Common Hall had been intent on preserving their own right, insisting that the members had still to fill both places, and rejecting the arguments of the common serjeant that Hockenhull must be accepted because the mayor had drunk to him. Eventually the Whigs had had their way and elected two of their own partisans, Clayton acquiescing. In 1681 the Whigs defeated another attempt at nomination, although both the mayor and the man he tried to nominate were reliable Whigs.[3] They saw that the rights of the City must be defended, and that this claim of nomination could be used by the Tories in the future to restrict popular election. Pilkington, the man whom the mayor tried to

[1] Luttrell, i. 186.

[2] The disputed election in 1682 aroused a furious pamphlet controversy; among the Whig publications (all in the Guildhall Library) were *The Right of Electing Sheriffs Stated*. *A Modest Enquiry concerning the Election of the Sheriffs of London*. *True Account of the Proceedings*.

[3] *Impartial Protestant Mercury*, 19, 24–28 June 1681.

nominate, refused to become sheriff in any way except by election, and explicitly declared that the election in the poll was the
source of his authority, and not merely confirmation of the choice
of the Lord Mayor.

The Whigs were therefore fully aware of the danger of one of
the sheriffs being nominated by a Tory mayor, but in the clash
which ensued in 1682 the advantages were all with the Tories.
After receiving personal encouragement from the King, Moore
persisted in his claim that North must be one of the sheriffs in
virtue of his nomination. To make sure that he did not waver a
succession of ministers dined with him, and assured him of their
support. When the poll began the outgoing Whig sheriffs, Shute
and Pilkington, persisted in polling for all four candidates for two
places. The mayor ordered the Court to adjourn, but the sheriffs
declined to recognize that he had any authority to do so. Encouraged by the presence of Whig leaders in the balcony in Guildhall they continued the poll, and were thereupon committed to
the Tower for riot. This did not intimidate the Whigs, who in
their turn tried to frighten the Court candidate into withdrawal.
Treby, the Whig recorder, almost succeeded in betraying the
mayor. When he was told to direct the sheriffs in the name of
the mayor to adjourn the poll forthwith, he deliberately falsified
the message, telling the sheriffs that they were merely requested
to adjourn. They of course referred the matter to their supporters,
knowing that they would be in favour of continuing the poll.[1]

The election was violent and farcical. Both sides proceeded to
poll only their own supporters, and thereupon declared their own
candidates elected by large majorities. The struggle was recognized as a trial of strength, both sides realizing the importance of
having 'right' men as sheriffs. The result was a Tory victory, but
it was by any standards a bare-faced swindle. The Tory candidate
who was declared elected by the mayor as a result of the first poll
had no wish to serve in such a contentious office. He fined off.
The second poll conducted by the Lord Mayor was held in private;
the bitter, baffled, and riotous Whigs being excluded by force

[1] Carte, 216, f. 86, Longford, 27 July; f. 113, Sir W. Steward to Arran, 22 July;
f. 119, Longford, 25 July. Luttrell, i. 206. *A Modest Enquiry*.

from the Guildhall by the stationing of the train bands outside. Still the Whig leaders would not admit defeat, but by attempting to arrest and prosecute the mayor for his allegedly illegal actions they were merely exposing themselves to future partisan Tory justice.[1]

By employing a different variety of tactics the Court was equally successful in carrying the election of another Tory to follow Moore as Lord Mayor. Here there was no doubt as to where the right of election lay. At first the Court considered the possibility of extending Moore's term, but this was hardly practicable since the only precedents dated from the interregnum. Instead they chose to follow the ordinary form of election, making intense efforts to rally support and deter the Opposition. Through the Bishop of London the clergy were ordered to use their influence on the laity. All keepers of ale and coffee houses were warned that their licences would not be renewed unless they appeared and voted for the Tory. The Whigs alleged that new liverymen were created, particularly in the Stationers' Company. The result of the poll was extremely close, but Pritchard the Tory was at the bottom of the poll.[2]

This meant that a new tactic had to be employed. In order to secure his return an examination of the poll was ordered, with the object of invalidating a sufficient number of Whig votes for Pritchard to be declared elected. The scrutineers were chosen by both sides, but the Whig representatives found themselves powerless, and when their protests were disregarded they withdrew. This merely facilitated the task of the Tories. They invalidated the votes of all Quakers, persons under excommunication, those who had omitted to take the oaths, newly transferred liverymen, and those alleged not to possess residence in the City. They made a particularly searching examination of the books of the Merchant Taylors and Farriers, and the refusal of the Glovers to allow a perusal of their books did not prevent some of the members

---

[1] Luttrell, i. 224, 319. *CSPD*, 1684/5, 177, 200. *A Display of Tyranny* (1689), 137–43. *HMC*, 13th *Report*, v. 49 ff.

[2] *CSPD*, 1682, 302, 557. Luttrell, i. 226, 230. The figures were Gold, 2,289; Cornish, 2,258; Pritchard, 2,233.

having their votes disallowed. On the other hand, the members of the Musicians' Company were admitted although they had never been allowed to vote before. Some Tory votes were struck out, but as might be expected the Tory scrutineers accomplished their task. Enough objections were made against Whig votes to give Pritchard the majority.[1]

To the Whigs this election of another Tory Lord Mayor was, of course, another blatant swindle, one that was long resented and had repercussions after the Revolution. But the Tories justified their conduct, claiming that the scrutiny exposed the Whig machinery of fraud which had given the party dominance in the City. Now that their admittance of 'mean and ill principled men into the Livery' had been exposed, Whig control over the City was at an end. Thus even before the successful outcome of the *Quo Warranto*, which forfeited the charter into the hands of the King, the Tories had gained control over the City for the Court.

IV

The loss of the City was the decisive stage in the slow but effective grinding down of the Whigs. Shaftesbury left his house in Aldersgate on the day after the new sheriffs were sworn.[2] The Whigs now lay at the mercy of juries packed by Tory sheriffs, and as a Tory commented many of them had now little thought but to save their bacon. There could now be no doubt that the Whigs were fighting a losing battle. In September, discouraged by the events in the City, but encouraged by the recent readmission of Sunderland to favour, some of the Whigs made an attempt at a general political settlement and personal accommodation.[3] The terms which they offered showed how far they realized the increasing weakness of their cause. They promised the King as much money as he wanted if he would call a Parliament, and

---

[1] Luttrell, i. 230. *An Exact Account of the Proceedings* (1682). Carte, 216, ff. 214, 218. After scrutiny the figures were Pritchard 2,138, Gold 2,124, and Cornish 2,093.
[2] Carte, 216, f. 216. Longford, 17 Oct.
[3] Ibid., f. 123, Colonel Fitzpatrick, 29 July; f. 157, Longford, 2 Sept.

agree to an act of indemnity. Guarantees would be forthcoming that no attacks would be made on the Duke of York or the ministers. The fact that Shaftesbury was not a party to this offer, and had gradually become separated from most of his former associates, was a further guarantee. But this effort at a settlement, based on a compromise, was bound to fail. The King's position was now so strong that he could afford to disregard all such over-tures. Moreover his ministers, and the Tories also, were suspicious of the possible results. They were already alarmed at the possible consequences of Sunderland's return to favour. When by chance Monmouth met his uncle in the Park he behaved to him with respect, but when he tried to make his peace at Court he found that politeness was not enough. The Tories urged that neither he nor the other Whigs should be readmitted to favour, 'without such submissions as will be most advantageous to the King's affairs'.[1]

Significantly this attempt at compromise was made at a time when all the preparations had been made for Monmouth's pro-gress to the north-west. He was offering to make his peace at a moment when he could expect that the Court would be more than ordinarily willing to buy him off, and so to concede better terms. This tour or progress, to Staffordshire, Cheshire, Shrop-shire, and Liverpool, was a popular triumph on the same scale as the visit to the west country in 1680, despite the decline in Whig fortunes. In the face of deliberate affronts from the Tory gentry and organized attempts to provide counter-attractions, Monmouth was everywhere acclaimed by the common people to whom he was still a hero and the Protestant champion.[2] But popularity by itself was of no value unless an insurrection was contemplated. Later, and on rather unreliable authority, it was said that before Monmouth left on his journey Shaftesbury had urged him to set up for a free Parliament in Cheshire if he received a sufficiently encouraging reception. When Monmouth was arrested on his return journey Shaftesbury was again reported to have advised him to escape and set up on his own in Cheshire. Logically

---

[1] Carte, 216, ff. 141, 157; this was their first meeting since 1679.
[2] CSPD, 1682, 370–1, 380–1, 383, 386–8, 392–3, 395–8.

Shaftesbury was right. Monmouth's return to London in custody, on a trumped-up charge, demonstrated again the fact that the Whigs were certain to get the worst of any legal struggle with the King, who had at his disposal all the prerogative powers and had repeatedly shown that he was ready to use them.[1]

Nevertheless, any rebellion at this time would soon have been crushed. Had Monmouth declared for a free Parliament his rebellion would have been as futile, isolated, and short-lived as Booth's rising in the same district in 1659. As then, the Government had made careful preparations, for as Monmouth was setting out from London Ormonde was instructing his son to collect men and ships in Dublin to cross the Irish Sea at short notice.[2] Moreover, unlike Booth twenty-three years before, the Whigs had no plans ready; the chances of Monmouth's welcome being transformed into a spontaneous mass rising were slight. Many of those who welcomed him had been led to believe that he was again in his father's favour. Certainly the prospect of defeat and the certainty of relentless punishment would deter many from joining a rising in its early stages.

Shaftesbury blamed Monmouth for his irresolution, but at this time only a few Whigs began to turn to ideas of resistance. Most of those who had sat in the Exclusion parliaments, or had been prominent outside, found it expedient to subside into inactivity. Even before the election of the Tory sheriffs in the City a number of prosecutions had been directed against prominent Whigs. In the country the dissenters were once again subjected to persecution. The effects of this repression were seen in the surrender of the municipal charters. Intimidated by the pressure of the Court and of local magnates, most towns offered surprisingly weak resistance. But when, as at Nottingham, a determined effort was made to prevent the subversion of the rights of the corporation, those who defied the Tories suffered severely at the hands of partisan justice for their temerity.[3]

The tyrannical actions of the Court, and the ascendancy of the

---

[1] *State Trials*, ix. 395–6; evidence of West. Carte, 216, ff. 181, 189; Longford 23, 26 September 1682. Lord Grey, *Secret History of the Rye House Plot*, 27.

[2] Carte, 219, f. 387.   [3] Morrice, f. 439.

Tories, forced the hard core of Whigs to consider some form of resistance. Their plans culminated in the so-called Rye House Plot of 1683. Much of the evidence given in the trials which followed can be seen as contradictory, unreliable, fabricated, and perjured. It is impossible here to go into all the details, but they can perhaps best be summarized by saying that there was as much, and as little, truth in the Rye House as in the original Popish Plot. The evidence of the informers, and of those Whigs who were trying to save their necks, was usually exaggerated, sometimes grotesquely so, but they revealed enough to show that some plans for the use of armed force had been made.

Shaftesbury seems to have been the first advocate of the use of force. His heat, his evident impatience with Monmouth, and the character of those with whom he now chose to associate, produced a rift between him and the other Whig leaders. Monmouth feared the consequences of precipitate action, and began to distrust Shaftesbury's judgement. His death, in exile in Amsterdam, was greeted with relief by the other leaders.[1] It left the Whigs divided into two sections. The surviving leaders of the City Whigs formed the more extreme section. Of the old leaders in the City some, like Clayton, had made their peace with the Court, others had already been intimidated, imprisoned, or driven abroad into exile. Those who remained, the hot-headed men with whom Shaftesbury had been associated during his last months, were men of less standing and often obscure origin, some being lawyers and old soldiers who had been employed as under-officers and Whig agents in the City. There was little sympathy, and not very much connexion, between these men—who were allegedly concerned in the assassination plot—and the smaller but politically more aristocratic and important group centred around Monmouth.

Nevertheless, the logic of events, and the deterioration of their own position, forced Monmouth and his friends to consider the use of force. At a time when, as it was said later, *quod Principi placuit, Lex esto*, all political activity and even moderate criticism of the King, the Duke, Court, and ministers involved savage

[1] Carte, 147, f. 144. *State Trials*, ix. 432; evidence of Lord Howard of Escrick.

punishment.[1] The lives of those who had been Whig leaders lay at the mercy of their enemies whenever it should suit the ministers to renew the management of perjured informers. The King's promises to maintain religion and the laws could hardly be reconciled with his actions, particularly the attack on the charters. It appeared that in the near future the Crown would be able to return Members of Parliament as easily as jurors. Moreover, this governmental influence would be employed, not to carry on the administration as it was to be in the eighteenth century, but in order to subvert the constitution and the liberties and properties of the nation.

Even in the face of this danger, most Whigs found it to be expedient to remain inactive. Many, it is true, were presented as disaffected by Tory grand juries, but this should be taken as evidence of party rancour on the part of opponents rather than of their continued Whig political activity. However fervently all exclusionists had sworn to stand by the Protestant religion with their lives, few Whigs were physically or psychologically ready to rise in rebellion in 1683 and 1685. Men expressed their horror at the news of the Rye House discoveries, regretting that they had ever associated with the Whigs. Even the more staunch shrank from the use of violence; Colonel Mildmay had been regarded as a very hot Whig in 1681 but Lord Grey discovered that he was unwilling to join in any plans for an insurrection.[2] John Trenchard, accused by the informers as being the leader of the intended rising in Taunton, actually left the country in 1685 so as to avoid being involved in Monmouth's rebellion. In fact although many searches were made of Whig houses in 1683, and many former exclusionists were placed in preventive custody in 1685, the authorities found little real and material evidence of nation-wide plans for the use of force. Yet, if the main leaders failed, Monmouth succeeded in building up a considerable, if ineffective, army. When everything else failed him, including his powers of leadership, Monmouth still received the popular support which the Whigs had always claimed.

[1] Noted on the title-page of *A Display of Tyranny*. According to a note on the copy in the Guildhall Library the author was Thomas Percivall (see above, Chapter 6, p. 168).   [2] Lord Grey, *Secret History of the Rye House Plot*, 25.

8

CONCLUSION

FROM this survey of the Exclusion crisis it can be seen that after
the dissolution of the Oxford Parliament the Whigs were forced
on the defensive. Their strength declined catastrophically even
before their loss of control over London and the repression which
followed the 'discovery' of the Rye House Plot. Without a Parliament, or the prospect of another in the foreseeable future, they
could no longer maintain significant pressure on the Crown. Once
popular passions subsided, when fears of violence and civil war
began to replace the feelings against Popery and absolutism, the
Whigs could no longer preserve an atmosphere of crisis. This is
the main explanation of the rapid crumbling of the Whig position
which Shaftesbury could do little to prevent or check. The elections of 1681 saw Whig organization at the highest pitch of
efficiency, yet six months later Charles felt strong and secure
enough to take openly repressive action against the Whigs, and
subsequently eliminated the bases of their strength and organization.

The defeat of the first Whigs, who were essentially a parliamentary party, was due primarily to the superior power of the
royal prerogative. Their domination of successive parliaments
proved to be inadequate because Parliament was still not an
essential part of the government of the country: the experience
of the years 1681–5 and 1686–8 showed that the King could
easily dispense with parliaments. After 1688 this was no longer
possible. By making it obligatory for the King to rule with the
assistance of Parliament, the Revolution changed the structure
of politics and the circumstances under which they were to be
conducted in future.

Exclusion was the drastic response to an apparently imminent and appalling danger which put liberties, religion, and property in peril, and forced the Whigs to unite in self-preservation. The revolution of 1688 finally eliminated the danger; extreme and extraordinary methods became unnecessary. The crisis was more acute, and raised questions of more fundamental importance than any which the eighteenth century was to experience; hence there was to be no concentration on a single issue like Exclusion, and nothing like the same popular interest in, and support for, a single cause until at least 1832. Nothing in the eighteenth century justified and demanded the discipline, organization, ruthlessness, and mass effort which, under Shaftesbury's leadership, made the first Whigs such a formidable force.

In this context the word party can be substituted for force, if only to emphasize the difference between the first Whigs and their post-revolutionary successors, to stress how different were the conditions of political life before 1688 from those of the ages of Walpole and George III. The first Whigs had necessarily to possess, or rather develop, the organization, cohesion, discipline, and mass appeal which made them a party, because of the intensity of the crisis through which they were living.[1] But all this was from necessity, not choice, and it is most doubtful whether they would have remained united and organized had they achieved power. The struggle for Exclusion required restrictions on their independence which most Whig peers and members would ultimately have found intolerable. They acquiesced, when their leaders employed such potentially dangerous methods as the mass petitions, only because the alternative was defeat or submission to the King and, even more hateful, to their local, Tory rivals. They followed Shaftesbury's somewhat autocratic leadership and subordinated their particular grievances and interests to the common cause. At the height of the crisis they remained surprisingly acquiescent when, during the 1681 elections, members were presented with instructions which although presented in the name of the electors

[1] In rejecting the right of the first Whigs to the title of 'party', John Carswell, *The Old Cause*, 2, stipulates as a test: 'there will be a directing committee, membership cards, a programme, a platform, a leader.' With the exception of the cards, hardly an essential, the first Whigs had all these qualifications.

had in fact been centrally organized by the Whig leaders, a move which threatened to undermine even the local influence of the individual Whig member.

Shaftesbury had, in reality, no intention of permanently subverting the independence of the individual members or of establishing a dictatorship based on popular support. He was forced to use the people in order to maintain pressure on the King, he had to establish close relations with the radicals, but he did not intend to share power with them. He used the most unscrupulous methods—subsidizing perjurers and an inflammatory press, appealing to the masses with a daring and an ability unmatched in the next century and a half, because of the long odds which he faced. The party machine which he developed might appear to be revolutionary and unprecedented (with the ominous exception of Pym's), Shaftesbury might seem to be a real demagogue, a veritable Tribune of the people, but his ultimate objectives were essentially conservative. His theoretical proposals for the reform of the representative system, involving a drastic reduction in the size of the electorate, would have strengthened the independence of the individual member and established an oligarchy even more secure than that which was to rule in the eighteenth century.[1]

Whig organization and tactics were entirely geared to the immediate purpose of forcing through Exclusion at all costs; they were evolved as instruments in the struggle, not as a means permanently to transform the structure and conditions of politics. The same immediate and polemical purpose was also characteristic of Whig political thought. It would not be unfair to say that

---

[1] These proposals were published in 1689, *Some Observations concerning the Regulating of Elections for Parliament.* Shaftesbury suggested redistribution according to population, a uniform franchise in which the forty-shilling qualification would be reassessed in terms of the present value of land, thereby reducing the electorate to a quarter of its existing size, a law against treating, the prevention of Crown interference by means of *Quo Warrantos*, and a minimum age of 40 for Members of Parliament. He also elaborated a more utopian scheme which would have entirely remodelled the system of representation. Householders in each parish were to elect a voter from a list compiled by the churchwardens. These voters, in turn, would elect members for the county from a list drawn up by the sheriff of all gentlemen over the age of 40 who possessed property worth £10,000. Voting was to be secret.

the Whigs had no developed, definite, or coherent political philosophy, and that for the most part they merely borrowed and repeated in an indiscriminate fashion the theories and arguments of those who had opposed Charles I. But if they possessed no more than certain common principles, assumptions, and prejudices, this is as much as most working British politicians have ever had. It was a source of immediate strength that the Whig case for Exclusion satisfied most of the assumptions about government and the constitution which had been held by the country Opposition earlier in the century.

Like Pym and Eliot, the Whigs tended to believe that the only thing which prevented harmony between King and Parliament, and provoked popular grievances, was the presence in high office of evilly disposed men. This belief fitted into their conveniently simplified version of what had happened at, and since, the Restoration. Asserting that this should, and could, have been the occasion for a reconciliation of all sections of the nation, they alleged that it had been turned into a partisan and vindictive act of revenge by self-interested courtiers and clerical crypto-Papists.[1] These same elements, with James at their head, were blamed for every subsequent act of oppression, for all the grievances of the people, and for the Popish Plot and the existing crisis.

The conclusion to be drawn from this analysis was that by the single act of Exclusion, by the elimination of James and so of his supporters, every problem would be on the way to solution. This one measure would enable the nation to preserve intact its liberties, property, and religion, without having to consider further and sweeping political reforms and changes—which the radicals alone wanted. Most Whigs thought that their task was to preserve the constitution from further encroachment, to repair the damage already done, and to restore it to its former state of perfection.[2]

[1] The Whig author of *A Modest Account of the Present Posture of Affairs in England* (1683) claimed that he had often heard Shaftesbury say 'that the Act of Oblivion was an Act of the King's honour and justice, as well as his mercy, it being a Treaty, and Agreement, much more sacred than any Act of Parliament', and ask how well the promises had been kept.

[2] A view well expressed by Henry Booth, later Earl of Warrington, *Works* (1694), 38: 'changes seldom happen for the better, and therefore the people will

There was little of the zeal for constitutional and social experimentation which had existed in the early years of the interregnum.

Intense pre-occupation with immediate political issues produced the superficial character which marked Whig thought and writing during the crisis. Whig pamphleteers and debaters were primarily polemical and controversial, more concerned to refute the arguments of their opponents than to construct a complete and coherent political theory or argument; Sidney's *Discourses on Government* was written as a refutation of Filmer, Johnson's *Julian the Apostate* as a counter to the divine-right preaching of the clergy. It was to be left to Locke to publish (if not to write) after 1688 the classical Whig exposition of the origin, nature, and purpose of political institutions. There were other serious weaknesses in much Whig political writing. Their appeal to history was profoundly unhistorical, and often ludicrous.[1] Some Whigs ransacked the past for precedents, which they used quite indiscriminately to assert the independence, and inflate the importance, of those institutions which served their purpose, such as Parliament and juries. Others, like Sidney, thought that natural law (ascertained by reason) overrode the law established by precedents.

None of the Whig political writings produced during the crisis bear close and critical examination.[2] Their zest in attacking individuals, James in particular, as responsible for all the evils and grievances in existence betrays a readiness to take short cuts, to evade thinking out the fundamental causes of the crisis, and the defects of the constitution. The Whigs used all grievances as

not be much delighted with the discontinuance of Parliaments', they being 'the only physic to purge out those peccant humours that are contracted by time or accident.'

[1] J. G. A. Pocock, 'Robert Brady', *Cambridge Historical Journal*, x. 2 (1951), 189–90.

[2] This subject is comprehensively dealt with by Miss B. Behrens, 'The Whig Theory of the Constitution in the Reign of Charles II', *Cambridge Historical Journal*, vii. 1 (1941), 45. She points out that most Whigs 'maintained a valiant but increasingly unsuccessful attempt to reconcile two irreconcilables—the historical argument which was conservative, and the argument from "reason" which, in their hands, was revolutionary'. See also C. Robbins, *The Eighteenth Century Commonwealthman* (1959), 26–27.

ammunition to be directed against the Court, but had they gained power they could have done little to rectify them in order to satisfy their supporters. But in the short run these defects and inconsistencies hardly mattered; the Whig objective was to mobilize the maximum amount of support for Exclusion, without much regard to what would happen afterwards. If they evaded the fundamental causes of the crisis, and over-simplified the issues, this very crudity or simplicity of their approach increased its appeal. The assumptions which the Whigs relied upon were so strongly and universally held as to be almost self-evident. All hated Popery, nearly everyone connected it with absolutism, most people had come to distrust the Court. Exclusion, and the reasons for it, could be understood by all.

The overriding unity which the crisis forced the Whigs to develop, with its organization, cohesion, and discipline, could not have lasted. The majority of the Whigs in Parliament was drawn from the country gentry, the section who so valued their independence but acquiesced in the use of extreme measures and accepted a degree of subordination only because the alternative was the establishment of Popery and absolutism. It is clear that Whig unity would not have lasted if they had won their objectives, and in fact it did not survive defeat. Not merely were the Whigs forced into total submission and inactivity in the years after 1683, but after 1688 those who called themselves Whigs explicitly repudiated Shaftesbury's example. To them, in retrospect, he appeared to have been a dangerous incendiary, another Pym. They revered Russell and Sidney as martyrs put to death by a tyrant, but they would not acknowledge Shaftesbury as their political ancestor. The frequent changes in his long career pointed to insincerity and opportunism, and his final conversion seemed to have been a tactical change of front rather than a genuine change of heart. It was not an accident that Shaftesbury had to wait so long for a biographer and apologist; he retained too much of the character of the age and circumstances which had produced Pym and Cromwell.[1] And although the reputation of the first Whigs

[1] Apart from the laudatory, inaccurate, and propagandist Whig life, significantly entitled *Rawleigh Redivivus* (1683), Shaftesbury had to wait until the nine-

in general stood higher than that of their leader during the eighteenth century, it suffered a crippling blow with the publication
of Dalrymple's *Memoirs*. His revelation of the links between
Louis XIV and many of the Whig leaders destroyed the legend
of their heroic virtue, and showed that morally they had been no
better than the corrupt ministers of the King.[1]

It is a fair verdict to say that the first Whigs were true sons of
their own time and political environment. Only a section was
thoroughly corrupt, but all can be condemned for their reliance
on unworthy agents and indefensible methods. But it should be
remembered that the Glorious Revolution, so-called, was the
result of equally deplorable but more successful tactics and propaganda.

In retrospect the Revolution justified the policy of Exclusion.
The events of the reign of James II fulfilled Whig predictions,
proving that Popery was incompatible with the liberties as well
as the religion of the nation. His conduct demonstrated to all
that the Crown could not be allowed to retain those prerogative
powers which had brought about the defeat of the Whigs, but
which James had then turned against the Tories and the Church
of England. Later generations disowned Shaftesbury, but they
did not repudiate the principles on which the case for Exclusion,
as well as the Revolution, rested—that political power should
reside with those who possessed the greatest weight in society,
and that in the last resort sovereignty rests with the people, the
interests of the nation taking precedence over those of the Crown.

teenth century for a biography. His steward and confidant, Stringer, started one
but died before it could be completed. The halting and unsatisfactory *Life* begun
by Martyn in the 1730's was continued by Kippis but not published until 1836,
edited by G. W. Cooke. Two further biographies by Christie (1871) and Traill
(1888) both failed to make him appear as a living character, the former depicting
him as a respectable Victorian born before his time, while the latter regards him
as no more than an adept intriguer. Nor has the most recent biography, L. F.
Brown, *The First Earl of Shaftesbury* (1933), come much nearer success. It is only
fair to add that there appears to be insufficient material for a convincing life.

[1] Sir John Dalrymple, *Memoirs of Great Britain and Ireland* (1771). Using the
archives, then at Versailles, Dalrymple showed how the leaders of the country
Opposition had accepted French money during the summer session of 1678.
Most of them later became fervent exclusionists, but only a few maintained these
links with the French ambassador.

INDEX

Albemarle, second Duke of, 97–98, 165.
Aldborough, 41, 45.
Alington, third Baron, 39.
Alsace, 147.
Anglesey, first Earl of: votes for Exclusion, 141; on Stafford's trial, 144.
Arlington, first Earl of, 34, 131, 190–1.
Armstrong, Sir Thomas: associate of Monmouth, 14; and the Black Box, 82; activities, 88; wins the Stafford election, 104–5; summer 1680 activities, 124.
Arnold, John: Monmouth election, 102; is attacked, 124, 197.
Ashe, Edward, 70 n.
Association, 56, 146–7.
Aylesbury, 46, 99.

Baber, Sir John, 84.
Barrillon, French ambassador: contacts, 13 n.; and army, 23 n.; organizes attack on Danby, 28; on elections, 48; on Exclusion, 69, 71; on William's interest, 83; on Meal-tub plot, 114; on Charles and James, 131; on 1680 session, 133; influence, 147–9; on English politics, 150; negotiates with Charles, 155; on Charles and Exclusion, 156.
Bath, seventh Earl of, 88, 99.
Bedford, seventh Earl of, 18, 103.
Bedlow, informer, 22, 166.
Bennett, Thomas, 35, 56.
Bernardiston, Sir Samuel, 192 n., 193, 198 n.
Bertie, Charles, 29, 41, 73.
Bethell, Slingsby, 127, 174 n.
Beverley, 13.
Birch, John, 13, 50, 136, 142.
Bletchingly, 104.
Bodmin, 12.
Booth, Henry, 135, 173, 174, 214 n.
Booth, John, 193–4.
Boscawen, Hugh, 11, 30 n., 104, 198 n.
Bothwell Brig, 80, 116.
Bridgwater, third Earl of, 45.
Brentford, 99.

Buckingham, 39, 46, 99.
Buckingham, second Duke of, 11, 15, 17, 34, 60, 101, 103, 109, 111, 149, 152; jealous of Shaftesbury, 18, 32; on Charles, 86; and Bucks. elections, 47, 99–100; and Oxford elections, 41, 164; on Shaftesbury's trial, 189.
Burnett, Bishop: quoted, 17, 76.
Byde, Sir Thomas, 118.

Cambridge, 39.
Cambridge University, 37–38.
Camelford, 42.
Cann, Sir Robert, 135 n.
Capel, Sir Henry, 10 n., 11, 51; assists Montagu, 29; goes over to Court, 57 n.; Court speaker, 63, 65; resigns from Privy Council, 92, 122; moves Exclusion, 134; supports Exclusion, 138–9.
Carew, Sir Nicholas, 11, 12, 178.
Castle Rising, 41.
Cavendish, Lord, 18; assists Montagu, 28–29; goes over to Court, 57 n; opposes Monmouth's pretensions, 81; resigns from Privy Council, 92, 122; supports Exclusion, 139; on Halifax, 142; suggests association, 146 n.
Celier, Mrs., 75, 109–111.
Chandos, eighth Baron, 98.
Charles I, 5, 59, 177, 214.
Charles II, 1, 4, 5, 6, 7, 8, 17, 20, 33, 36, 37, 45, 57, 64, 71, 72, 75, 82, 100, 107, 129, 142, 143, 145, 147, 151, 159, 167, 168, 181, 183, 184, 211, 213; ill, 14; on Popish plot, 23; electoral influence, 36–38, 93; letters of recommendation, 38; attitude to James, 55; changes policy, 57–58; Shaftesbury's comments on, 59–60, 75; new Privy Council, 61–62; uses, 62–63; prorogues first Whig Parliament, 73; and Halifax, 77–78, 90; and covenanters, 79; and Lucy Walter, 80–81, 126; Sunderland's estimate of, 84; negotiates with

Charles II (*cont.*)
France, 8, 86, 147, 155, 176; illness causes crisis, 86–87; sends Monmouth abroad, 88–89; under James's influence, 89–91; refuses to let Parliament sit, 92, 114; on Monmouth, 113; and Mildmay, 118; attitude to petitions, 119; purges J.P.'s, 120; attitude, 1679–80, 122–3; visits City, 123; second illness, 123; orders Monmouth abroad, 125; on Exclusion, 126, 131, 133, 137, 140–1, 150, 179–80; Sunderland's misjudgement of, 140; on Stafford, 144; distrusted by France, 148; and Montagu, 153–4; uncertainty of intentions, 156–7; and Oxford Parliament, 176; offers limitations, 177; at Oxford, 179–80; on Shaftesbury's trial, 189–91; not to call Parliament, 196; and City, 200–2.
Charlton, Francis, 191.
Chester, 169.
Chetwind, Walter, 105.
Cholmley, Sir Henry, 87–88.
Christchurch, 165–6.
Clarendon, second Earl of, 143, 165.
Clarges, Sir Thomas, 28, 29 n., 57 n., 64, 71.
Clarges, Sir Walter, 165.
Clayton, Sir Robert, 104, 178, 198 n., 203, 209; and Meal-tub plot, 112; and City petition, 119; welcomes Charles, 123; withdraws from politics, 202.
Clifford of Chudleigh, 68.
Clifford, Lord Charles, 44–45, 163.
Colchester, 164–5.
Colchester, Lord, 14.
Coleman, Edward, 25, 26, 51, 56, 68, 70, 135, 160.
College, Stephen, 186, 188–9, 192, 193.
Colt, J. D., 142.
Conway, first Earl of, 14 n., 140.
Copley, Sir Godfrey, 41 n.
Cornish, Henry, 127, 174 n., 205 n.
Cornwallis, third Baron, 165.
Corporation act, 120, 144, 198, 201.
Coventry, 102.
Coventry, third Baron, 102, 162.
Coventry, Henry, 26 n.
Coventry, Sir John, 12, 26.
Cowper, Sir William, 118, 178.
Cricklade, 12, 106.

Danby, first Earl of, 3, 5, 6, 14 n., 20–21, 34, 69, 71, 72, 73, 76, 81, 97, 148, 149, 175; and Popish plot, 23; whether to defend James, 25, 26; attacked by Montagu, 27–29; in Parliament, 29–30, 51–53; and Holles, 35; in elections, 38–39, 40, 44, 46; advice to Charles, 57–58, 93; represented at Shaftesbury–Monmouth meetings, 88; William and asylum for, 129; and Fitzharris, 174 n., 175.
Dangerfield, Thomas, 110–12, 134, 167.
Denbigh, third Earl of, 96.
Dennis, informer, 188.
Dering, Sir Edward, 139.
Dering, Edward, 163.
Digby, Lord, 102.
Dover, 37, 102.
Dover, treaty of, 148.
Downton, 165.
Duckett, Lionel, 158 n.
Dugdale, informer, 166, 188, 193.
Dumblane, Lord, 39, 46.
Dunwich, 98.

Election regulation bill, 53–54.
Eliot, family, 13, 41, 104.
Ellis, Sir William, 51.
Ernle, Sir John, 28, 38.
Essex, 97–98, 169.
Essex, first Earl of, 11; in Lords, 32; denounced by Shaftesbury, 78; and Monmouth, 81–82; and William, 83, 195; for Dutch alliance, 84; recalls James, 87; in eclipse, 90; position, 91; wants Parliament to meet, 92; resigns from Treasury, 92; but not from Privy Council, 122; and Irish plot, 187; rumours of arrest, 189.
Evelyn, George, 43.
Exclusion, bills, 4, 6, 214, 216–17; moved, 65–66; reasons for, 67–69; and succession, 69–70, 136–7; vote on, 71; re-introduced, 135; passes commons, 138–9; defeated in Lords, 140–1; provisions, 146; at Oxford, 178–80.
Exeter, 41.
Exeter, fifth Earl of, 41.

Fairfax, fourth Baron, 38, 44, 45, 163.
Fauconberg, second Viscount, 72.

Fell, Bishop, 40.
Ferguson, Robert, 15.
Feversham, second Earl of, 89, 143.
Finch, Daniel, 105, 136.
Fitzharris, Edward, 174–6, 183.
Fleetwood, Major-General, 43.
Foley, Paul, 66.
Foley, Thomas, 162.
Fox, Sir Stephen, 73.
Freke, Thomas, 165.

Garroway, William, 63, 135.
Gatton, 12, 104.
Gerard, Lord Brandon, 82.
Godfrey, Sir Edmund Berry, 1, 21, 22, 23, 24, 70, 174, 175, 197.
Godolphin, Sidney, 141 n., 142.
Gold, Sir Thomas, 205 n.
Great Bedwin, 106.
Gregory, William, 50.
Grey, second Baron of Warke, 98, 99, 180, 210.
Grimstone, 13.

Habeas Corpus Amendment Act, 18 n., 54, 67.
Hackett, Sir Andrew, 47.
Halifax, first Marquis of: in 1678 session, 32; associates, 64, 72; joins Court, 77–78; for Dutch alliance, 84; recalls James, 87; James's attitude to, 90; eclipsed, 112; on Exclusion, 140; Sunderland on, 141–2; Whig attacks on, 142–3, 152, 157; and trial of Shaftesbury, 189, 191; influence declines, 196; in City, 202.
Hamilton, first Duke of, 80.
Hampden family, 18, 47, 103.
Hampden, John, 45–47, 99–100.
Hampden, Richard, 151, 152, 186.
Harbord, William, 13, 35, 41; joins Court, 57 n, 64; for William, 84; supports Exclusion, 139; attacks Halifax, 142, and Barrillon, 149; intrigues, 153–4.
Harris, Sir Arthur, 13.
Harris, Benjamin, 158.
Hartop, Sir Arthur, 43–44.
Harwich, 37.
Herbert, Lord, 101–2.
Herne, Sir Nathaniel, 22 n.
Hetherington, 124, 188.
Hickman, Sir William, 64, 65, 135.

Higham Ferrers, 13.
Hobart, Sir John, 97, 182.
Hockenhull, 203.
Honeywood, J. L., 98.
Holles, first Baron, 11, 30 n., 35, 132, 150.
Hotham, Sir John, 12.
Howard, Sir Robert, 10 n., 52, 136, 139.
Huntingdon, seventh Earl of, 9 n., 10 n., 165, 190.
Hyde, Laurence, 131, 143, 189, 191, 195, 196.

Ivey, informer, 188.

Jeffreys, George, 127, 143, 199.
Jenkins, Sir Leoline, 130, 135, 153, 177, 191.
Jenks, 15 n., 88, 101.
Johnson, Samuel, 215.
Jones, Sir William, 138, 146 n., 151; disparages Shaftesbury, 152; attacks limitations, 178; and William, 195.

Kaye, Sir John, 45.
Knight, Sir John, 50, 65, 136.
Konigsmarck, Count, 197.

Lane, informer, 109.
Latimer, Viscount, 38, 44.
Lauderdale, 52, 71, 76, 79, 91, 125.
Lee, Sir Thomas, 46, 51.
Legge, William, 38.
Lichfield, 105.
Limitations, 26 n., 64, 65, 90, 145, 177–8.
Littleton, Sir Thomas, 30 n., 178.
Locke, John, 9 n., 166, 170, 215; drafting addresses, 169; and Shaftesbury's trial, 190–1.
London, 15, 107, 211; elections, 42, 100–1, 161–2; proposals to disarm, 58, 107; petitions, 79, 116, 117, 119–20; shrieval elections, 126–7, 199; Whig demonstrations in, 88, 112; welcomes Monmouth, 113; Charles visits, 123; displaces Jeffreys, 143; address, 171; juries, 186–7, 188, 191–2, 193, 197; proposed visit by William, 196; services to Whigs, 198–9; royal attack on, 200–6.

Longford, first Earl of, 43, 92–93, 120.
Louis XIV, 5, 68, 147, 150, 160, 195, 196, 217.
Lovelace, third Baron, 46, 103, 164.
Ludgershall, 38, 106.
Lyme Regis, 163.

Macclesfield, first Earl of, 126, 181.
Macnamarra, John and Dennis, 188.
Maldon, 105.
Malmesbury, 46.
Manchester, second Earl of, 141.
Mansell, Colonel, 111, 112.
Mariet, Thomas, 96.
Mary of Orange, 69, 83, 137, 179.
Maynard, Serjeant, 51.
Meal-tub plot, 109–12.
Meres, Sir Thomas, 20 n., 51, 178.
Mildmay, Colonel, 97–98, 118, 210.
Monmouth, 101–2.
Monmouth, first Duke of: associates, 13–14; and 1679 elections, 37–38; pretensions, 18–19, 69–70; position causes uncertainty, 74; sent to Scotland, 80; relations with James, 80–81; and opposition, 81–82; and Sunderland, 82; in crisis, 87–88; loses offices, 88–89; and Shaftesbury, 88; popular, 99; banished, 106–7, 115; unauthorized return, 113–14; position summer 1680, 124–5; western tour, 125–6; rejects approach, 126; and William, 129; meets Duchess of Portsmouth, 132; Whig attitude to, 136–7; and Barrillon, 147, 150; and Montagu, 152; votes on his behalf, 155; and Regency, 179; rumours of arrest, 189; attempts reconciliation, 197, 207; visits north-west, 207–8; and use of force, 209–10.
Monmouthshire, 171.
Montagu, Ralph: position, 6, 13, 14, 17; rival to Shaftesbury, 18; elected for Northampton, 27; betrays Danby, 27–29, 33; in elections, 38, 41; left out of Privy Council, 62; on Monmouth, 82, 125; attacks Halifax, 142; with Barrillon, 149; intrigues for office, 151–4.
Moore, Sir John, 200, 201, 203, 205.
Morley, Bishop, 94.
Mowbray, Lawrence, 188 n.
Musgrave, Sir Christopher, 135.

Nanfan, Bridges, 162.
Newcastle, second Duke of, 38.
Netherlands, Spanish, 147.
Newport, first Viscount, 72.
Noel, Edward, 100.
North, Dudley, 203, 204.
North, L.C.J., 143.
Northampton, 27, 98.
Norwich, 40.

Oakhampton, 13.
Oates, Titus, 1, 6, 111, 112, 117, 144, 186, 187; why so influential, 21–23; accuses Queen, 32; and Irish witnesses, 124.
Onslow, Arthur, 43.
Ormonde, first Duke of, approaches Shaftesbury, 76–77; attacked by Essex, 91; and Irish plot, 187; and trial of Shaftesbury, 189–90; in City, 202; prepares against rising, 208.
Owen, Thomas, 168.
Oxford, 41, 164.
Oxford, twentieth Earl of, 165.

Paget, seventh Baron, 99.
Papillon, Thomas, 102, 127, 198 n.
Pemberton, Sir Francis, 191.
Pembroke, seventh Earl of, 125, 165.
Pepys, Roger, 39.
Pepys, Samuel, 38, 39, 41.
Percivall, Thomas, 168, 210 n.
Peterborough, second Earl of, 16 n., 110–12.
Peyton, Sir Robert, 110, 168.
Peyton, Sir Thomas, 163.
Pilkington, Thomas, 65–66, 203–5.
Pitts, George, 75.
Player, Sir Thomas, 42, 51, 66, 107.
Plunkett, Oliver, 187.
Portsmouth, 37.
Portsmouth, Duchess of, 85, 89, 118, 125, 131, 156; indictment against her, 127–8.
Powis, first Earl of, 110.
Powle, Henry, 28, 51, 149; joins Court, 57 n.; Court speaker, 63; advocates limitations, 65; wants meeting of Parliament, 92; resigns from Privy Council, 92, 122.
Pritchard, Sir William, 205, 206.
Prodgers, Edward, 76.
Pulteney, Sir William, 178.
Pym, John, 59, 116, 156, 213, 216.

Queen Catherine, 32, 70, 174 n.
Queenborough, 37.

Radnor, first Earl of, 72, 112, 122, 131.
Ranelagh, first Earl of, 38.
Reresby, Sir John, 41.
Reynolds, Samuel, 164–5.
Roberts, Sir William, 167–8.
Rochester, 37.
Rochester, second Earl of, 72.
Rolle, Sir Francis, 100.
Roos, Lord, 43–44.
Rous, Francis, 191–2.
Rudd, Sir Rice, 13.
Rudge, Edward, 198 n.
Rushout, Sir James, 198 n.
Russell, Edward, 103.
Russell, Robert, 103.
Russell, Lord William, 8, 12, 82, 103,
    137, 152; Shaftesbury's lieutenant,
    18, 25–26; attacked by Danby, 29;
    in Privy Council, 63, 77; resigns, 92,
    122; elected in Hants, 100; attacks
    James, 135; on Tangier, 145; and
    William, 195; death, 216.
Rutland, eighth Earl of, 43.
Rye House plot, 8, 210, 211.

Sacheverel, William, 18, 26, 29 n., 35,
    51, 52, 70 n., 152, 163; attacks Powle,
    63; opposes petitioning, 118–19; his
    attitude after 1680, 158–9.
St. Germans, 41, 104.
Scroggs, L.C.J., 109, 127, 143, 184,
    186.
Seymour, Edward, 40, 49, 51, 143, 189.
Shaftesbury, first Earl of, 2, 4, 6, 7, 8,
    9, 11, 13, 14, 21, 22, 71, 86, 91, 96,
    159, 184, 185, 195, 196, 198, 212,
    214 n., 217; character, 16–18; on
    Popish plot, 23; in Lords, 31–33; and
    first Whig Parliament, 48–49; on
    Exclusion, 55, 62; on Charles, 59–60;
    case against James, 67–69; breaks
    with Charles, 73; as Lord President,
    74–75; not a courtier, 75–76; rejects
    office in 1674, 76; imposes conditions,
    76–77; and Ormonde, 76–77; and
    other ministers, 77, 83; and Halifax,
    77–78; and covenanters, 79–80;
    exploits Monmouth, 83; Sunderland
    on, 84–85; and William, 85; meets
    Monmouth, 88; dismissed, 89, 108;

and Sunderland, 89–90; in elections,
    103; attitude inflexible, 106–8; and
    Meal-tub plot, 112; and Monmouth's
    return, 113; negotiates with Charles,
    114; advises privy councillors, 121;
    and Irish plot, 122, 144, 187; indicts
    James, 127–8; needs Sunderland, 131,
    132; and Montagu, 149; attempt to
    displace, 152–3; appeals to Charles,
    157; 1681 elections, 165–6; and
    Monmouth, 179; position weakens,
    180; prosecution of, 189–93; goes
    into hiding, 206; split with friends,
    207; advises Monmouth, 207–8;
    death, 209; political objectives, 213;
    posthumous reputation, 216.
Shaftesbury, 165.
Sheldon, Sir Joseph, 42.
Sherrard, Lord, 43.
Shorter, Sir John, 201.
Shute, Samuel, 204.
Sidney, Algernon, 8, 9 n., 149, 215,
    216.
Sidney, Henry, 10 n., 83, 85, 90,
    139, 140, 148.
Speke, George, 11, 40.
Stafford, 104.
Stafford, first Baron, 144, 188.
Stamford, 13, 41.
Stamford, second Earl of, 165.
Stockbridge, 105.
Stokes, William, 102.
Stringer, Thomas, 55 n., 76 n., 217 n.
Suffolk, third Earl of, 141.
Sunderland, second Earl of: denounced
    by Shaftesbury, 78; and Monmouth,
    82; and William, 83; position at end
    of 1679, 84–85; and James, 89;
    negotiates with Shaftesbury, 89–90,
    108; with William, 89, 128–9, 140;
    thinks Whigs a spent force, 128, 123;
    renews Whig negotiations, 130–
    3; on Charles's intentions, 131,
    156; in disgrace, 141; on Halifax,
    141–2; on France, 148; working for
    William, 150; intrigues, 153; re-
    admitted to favour, 206.
Swinfen, John, 11, 18, 47–48.

Tamworth, 47.
Tangier, 145, 158.
Taunton, 170.
Temple, Sir Richard, 154

Temple, Sir William, 27, 28, 61, 83, 90, 92, 141 n., 142, 145, 148, 179.
Thetford, 42.
Thomas Thynne, 47, 105.
Thomas Thynne (d. 1682), 103–4, 118, 153, 197.
Titus, Silas, 26, 51, 135, 145, 153.
Townshend, first Baron, 75, 97, 182, 197.
Treby, Sir George, 25 n., 51, 70 n., 135, 143, 199, 204.
Tregoney, 12, 104.
Trenchard, John, 51, 138, 210.
Truro, 104.
Turberville, 188.
Turgis, Thomas, 104, 198 n.

Vane, family, 39.
Van Leuwen, 194, 195.
Vaughan, Edward, 51, 178.
Vernon, Edward, 142, 163.

Wakeman, Sir George, 94, 109, 184, 185.
Waller, Sir William, 22, 42, 175.
Walter, Lucy, 80, 82, 126.
Ward, Sir Patience, 198 n.
Wendover, 46.
Westbury, 46.
Westminster, 163, 168.
Wharton, fourth Baron, 9 n., 10 n., 12–13, 45–47, 103.
Wharton, Thomas, 12, 45–47, 99–100.
Whitley, Roger, 12.
Whorwood, Broome, 41, 63, 164.
William, Prince of Orange: interest of, 83; Sunderland plans visit by, 85; dangers to, 90; did not know of Monmouth's return, 113; position in 1680, 128–30; Whig attitude to, 136, 151; refuses to come over, 140;

Barrillon on, 150; hunts on Sundays, 151; and Regency, 179; visits England, 194–6.
Williams, William, 50, 169 n.
Williamson, Sir Joseph, 26.
Winchelsea, 171.
Winchester, sixth Marquis of, 32, 100, 103, 165.
Windsor, 37, 104.
Windsor, seventh Baron, 162.
Winnington, Sir Francis, 13, 30 n., 51, 64, 134, 138, 139, 142, 146, 153–4, 185–6.
Worcester, third Marquis of, 101–2, 143.
Wright, William, 164.
Wythens, Sir Francis, 135 n.

Yarmouth, first Earl of, 40, 96, 112.
Yonge, Sir Walter, 13.
York, 44, 119, 121.
York, James Duke of, 1, 3, 4, 6, 20, 26, 51, 59, 84, 91, 94, 106, 107, 110, 115, 124, 146, 160, 163, 169, 178, 180, 185, 196, 214, 217; and plot, 25–26; exempted from test, 27; negotiates with Shaftesbury, 23, 31; exiled, 35; reasons for excluding, 4, 55, 67–69; attacked, 56; fears abandonment, 64, 131; exclusion moved, 65–66; on Shaftesbury's appointment, 74–75; and Monmouth, 80–81; and Sunderland, 85; recalled, 88–89; and Halifax, 90; and second Whig parliament, 92; and City, 101; and York, 121; petitioned against, 121; indicted, 127–8; corresponds with William, 129–30; Dangerfield's evidence against, 134; vote against, 155; addressed against, 169; and Fitzharris, 174 n., 175; Whigs promise immunity, 207.